D0848047

THE
GREAT FIRE
OF ROME

THE
GREAT FIRE
OF ROME

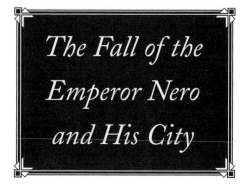

*The Fall of the
Emperor Nero
and His City*

STEPHEN DANDO-COLLINS

DA CAPO PRESS
A Member of the Perseus Books Group

Designed by Brent Wilcox
Set in 11.25 point Adobe Caslon by the Perseus Books Group

Library of Congress Cataloging-in-Publication Data
Dando-Collins, Stephen.
   The great fire of Rome : the fall of the emperor Nero and his city /
Stephen Dando-Collins.
      p.   cm.
   Includes bibliographical references and index.
   ISBN 978-0-306-81890-5 (alk. paper)
   1. Rome—History—Nero, 54–68.   2. Nero, Emperor of Rome, 37–68.
3. Great Fire, Rome, 64.   I. Title.
   DG285.3.D36 2010
   937'.07—dc22

                                                      2010013443

First Da Capo Press edition 2010

Published by Da Capo Press
A Member of the Perseus Books Group
www.dacapopress.com

Da Capo Press books are available at special discounts for bulk purchases in the U.S. by corporations, institutions, and other organizations. For more information, please contact the Special Markets Department at the Perseus Books Group, 2300 Chestnut Street, Suite 200, Philadelphia, PA 19103, or call (800) 810-4145, ext. 5000, or e-mail special.markets@perseusbooks.com.

10 9 8 7 6 5 4 3 2 1

Contents

Acknowledgments

My sincere thanks go to Bob Pigeon, executive editor with Da Capo Press, for commissioning this work. It turned out that Bob and I had shared a fascination with the Great Fire of Rome for many years.

I also extend grateful thanks to my New York literary agent, Richard Curtis, for putting Bob and me together.

And, as always, I record my gratitude to my wife, Louise. She has been the great fire in my life for the past twenty-eight years.

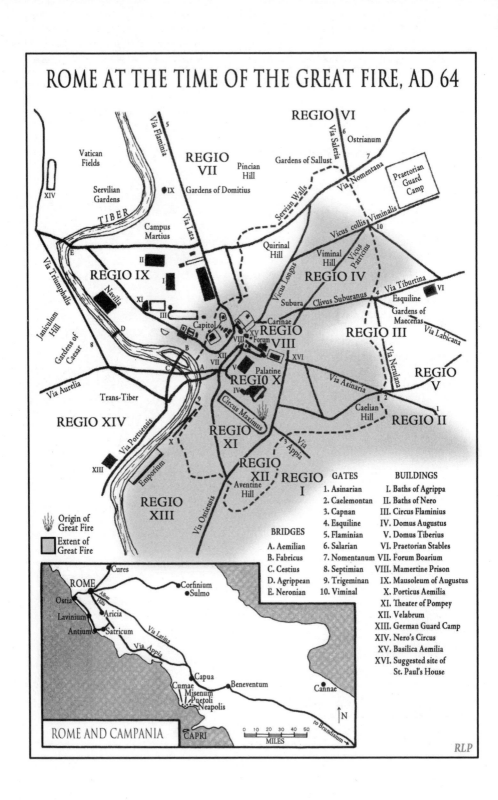

ROME AT THE TIME OF THE GREAT FIRE, AD 64

Via Flaminia
REGIO VI
5
Via Salaria
6
Ostrianum
7
REGIO VII
Pincian Hill
Gardens of Sallust
Vatican Fields
Gardens of Domitius
IX
Via Lata
Via Nomentana
Praetorian Guard Camp
Servilian Gardens
XIV
TIBER
Campus Martius
Servian Walls
Vicus collis
Viminalis
10
E
Quirinal Hill
Vicus Patricius
Via Triumphalis
II
REGIO IX
I
Viminal Hill
Vicus Longus
REGIO IV
Via Tiburtina
VI
Navelia
XI
III
Subura
Clivus Suburanus
Esquiline
Gardens of Maecenas
Via Labicana
Janiculum Hill
Capitol
Carinae
Forum
REGIO VIII
REGIO III
Gardens of Caesar
D
8
B
VIII
XV
Via Nerulana
REGIO V
Via Aurelia
C
A
XII
VII
XVI
Via Asinaria
2
Trans-Tiber
V
Palatine
Caelian Hill
REGIO II
REGIO X
REGIO XIV
IV
Circus Maximus
1
9
REGIO XI
3
Via Appia
X
REGIO XII
REGIO I
Via Portuensis
Aventine Hill
Emporium
REGIO XIII
XIII
Via Ostiensis

GATES	BUILDINGS
1. Asinarian	I. Baths of Agrippa
2. Caelemontan	II. Baths of Nero
3. Capnan	III. Circus Flaminius
4. Esquiline	IV. Domus Augustus
5. Flaminian	V. Domus Tiberius
6. Salarian	VI. Praetorian Stables
7. Nomentanum	VII. Forum Boarium
8. Septimian	VIII. Mamertine Prison
9. Trigeminan	IX. Mausoleum of Augustus
10. Viminal	X. Porticus Aemilia
	XI. Theater of Pompey
	XII. Velabrum
	XIII. German Guard Camp
	XIV. Nero's Circus
	XV. Basilica Aemilia
	XVI. Suggested site of St. Paul's House

BRIDGES
A. Aemilian
B. Fabricus
C. Cestius
D. Agrippean
E. Neronian

Origin of Great Fire
Extent of Great Fire

ROME AND CAMPANIA

Cures
ROME
Corfinium
Sulmo
Ostia
Allien
Tilia
Lavinium
Aricia
Antium
Satricum
Via Latina
Via Appia
Capua
Beneventum
Cannae
Cumae
Misenum
Puetoli
Neapolis
CAPRI

0 10 20 30 40 50
MILES

N

to Brundisium

RLP

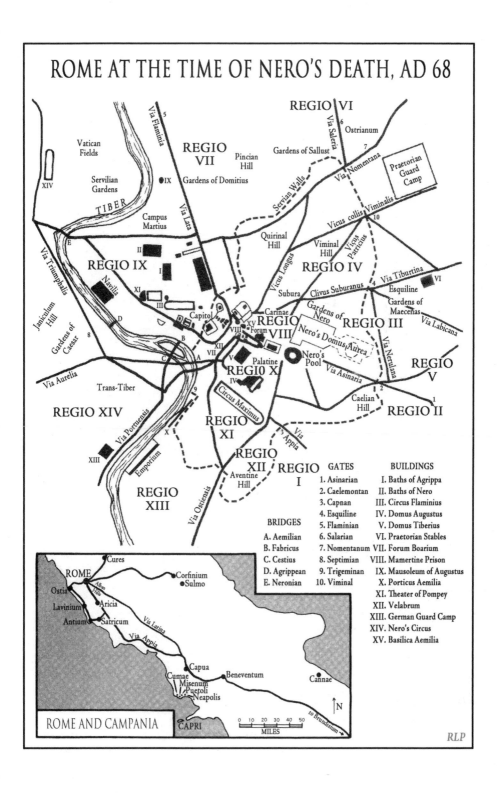

ROME AT THE TIME OF NERO'S DEATH, AD 68

Vatican Fields

Via Flaminia 5

REGIO VI

REGIO VII

Pincian Hill

Gardens of Sallust

Via Salaria 6

Ostrianum

7

Via Nomentana

Praetorian Guard Camp

Servilian Gardens

IX

Gardens of Domitius

Servian Walls

XIV

TIBER

Campus Martius

Via Lata

Vicus collis Viminalis

10

Quirinal Hill

Viminal Hill

Vicus Patricius

E

REGIO IX

II

I

Vicus Longus

REGIO IV

Via Tiburtina

VI

Navilia

XI

III

Capitol

Subura

Clivus Suburanus

4

Esquiline

Gardens of Maecenas

Via Labicana

Janiculum Hill

Gardens of Caesar

8

D

B

C

A

XII

VII

Carinae

Gardens of Nero

xv Forum

VIII REGIO VIII

Nero's Domus Aurea

REGIO III

Via Neronian

REGIO V

Via Triumphalis

Via Aurelia

Trans-Tiber

9

V

Palatine

REGIO X

IV

Nero's Pool

Via Asinaria

Caelian Hill

2

REGIO II

1

REGIO XIV

Via Portuensis

X

Circus Maximus

REGIO XI

3

Via Appia

Emporium

XIII

REGIO XIII

REGIO XII

Aventine Hill

REGIO I

Via Ostiensis

GATES

1. Asinarian
2. Caelemontan
3. Capnan
4. Esquiline
5. Flaminian
6. Salarian
7. Nomentanum
8. Septimian
9. Trigeminan
10. Viminal

BRIDGES

A. Aemilian
B. Fabricus
C. Cestius
D. Agrippean
E. Neronian

BUILDINGS

I. Baths of Agrippa
II. Baths of Nero
III. Circus Flaminius
IV. Domus Augustus
V. Domus Tiberius
VI. Praetorian Stables
VII. Forum Boarium
VIII. Mamertine Prison
IX. Mausoleum of Augustus
X. Porticus Aemilia
XI. Theater of Pompey
XII. Velabrum
XIII. German Guard Camp
XIV. Nero's Circus
XV. Basilica Aemilia

Cures

ROME

Corfinium
Sulmo

Ostia

Alban Hill

Aricia

Lavinium

Antium

Satricum

Via Latina

Via Appia

Capua

Beneventum

Cannae

Cumae
Misenum
Puteoli
Neapolis

N

ROME AND CAMPANIA

CAPRI

to Brundisium

0 10 20 30 40 50
MILES

RLP

Nero Claudius Caesar Augustus Germanicus, 37–68 AD
(Antiquarium of the Palatine)

INTRODUCTION

Rome's Great Fire is one of the best known of all historical events. Yet, strangely, few books have been written about the fire and the events surrounding what came to be one of history's great turning points—the end of the Roman dynasty created by Julius Caesar.

Could it be that we think we know all there is to know about that great catastrophe? Who, after all, has not heard the story about the mad emperor Nero setting fire to Rome and then fiddling while the city burned around him, only for him to blame the Christians for the fire and to make human torches of them? Ah, but was Nero mad, did he set the fire, did he fiddle, and did he in fact burn a single Christian? Was there much more to the Great Fire than previously believed?

In the twentieth century, many scholars and historians began to reappraise Nero the ruler. Has Nero been misrepresented down through the ages? Certainly, the fiddling incident can quickly be consigned to myth. The fiddle was an instrument that did not emerge in Europe until a millennium after Nero. So, Nero did not fiddle while Rome burned. Did he perhaps play some instrument? The lyre, for example? Yes, he was a noted player of the small, harplike lyre, the only stringed instrument used by Romans in classical times. But did he play the lyre at Rome on July 19, AD 64, or during the following days, while Rome burned?

If we are to believe Tacitus, one of Rome's more reliable first-century historians, who lived through the Great Fire as a nine-year-old, Nero did not play the lyre at Rome while the city burned. But he did play the

1

lyre on the night the fire broke out—Tacitus put Nero at the city of Antium, modern-day Anzio, on the west coast of Italy, playing the lyre.
Not that this would preclude Nero from having ordered the lighting of
the fire.

Nero, said Tacitus, played the lyre in a musical competition at Antium, the emperor's birthplace, on the evening of July 19. After he was
informed of the fire, he returned to the capital, where he industriously
directed firefighting operations and the provision of shelter and food for
the population. It was another Roman historian, Cassius Dio, a senator,
onetime consul, general, and governor of several Roman provinces, who
wrote that Nero gleefully played the lyre at Rome while the city burned,
and it is primarily from him that the fiddling-while-Rome-burned story
has come down to us. But Cassius Dio wrote his version of events some
165 years after the Great Fire. And in writing what he did about Nero
and the fire, Dio evidently misinterpreted or misquoted Tacitus and another first-century Roman historian, Suetonius.

Here, in part, is what Dio said, in the third century, about the way
the Great Fire of Rome started, laying the blame for the conflagration
squarely at the feet of Nero: "He secretly sent out men who pretended to
be drunk or engaged in other kinds of mischief, and caused them to first
set fire to one or two or even several buildings in different parts of the
city, so that the people were at their wits end, not being able to find any
beginning of the trouble nor to put an end to it."[1] This claim by Dio, that
the fire of AD 64 was deliberately set in a number of buildings in different parts of the city, is at variance with the information from Tacitus.
The Tacitus version, which is widely accepted by historians, says that the
Great Fire began at a single location, the Circus Maximus. But let us follow Dio's line a little further.

He also wrote, after graphically describing how the fire affected the
city's million or more residents and caused widespread grief: "While the
whole population was in this state of mind, and many, crazed by the disaster, were leaping into the very flames, Nero went up to the roof of the
Palatium [his palace on Rome's Palatine Hill], from which there was the
best general view of the greater part of the conflagration, and assuming
the dress of a lyre-player, he sang the 'Capture of Troy,' as he called the

song himself, though, to the eyes of the spectators, it was the Capture of Rome."[2]

To begin with, everything on the Palatine Hill, including the Palatium, was, as Dio himself would write, destroyed in the fire. Along with every other building on the Palatine Hill, the palace was consumed in the fire's first stage. Even if we assume that Dio meant that Nero ascended the Palatium roof to play his lyre during the early stages of the fire, before the flames reached the palace, no other Roman writer put Nero on the roof of his palace at Rome, playing the lyre, at any time during the Great Fire. Tacitus wrote that Nero only set off back to Rome when he heard that the fire was approaching his palace.

Dio clearly took his lead from Nero's biographer Suetonius, whose parents actually lived at Rome at the time of the Great Fire—Suetonius himself was born some five years later. Suetonius made Nero culpable for the conflagration, writing:

Pretending to be disgusted by the drab old buildings and narrow, winding streets of Rome, he [Nero] brazenly set fire to the city. Although a party of ex-consuls caught his attendants, armed with tow [the coarse and broken part of flax and hemp] and blazing torches, trespassing on their property, they dare not interfere.

Suetonius went on to say of Nero:

He also coveted the sites of several granaries, solidly built in stone, near the Golden House. Having knocked down their walls with siege engines, he set the interiors ablaze. The terror lasted for six days and seven nights, causing many people to take shelter in monuments and tombs. Nero's men destroyed not only a vast number of apartment blocks, but mansions that had belonged to famous generals and were still decorated with their triumphal trophies. Temples, too, vowed and dedicated by (Rome's) kings, and others during the Punic and Gallic wars. In fact, very ancient monuments of historical interest that had survived up to that time. Nero watched the conflagration from the Tower of Maecenas enraptured by what he called "the beauty of the flames," then put on his tragedian's costume and sang "The Sack of Ilium" from beginning to end.[3]

Here then was Suetonius' account, written several decades after the event, in which Nero was described as singing while Rome burned, but not from the roof of his palace. Cassius Dio wrote his history of Rome using the works of earlier writers, adding his own opinions, biases, and flourishes—such as changing the name of the tune supposedly played by Nero, apparently to give more emphasis to the claim that Nero celebrated the destruction of his capital. And, of course, Suetonius' account of the fire was one to which Dio would have had access long after it was written.

Even though Tacitus makes no mention of it, there is a high probability that when Nero arrived back at Rome from Antium, he did indeed observe the fire from the vantage point of the Tower of Maecenas, which stood on the Esquiline Hill, in the imperial gardens of Maecenas—the fire was eventually brought to a halt at the foot of the Esquiline. And perhaps Nero did sing a song or two during that fraught week of the fire. But did he celebrate the fire, and did he in fact set it, as Suetonius, alone among first- or second-century writers, claimed and as Dio much later echoed?

Some of Suetonius' "facts" in his book *De vita Caesarium*, or Lives of the Caesars, in which he wrote the above passages about the Great Fire, are demonstrably incorrect, while others are mystifyingly jumbled, and some, obviously invented. Suetonius apparently commenced writing this book during the reign of the emperor Hadrian, when the historian had charge of the imperial records held in the Tabularium, Rome's official archives. Suetonius seems to have only completed the first three sections of his book on the Caesars, covering Julius Caesar, Augustus Caesar, and Tiberius Caesar, when he fell out with the emperor and lost both his post and his access to the official records after acting impolitely toward the empress Sabina.

Up to that point, his book abounds with quotes from the letters, journals, and unpublished memoirs of the figures he wrote about. From that point on, Suetonius had to rely almost entirely on other sources for his information—mostly gossip. Consequently, in his biography about Nero, we often find attributions like "some say," "according to my informants," and "it is said," as Suetonius relates one sensational and scurrilous anecdote about Nero after another. To his readers, ancient and modern, Suetonius' revelations about Nero and his imperial subjects made for risqué reading. They do not necessarily make for reliable history.

Flavius Josephus, the Jewish rabbi, general, and author who became a favorite of the Flavian emperors, Vespasian, Titus, and Domitian, and who was at Rome at the time of the Great Fire, would write, some years later: "There have been a great many who have composed the history of Nero, some of whom have departed from the factual truth because of favor, having received benefits from him." Josephus would have been referring here to the likes of Cluvius Rufus and Pliny the Elder, both of whom are known to have written about Nero, although their works, to which Tacitus several times referred, are no longer extant. "While others," Josephus went on, "out of hatred for him [Nero], and the great ill will that they bore him, have so impudently raved against him with their lies, that they justly deserve to be condemned."[4]

One of the authors who fell into Josephus' latter category would have been historian Fabius Rusticus. Considered the "finest of modern writers" by Tacitus, Fabius had been raised to his "position of honor" through his friendship with and patronage by Seneca, and he would subsequently have resented Seneca's bloody end, giving him cause to hate Nero and to be among those who "impudently raved against him" after the emperor's demise. Even Tacitus had to admit that of all his contemporaries, Fabius was the only author who claimed that Nero had lusted after his own mother, Agrippina the Younger. Every other historian of the day, said Tacitus, had written that it was Agrippina who had attempted to seduce Nero, to regain her power over him, and that this was the accepted truth of the matter.[5]

Josephus himself had no reason to love Nero. It had been on Nero's orders and in Nero's name that Vespasian and his son Titus had gone to war against the Jews in Palestine in AD 67 and destroyed Jerusalem and the Temple. Yet Josephus, who claimed that his only interest was in the truth, had no time for those who falsely vilified Nero. Suetonius fitted into the category of those "impudent liars" who wrote falsehoods about Nero. It is easy to suspect Suetonius' fabrications, which seem far-fetched even for the political and moral climate of that time, but it is not as easy to prove them. "Nor am I surprised by those who have written lies about Nero," Josephus continued, "since in their writings they have not preserved the historical truth regarding those events that took place in prior times, even when the subjects [of those works] could have in no way incurred their hatred, since those writers lived long after their day." Josephus may have died before Suetonius published his Lives of the Caesars, with its sensational claims about the habits, lifestyles, and peccadilloes of earlier Caesars, as well as those of Nero. So, other authors were equally scurrilous. "As far as those authors who have no interest in the truth are concerned," Josephus went on, "they can write what they like, for that is what they delight in doing."[6]

The question of veracity in the works of Roman authors brings us to the widespread modern belief that in an effort to find scapegoats for the fire, Nero martyred the Christians of Rome, a belief that has become embodied in Christian legend. Where did that belief originate? In Suetonius' *Nero*, we find the brief reference in his description of Nero's overall life and career: "Punishments were also inflicted on the Christians, a sect professing a new and mischievous religious belief."[7] This lone sentence appears out of context and without any reference to or connection with the Great Fire and can almost certainly be dismissed as a later fictitious insertion in Suetonius' original text by a Christian copyist.

Surprisingly, Tacitus, in his *Annals*, claims that Nero specifically punished the Christians at Rome for the Great Fire, though the *Annals* can be regarded as an otherwise quite reliable work in terms of historical fact. As typified by the listing for "Nero" in recent editions of *Encyclopaedia Britannica*, many modern-day historians believe that this tale of Christian persecution was apocryphal and was inserted in Tacitus' *Annals* by a Christian copyist, centuries later.[8]

None of the copies of the great Roman books such as the *Annals* that exist today are originals. All are later copies, often created centuries after the first edition, in the laborious, handwritten production process that all books went through prior to the invention of the printing press, making the insertion of invented interpolations simple and, unless a reader was in possession of the original text, undetectable. These copies of ancient Roman works were found, over the past several hundred years, in the libraries of Christian monasteries and institutions (the task of writing books by hand became the province of monks in Christian society) and in the private libraries of devout Christian aristocrats.

One of the reasons for suspecting the authenticity of the Christian reference in Tacitus, and the reference in Suetonius, is that the term *Christian* makes no other appearance in Roman literature of the first century. Tellingly, neither Saint Paul nor Saint Peter, who are believed to have died during Nero's reign, describe their followers as Christians in their Gospel letters. Neither does the New Testament's Acts of the Apostles, thought to have been written by Saint Luke. Many early followers of Jesus Christ, a Jew, were Jewish, like Paul and Peter. To the Roman masses, this religion based around the Nazarene was nothing more than a Jewish cult, and so its followers were, for a long time, labeled Jews.

Cassius Dio, writing in the third century, described how, in AD 95, the emperor Domitian had a number of people arrested, including the emperor's own cousin Flavius Clemens, and Clemens' wife Flavia Domitilla—who was also related to the emperor, being the daughter of Domitian's sister. "The charge brought against them both was that of atheism, a charge on which many others who drifted into Jewish ways were condemned," said Dio.[9] Many later Christian scholars believed that "Jewish ways" was a reference to the Christian faith. They cited the case of another leading Roman arrested at this same time—according to Dio, on the same charge—and who, like Clemens, was executed. The man in question was Manius Acilius Glabrio. In support of Glabrio's supposed adherence to Christianity, some scholars have claimed that his remains were found in a Christian catacomb at Rome. Critics of this supposition point out that this catacomb was only first used several centuries after Glabrio's death.

Nowhere in Dio's text are these people referred to as Christians, a term in common use by Dio's time in the third century. To further erode the claim that Glabrio was a Christian, and a Christian martyr at that, Suetonius, who was a man of twenty-six or so and living at Rome at the time of Glabrio's execution, makes no reference to any charge of atheism against the man. In fact, according to Suetonius, Glabrio was one of three former consuls executed by Domitian because they were "accused of conspiracy," not for atheism or "drifting into Jewish ways," as Dio wrote more than a century later. Suetonius did, however, write that Glabrio was initially exiled before being executed in exile for conspiracy.[10] As was the case in the reign of Nero, frequently a person initially exiled for conspiracy would ultimately be executed as a consequence of the original charge.

Less important, perhaps, is that passages in the *Annals* refer to Pontius Pilatus (Pilate) as a "procurator," a title always accorded Pilate in Christian literature. Pilate actually held the lesser rank of prefect in Judea, something that Tacitus, who had access to the official records at Rome's Tabularium and frequently quoted from them in his *Annals*, should have known.

After explaining that there was a widespread "sinister belief that the conflagration was the result of an order" from the emperor, the *Annals* go on:

> Consequently, to get rid of the report, Nero fastened the guilt and inflicted the most exquisite tortures on a class hated for their abominations, called Christians by the populous. Christus, from whom the name had its origin, suffered the extreme penalty during the reign of Tiberius at the hands of one of our procurators, Pontius Pilatus, and a most mischievous superstition, thus checked for the moment, again broke out not only in Judea, the source of the evil, but even in Rome, where all things hideous and shameful from every part of the world find their center and become popular.
>
> Accordingly, an arrest was first made of all who pleaded guilty. Then, on their information, an immense multitude was convicted, not so much of the crime of firing the city, as of hatred against mankind. Mockery of every sort was added to their deaths. Covered with the skins of beasts, they were torn by dogs and perished, or were nailed to crosses, or were doomed to the flames and burnt, to serve as a nightly illumination, when daylight had expired. Nero offered his gar-

dens for the spectacle, and was exhibiting a show in the circus, while he mingled with the people in the dress of a charioteer or stood aloft in a chariot. Hence even for the criminals who deserved extreme and exemplary punishment, there arose a feeling of compassion. For, it was not, as it was portrayed, for the public good, but to satisfy one man's cruelty, that they were being destroyed.[11]

That "an immense multitude" was arrested is another cause to doubt that these people were Christians. Even the Christian Church acknowledges that the Christian community at Rome in AD 64 would have been quite small. The Apostle Paul, in his letters, usually listed the many leading Christians of the city or town where he was staying; in his letters from Rome of AD 60–62, he named not a single local Christian. In a letter apparently written in AD 66, while he was incarcerated at Rome for the second time, he specifically named just three male and one female Christians living at Rome; from their names, those four appear to have been noncitizens, probably former slaves.[12]

That there were indeed Christians at Rome at the time is affirmed by Acts of the Apostles, which referred to a small party of Christians coming out of the city to meet Paul at his last stop outside Rome while on his way to the capital in the spring of AD 60.[13] But for Tacitus to describe this small community as a "class" at Rome does not ring true. The observation that some of these people were executed on crosses by Nero following the Great Fire tells us not that they were Christians, but that they were not Roman citizens. Crucifixion was the regular method of execution for noncitizens convicted of a crime throughout the Roman empire, for centuries before and after the crucifixion of Christ. The use of crosses for these particular prisoners' executions was not a deliberate allusion to, or a mockery of, Christianity. It had nothing to with Christianity.

Was this entire section of the *Annals* text a forgery, as some believe? Or did the person responsible for the interpolation merely change a word here and add a sentence there to distort Tacitus' original, for religious propaganda purposes? What if, for example, the original text had described those arrested and executed for starting the fire as followers of the Egyptian goddess Isis, and not as Christians? In that instance, all the interpolator had to do was replace "Egyptians," as followers of Isis were known, with the word "Christians."

The worship of Isis was among the most popular of the religious cults followed at Rome by noncitizens during the first century. The first altars to Isis appeared on the Capitoline Mount early in the first century BC. Destroyed by the Senate in 58 BC, they were soon replaced by a temple to Isis, the Iseum, which was leveled on Senate orders eight years later. The so-called First Triumvirate, Octavian, Antony, and Lepidus, had a new temple to Isis and her consort Serapis erected in 43 BC—the Iseum Campense—on the Campus Martius, on Rome's northern outskirts. Other large Isea, or temples to Isis, would eventually be built at Rome— one on the Capitoline Mount and another in Regio III, with smaller ones on the Caelian, Aventine, and Esquiline hills.

Isis, who was seen as a caring goddess welcoming both men and women, rich and poor, and who promised eternal life and aid with her followers' earthly woes, soon had thousands of followers among all classes at Rome, but particularly among the lower classes. The cult of Isis involved certain mysteries, which Isiacs were not permitted to reveal to nonbelievers. There were even a number of similarities between the cult of Isis and the later Christian faith, not the least being initiation by baptism in water, the belief in resurrection, and the adoration of a holy mother and son—Isis and Horus. Later statues of the Virgin Mary nursing the infant Jesus Christ bear a striking resemblance to the earlier statues of Isis nursing her son Horus, which may well have inspired them.

By AD 64, the cult of Isis had been in and out of favor at Rome for a century. In 21 BC, Augustus' efficient right-hand man, Marcus Agrippa, forbade the rites of the cult of Isis to be practiced within a mile of Rome. In AD 18–19, during the early years of the reign of the next emperor, Tiberius, four thousand "Egyptians" and Jews, all of them freedmen of military age (18 to 46), were rounded up at Rome and sent to repress brigands on the island of Sardinia.

The remaining Egyptians and Jews at the capital, including those who held Roman citizenship, were required to either abandon their faith or depart Italy by a given date. In addition, said Suetonius, Tiberius forced "all citizens who embraced these superstitious faiths to burn their religious vestments and other accessories."[14] Those priests of Isis who failed to give up their faith were crucified, on Tiberius' orders. According to the author Philo Judaeus, a first-century Jewish elder at Alexandria, this pre-Christian persecution of the Jews was driven by Tiberius' Praetorian prefect, Sejanus, who possessed, in Philo's words, a "hatred of, and hostile designs against, the Jewish nation."[15] Tiberius, meanwhile, was said to have personally cast a statue of Isis into the Tiber River.

Under the next emperor, Gaius—Caligula, as we know him—both Egyptians and Jews returned to Rome, and Isis was officially adopted into the Roman pantheon. Caligula even dedicated his new palace on the Palatine Hill to the goddess, calling it the Aula Isiaca, or Hall of Isis. But his successor Claudius expelled all followers of Isis from Rome for, according to Suetonius, "creating disturbances." Jews were separately banned from the city by Claudius for similar "disturbances."[16] Under Nero, not only was the cult of Isis permitted at Rome, but the emperor also added several Isiac feast days to the official calendar. Nero was going through a period in which he was obsessed with all things Egyptian, and it has been suggested that his interest in Isis came about through the influence of Chaeremon, former librarian at the Sarapium, the temple of Sarapis, at Alexandria. This Egyptian Stoic was said to be briefly Nero's tutor when he was a boy.

It has also been suggested that once Nero became emperor, Apollonius of Tyrana, a client of Nero's who, guided by Egyptian priests, professed himself to be a teacher from heaven and was a follower of Isis, influenced Nero's beliefs. Many scholars believe that Nero, wracked by guilt after he brought about the murder of his mother in AD 59, began a search for spirituality that saw him, for a time at least, personally embrace the cult of Isis, the mother goddess. While his interest in Egypt and Egyptian customs had not waned by AD 64, Nero seems to have moved on from Isis in his restless quest for spiritual relief.

Some Christian legends even suggest that Nero consulted the Apostle Paul while the evangelist was at Rome, and that Nero's freedwoman mistress Acte and his official cup-bearer at the Palatium were converted to Christianity by Paul. It was through this pair's influence, so legend has it, that the emperor consulted Paul. The traditional belief that Acte was a Christian, or certainly the modern perpetuation of it, stems from the 1895 novel *Quo Vadis* by Nobel Prize–winning Polish author Henryk Sienkiewicz, who made the character of Acte a Christian. Part of the attraction of Paul's creed to Nero supposedly was the belief in a holy mother and a virgin birth—a belief shared by Christianity, the cult of Isis, and other Eastern religions—but this is contradicted by the fact that the Virgin Mary never featured in Paul's teachings.

Tacitus makes it clear that despite every benevolent act by Nero immediately following the Great Fire, which, Tacitus says brought him great short-term popularity with the public, he could not overcome the power of the rumor that swept through the city even faster than the all-devouring flames: that he had caused the disaster. It was in character for Nero, a twenty-six-year-old dominated by others all his early life, wracked by major self-confidence issues, and plagued by a perplexing rumor campaign that set the blame for the fire at his feet, to find scapegoats, to shift the blame from his own shoulders.

The cult of Isis, while initially attracting Nero, had come to disappoint him. In the end, he very publicly scorned the cult. In laying blame for the Great Fire at the feet of the followers of Isis, he could have been sure of tapping into widespread public distaste for the cult. The followers of Isis were generally disliked by other Romans, particularly those of the upper classes. The poet Juvenal, for example, ridiculed followers of Isis. His contemporary, Plutarch, the Greek historian who served as a priest at the Temple of Apollo at Delphi at one time, considered the cult of Isis detestable. Suetonius, writing early in the second century, described the cult of Isis as "that rather questionable order."[17]

One of the criticisms that most Romans had of the cult was its adoration of animals—the crocodile, the ibis, and the long-tailed ape among them. Isis herself was depicted with the horns of a bull jutting from her head, while her male consort, Sarapis, god of the underworld, was often represented as a bull. In the Navigium Isidis, the festival of Isis that took place on March 5, which became part of the Roman calendar as the opening of the Mediterranean sailing season each year with the blessing of the fleets, a priest wearing the dog head of Anubis, the Egyptian god of death, took part in the official procession that opened the festivities. These animal gods were hideous to Romans accustomed to worshipping deities that took human form, while participation in the cult was considered shameful.

Other evidence hints at the identity of those who were executed on Nero's orders after the Great Fire. Look again at what the *Annals* says about them: "Mockery of every sort was added to their deaths. Covered with the skins of beasts, they were torn by dogs and perished." Consider also that followers of Isis were seen by Romans to worship animals, and that Anubis, the Egyptian god of the dead, had the head of a dog. Conversely, the priests of Isis eschewed all contact with animal products, which were considered unclean, and wore linen garments and sandals made from papyrus. For all these reasons, the mockery to which Tacitus refers—with the condemned made to wear animal skins as they were torn to pieces by dogs—strongly suggests that these people were followers of Isis.

There was one other connection: As Nero would have known, fire played a key part in Isiac religious observances. This made the burning to death of some of the prisoners another mockery of the cult, just as it would have made the connection between the worship of Isis and the Great Fire credible to Romans at the time. It is not impossible that followers of Isis were indeed guilty of either spreading the fire, to "cleanse" Rome, or of possibly setting the second-stage blaze in the Aemilian property.

The first part of the relevant passage from Tacitus, as he wrote it, may have originally read something like the following: "Consequently, to get rid of the report, Nero fastened the guilt and inflicted the most exquisite tortures on a class hated for their abominations, followers of the cult of Isis, called Egyptians by the populace, which had taken root at Rome, where all things hideous and shameful find their center and become popular."

All the indications are that the cult of Isis was subdued over the next few years after the Great Fire, before one of the first three of the four emperors of the tumultuous year of AD 68–69—Galba, Otho, or Vitellius—

again permitted the worship of Isis. So rehabilitated did the cult of Isis become under the Flavian emperors that in AD 71, Vespasian and his son Titus actually spent a vigil in the Iseum on the Campus Martius the night prior to celebrating their joint triumph for putting down the Jewish revolt in Judea.

Vespasian's second son, Domitian, last of the three Flavian emperors, owed his life to his disguising himself as a priest of Isis in December AD 69. He may have shaved his head as the priests did—they shaved their entire bodies every three days—and donned their simple, ankle-length linen robe, to effect his escape from the burning Capitoline complex, accompanied by his cousin Clemens, who was similarly disguised. They may also have worn the dog's-head mask of Anubis, as was the case when an aedile named Marcus Volusius used the same disguise, that of a priest of Isis, to escape the First Triumvirate's proscriptions that followed the murder of Julius Caesar. Domitian's escape came when men of the emperor Vitellius' bodyguard, the so-called German Guard, were besieging Vespasian's brother Sabinus, his family members, and supporters on the Capitoline Mount.

Once he ascended the throne, Domitian declared himself the incarnation of Isis' consort Serapis and actively encouraged and promoted the cult. He repaired the Temple of Isis on the Campus Martius, which was seriously damaged in the fire of AD 80, and he decorated several other temples to Isis and Serapis, including the one on the Capitoline Mount. Domitian is also believed to have erected a new temple to Isis at Beneventum, in AD 88.

Historian Tacitus, a senator during the reign of Domitian, despised the cruel, vindictive young emperor and everything that he stood for, but was ashamed of himself for acquiescing to Domitian's bloody rule. Without doubt, like fellow historian Suetonius, Tacitus also despised the cult of Isis and had no hesitation in branding it "hideous and shameful," if for no other reason than the fact that it had been adopted by Domitian. In reality, it is doubtful that Tacitus, a clearly dedicated adherent of the Roman gods, had ever heard much about either Christianity or Christ, while he would have lifelong exposure to, and some knowledge of, the cult of Isis. This all made it much more likely that he would describe Isiacs as "hideous and shameful," but not Christians.

Yet, for all this discussion of fiddles and Christians, and questions about the mystery of who lit the fire, much more complex historical questions relating to the Great Fire need to be explored. The Rome of AD 64 was a bustling, flourishing metropolis that famously never slept. It was experiencing boom times, as was Rome's empire as a whole. Military disasters in the east and in Britain several years before were now recent history. In Britain, the Celtic war queen Boudicca and her rebels had been bloodily quashed in AD 60–61, and it was business as usual for Roman commerce there. In Armenia, brilliant Roman general Domitius Corbulo had twice overrun Armenian and Parthian forces and in AD 63 had forced the Parthian-born king of Armenia, Tiridates I, to become a Roman ally.

More than that, Corbulo had wrung agreement from Tiridates that he would come to Rome, bow down to Nero, and acknowledge him as his sovereign lord—which he would do in AD 66. Never before had a Parthian bowed down to a Roman emperor. Nero's fame and popularity were at their zenith with the ordinary Roman people. How is it then, that within four years of the Great Fire, Nero would be deserted by his people and forced to flee his throne? What changed the public's attitude toward, dampened their ardor for, and destroyed their loyalty to their young emperor, the last member of the revered family of the Caesars?

There had frequently been serious fires at Rome prior to AD 64, and several more conflagrations would destroy significant portions of the city over the forty years that followed. The next major blaze would be a deliberately lit fire that destroyed the Capitoline complex in AD 69. Another fire caused widespread devastation on the Campus Martius in AD 80, while yet another did serious damage in the center of Rome in AD 104.

Nonetheless, the destruction of almost two-thirds of Rome by a raging fire was a disaster matched only by the destruction of much of the city by the Celts in 390 BC. It was an event that undoubtedly traumatized the population. And within months of the AD 64 fire, several plots by both Roman aristocrats and officers of Nero's own palace guard to overthrow him would be exposed. Within another year of those plots, major revolts against Nero's rule would explode in Judea and Gaul, and the die would be cast. Nero's inglorious end was nigh.

This book explores two aspects of the Great Fire—the physical fire that engulfed the capital of the Roman world in AD 64 and the political fire unleashed in its wake and which led to the destruction of the Caesar dynasty. Using the texts of numerous classical authors as its sources, this book faithfully follows the lives of Nero and many of the figures whose fortunes would be affected by the Great Fire. The narrative begins as the year AD 64 began, on New Year's Day.

THE JANUARY OATH

Silence. The winter wind ruffled the golden-yellow horsehair parade plumes on their gleaming helmets. Large, curved, wooden shields bearing the thunderbolt emblem sat on their left arms. Right hands rested on the hilts of the Roman short sword, the *gladius*, sheathed on each man's right side. Rank upon rank upon rank of men in segmented body armor and blood red tunics. Recruited exclusively from Rome and central and southern Italy, the best-paid men in the Roman army. The Praetorians.

A young man of twenty-six stepped out onto the raised tribunal in front of them, wearing gold-embroidered white robes. Of average height, he was blue-eyed and blond-haired. Many here would have remembered him as a youth of sixteen, when first he stood before the Praetorians, nine years before, and won their approbation. Back then, he was handsome—pretty, even, despite the thick bull neck that he had inherited from his great-great-grandfather Mark Antony. Now, this first day of AD 64, he was pudgy, had a pot belly, and was going bald. This was Nero Claudius Caesar Augustus Germanicus, grandson of Germanicus Julius Caesar, son of Agrippina the Younger, and nephew and adopted son and heir of the emperor Claudius. This was the emperor Nero Caesar.

"Hail, Caesar!" The cry, bellowed by fourteen thousand voices, boomed around the thick walls of the Castra Praetoria, the castle-like barracks of the Praetorian Cohorts, or Praetorian Guard as later writers would call them, in Regio VI, the city of Rome's Sixth Precinct. And then the soldiers broke into applause, as was the custom when a Roman commander in chief came before his men.

Nero smiled and waved a hand in thanks, looking down at the Praetorian standard-bearer proudly holding aloft his standard with its golden representation of Victoria, winged goddess of victory. Behind the standard, the tribunes of each of the fourteen cohorts stood in front of their men in parade armor, which glowed with gold and silver. These officers of upper-class Equestrian Order rank—misleadingly called "knights" by latter-day authors—were career soldiers, the best of the best, men such as Subrius Flavus, Gavius Silvanus, and Statius Proximus. Just fourteen men held the rank of tribune of the Praetorian Cohorts at any one time, and many occupied their powerful posts for decades. Nero lifted his gaze to the cohorts, each of a thousand clean-shaven, physically imposing conscripts headed by standard-bearers clad in lion-skin capes. And he saw their centurions, officers promoted from the ranks after proving their worth on active service.

Several men stood behind the young emperor on the tribunal, also attired in their best armor—among them the two Praetorian prefects, Sophonius Tigellinus and Faenius Rufus, and, in their purple-bordered white senatorial robes, the two new consuls for the year, Gaius Laecanius and Marcus Licinius. All joined the applause until it faded away. Silence returned. The white-cloaked Praetorian tribune of the duty cohort, charged today with the duty of narrator, now stepped to the front of the balcony and barked a command. He then proceeded to lead all the men in reciting an oath. Again, thousands of voices sounded around the colonnaded parade square in a unified chant:

> I swear, that I will obey the emperor willingly and implicitly in all his commands, that I will never desert, and that I will always be ready to sacrifice my life for the empire of Rome.[1]

It was New Year's Day, AD 64, and the men of the Praetorian Cohorts, Roman citizens all, Italians all, were renewing the oath of allegiance that all citizen soldiers around the Roman Empire took on January 1 every year.

Nero was in good spirits as he departed the barracks after the oath-taking ceremony, carried in a litter by brawny young slaves, with a cohort of tall, blond, bearded men of his bodyguard of the *Germani corporis custodes*, the so-called German Guard, marching in close order around him. The men of the ten "German" cohorts came from along the Rhine, primarily from the old kingdom of Batavia, modern-day Holland. They wore the same armor and helmets that the Praetorians wore, but the "German" shields were flatter and carried a different emblem, and their cavalry-style swords were longer.

Cheering, applauding members of the public lined the street. Children looked in awe as the closed litter of their emperor passed. An entourage of imperial freedmen and slaves trailed along behind the litter. The emperor was heading back to his palace, the Palatium, on the Palatine Hill in the center of the city, to conduct his business for the day before preparing for a lavish banquet with his most intimate friends. Before the sun had risen that morning, Nero had gone to the Capitoline Mount, where a great crowd of plebeians had gathered to declare their allegiance to him and offer prayers for his health, safety, and prosperity in the coming year, as was the custom each New Year's Day.

At dawn, in his capacity as *pontifex maximus*, chief priest of Rome, Nero had presided when the special New Year sacrifice was conducted in the Arx, the most sacred area on the Capitoline Mount, in the presence of the augurs and the priests of Rome's various religious orders. The organs of the sacrificial bird had been unblemished, and the haruspex, the chief augur, had declared that the omens were auspicious for a good year for Rome and for the emperor. All was well in Nero's world. All was well in the Roman world.

"Never had there been so profound a peace," historian Tacitus said of this period.[2] A revolt in Britain that had almost seen the province overrun by the Celtic war queen Boudicca and her hundreds of thousands of rebel Britons had been brutally put down three years before, and Roman rule and Roman commerce were again flourishing in Britain. Trouble in the east, which had seen the Parthians occupy Armenia and threaten Syria and other Roman provinces, had finally and convincingly been terminated just a year back by Nero's doughty, determined general Lucius Domitius Corbulo. Not only had the Parthians been thrown back, but Corbulo had forced the Parthian-born king of Armenia, Tiridates I, to become a Roman ally and promise to come to Rome to bow down to Nero and acknowledge him as his sovereign lord. What a boost to Nero's prestige that would be!

For several years now, Nero had been expressing his artistic side, on a limited scale. "Nero from early boyhood turned his lively genius" to the arts, said Tacitus. "He carved, painted, sang." Nero also exhibited some ability as a poet. Tacitus begrudgingly credited him with "occasionally composing verses that showed that he had the rudiments of learning."[3] Nero's biographer Suetonius would write that Nero "would dash off verses enthusiastically, without any effort," and that after Nero's death, his enemies would claim that he had stolen his best poems, which were published in Nero's lifetime, from other authors. But, said Suetonius, Nero's notebooks, in his own handwriting and complete with his corrections, came into the biographer's possession, and they proved, to him, that Nero was indeed the original creator.[4]

Nero possessed a singing voice of which he was proud, and he had become an accomplished player of the lyre, a stringed instrument like a small harp, with which he accompanied himself. "Music formed part of his childhood curriculum," said Suetonius, "and he developed a taste for it early."[5] Not long after he came to the throne, Nero had summoned the greatest lyre player of the day, Terpus, to sing to him after dinner at the Palatium. For several nights, Terpus had performed for the emperor, singing and playing until a late hour. Inspired by Terpus, Nero himself had taken up the study of the lyre and mastered it.

Nero had made his first public appearance as a singer by competing in the Juvenile Games as an adolescent, prior to becoming emperor. Since taking the throne, he had sung in the houses of friends and in the imperial gardens, before small but appreciative audiences made up of his intimates and retainers. These performances, he decided, were "on too small a scale for so fine a voice."[6] Now, with the coming of the new year, Nero had made a resolution—to take his talent to a much broader audience and compete in public singing contests.

Yet, for all his confidence in his own singing prowess, Nero was nervous of how the ordinary people of Rome would receive their emperor's performing on the public stage. Such a thing had never before occurred. He was not alone in this concern. When, back at the Palatium, Nero informed his senior advisers of his intention, they expressed fears that it would demean the emperor and detract from his authority. He would not give up the idea entirely, but the advisers were able to convince him to at least make his first public singing appearances away from the capital.

Public opinion was very important to Nero. He cared little for the ambitious, fickle, back-stabbing Roman nobility; his most intimate friends were almost entirely Equestrians and freedmen. The esteem of the ordinary people, on the other hand, mattered to him greatly. Suetonius said that Nero had "a thirst for popularity."[7] It was not so much a thirst as a perceived need. At the commencement of his reign his sage adviser, Seneca, would have counseled him to heed the mood of the masses if he wanted to retain his throne.

Augustus Caesar, Rome's first emperor, had been a master of gauging the public mood and pandering to it. Unlike Julius Caesar, who, in his determination to eclipse Pompey the Great, had ostentatiously celebrated every victory, accepted every honor, and paid the ultimate bloody price for his egotism. Augustus had known the limits of his people's tolerance and had died in his bed after a reign of almost half a century. His successor Tiberius, conscious of public opinion, had begun his reign with caution and restraint, but eventually lost touch with the man in the street and almost lost his throne to a usurper, Sejanus, as a result.

The next emperor, Gaius, or Caligula as we know him, had at the outset of his reign been buoyed by public expectations, as the son of the wildly popular Germanicus Caesar. This had, ironically, made him oblivious to public opinion. Caligula soon perished, dispatched by his own bodyguards and unmourned by his people. Claudius, Caligula's successor, had known how to keep the public amused and died popular because of it. To lose the goodwill of the people of Rome was a dangerous thing, and Nero was wise enough, or perhaps insecure enough, to know that an appearance by the emperor on stage at the capital before a public unprepared for such an unprecedented event could prove disastrous.

Nero now decided that once the season for competitions had begun, he would enter the annual contest held at Neapolis, modern-day Naples, on the west coast of Italy. Neapolis had been founded by Greek settlers in about 600 BC, and despite being captured by Rome in 326 BC, it had always retained a Greek flavor. The Greeks were considered by the Romans to be the great artists of their time, in all the arts, and Nero felt that an artist such as himself should appear among the Greeks and win their praise, and their prizes. Only then would he feel confident enough to appear on stage in front of the people who mattered, the public of Rome.

The idea of acclaim from the Greeks soon convinced Nero that after he made his debut at Neapolis, he would travel on to the province of Achaia, in southern Greece. There he would appear in all the major singing contests, which had been held for centuries, confident of "winning the well-known and sacred garlands of antiquity." Having won the Greek contests, Nero was convinced, said Tacitus, he could return home and to the stages of the capital, having evoked "with increased fame, the enthusiasm of the citizens" of Rome.[8]

THE RIVAL PREFECTS

The Praetorian prefect Tigellinus stood in the Forum, looking approvingly at the bustle of early-morning activity around the shops of the Aemilian Basilica. If business for the shopkeepers of the Aemila this winter's day was good, then that was good for Tigellinus. For, not only was Tigellinus one of the two prefects in charge of the Praetorian Cohorts. Tigellinus was also a man of business.

The first emperor of Rome, Augustus, had resumed the ancient practice of putting two prefects over the Praetorian Cohorts. Rome's oldest military unit had been created by the praetors of Rome as their personal protection force after the formation of the Roman Republic in 509 BC. Later, the two consuls elected to power each year had controlled the Praetorian Cohorts, with each appointing one senior officer to jointly command them. By the time of Julius Caesar, the Praetorian Cohorts had fallen into disuse, only to be reformed by Mark Antony in 44 BC in the wake of Caesar's assassination, again as a personal protection force. At that time, the most senior Praetorian officers were their tribunes. This changed with the coming of the emperors. Augustus made the Praetorians more than bodyguards. Employing the hand-picked auxiliary troops of the *Germani corporis custodes* for his close personal protection, he had turned the nine Praetorian Cohorts that then existed into his political police; they had become his enforcers and executioners, and via their muscle and steel, they and their commanders wielded enormous power.

It had been wise Augustus' intent that a check should be placed on the misuse of Praetorian power by emulating the old custom of putting not one but two men in overall charge of these household troops, with both men holding the equal rank of prefect. Augustus' successor, Tiberius, had learned the wisdom of this through bitter experience when his sole appointee, Sejanus, had attempted to usurp him. Later emperors adhered to the policy of appointing a pair of Praetorian prefects, but Claudius, several years before his death, and under the influence of his last wife, Agrippina the Younger, the mother of Nero, had appointed a single Praetorian prefect, Afranius Burrus.

Burrus, a physically imposing man, had overcome the disability of a withered left hand to become a soldier of great renown before he took command of the Praetorians. He proved to be an honest and able prefect and a clever military strategist, serving in the capacity of what in modern terms would be considered a secretary of defense. Retaining his post when Nero came to the throne, Burrus had been, in combination with Nero's chief of staff (the famed and flawed philosopher Lucius Annaeus Seneca), another of Agrippina's favorites, a steadying influence on the boy emperor for the first five stable years of Nero's reign.

In AD 62, Burrus had died from throat cancer, although the gossips would claim that Nero, tiring of the prefect's strict influence, murdered Burrus by sending him a poison-laced medicine for his throat. Following Burrus' death, Nero, on the advice of Seneca, had reverted to the custom of two Praetorian prefects. To satisfy Seneca and the public, he first chose Faenius Rufus, yet another favorite of Agrippina. Nero had earlier appointed Rufus to the post of commissioner of the corn supply. The poet Juvenal said that Romans would be content just as long as they were provided with bread and circuses, and there was much truth in this. The man who controlled the capital's supply of corn, most of which had to be shipped in from the wheat fields of Egypt and North Africa in vessels of the Mediterranean grain fleet, controlled the lives of the people of Rome. Some of the 150,000 tons of grain shipped into Rome each year was sold to bakers, but since the reign of Augustus, most was doled out free of charge to the poorer residents of Rome and sold to soldiers at a subsidized rate.

Some past holders of the post of commissioner of the corn supply had been lazy; others had been inept, and others still, corrupt. Rufus was an exception; he had gained "vulgar popularity," according to Tacitus, through "his administration of the corn supplies without profit to himself."[1] Yet, just as Rufus was widely known as a virtuous man, he was equally well known as a passive, if not downright timid man. And this admirably suited both Nero and his second choice for prefect.

This was Tigellinus, who, like Rufus, was by AD 64 a middle-aged man. A senator of lowly birth, Tigellinus had been banished from Rome by Caligula in AD 39 for having an affair with Nero's mother, Agrippina. Once Claudius came to the throne and Agrippina became his wife, Tigellinus was allowed to return to Rome. Early in Nero's reign, he had been appointed prefect of the Cohortes Vigiles, or the Night Watch. He had soon wormed his way into Nero's favor by encouraging and participating in the young emperor's worst vices, particularly his night revels around the taverns, brothels, and back streets of Rome. Tigellinus, who was famous for personally keeping a veritable harem of concubines, had gone on to become Nero's procurer; whatever Nero wanted, Tigellinus would organize.

It was Tigellinus' "inveterate shamelessness and infamy," according to Tacitus, that put him, and kept him, in Nero's most intimate circle of friends.[2] In return, Nero had heaped money, property, and favors on Tigellinus. On one occasion, when Tigellinus' son-in-law was banned from the Senate by a vote of the House for an undisclosed crime, Tigellinus, with Nero's support, had the ban overturned.

Tigellinus' co-prefect Rufus, once appointed to head the Praetorians, "enjoyed the favor of the people and the soldiers."[3] Tigellinus, meanwhile, began office universally despised and devoid of respect at all levels of society. Rufus' popularity meant that Nero dare not antagonize the men of the Praetorian Cohorts by removing him, so Tigellinus set to work to undermine his fellow prefect. After Seneca had retired from the post of chief secretary in AD 62, within months of the death of Burrus, Tigellinus launched his campaign. He began by discreetly reminding people that Rufus had been a favorite of the emperor's mother. Officially, Agrippina's name had been mud ever since her murder, on Nero's orders in AD 59, with the Senate declaring Agrippina guilty of conspiring to kill her son. Still, association with the disgraced Agrippina alone was not enough to destroy Rufus' reputation or his popularity. Tigellinus had more work to do to increase his power at his colleague's expense.

Tigellinus progressed to hatching plots against leading men of Rome. According to Tacitus, Tigellinus thought that "wicked scheming" was all he needed to bring him power and that his schemes would be all the more successful if he "could secure the emperor's complicity in guilt."[4] To do this, Tigellinus would, at dinner with the emperor or while out carousing with him, delve into the young man's most secret fears. And fears he had aplenty. Having grown up in a Palatium rent by intrigues and sullied by murder, Nero was, not surprisingly, insecure.

Like many an emperor before and after him, Nero above all feared being overthrown. Seneca, while serving as his chief secretary, had counseled him not to live in fear, for he could never execute his successor; it did not matter how many men he executed, someone would take his place. But with Seneca out of the picture, no such wise counsel existed, and Tigellinus was able to play on his employer's insecurities.

Crafty Tigellinus identified the two men whom Nero dreaded most. Rubellius Blandus Plautus had several marks against him. Plautus' mother was, like Nero, a member of the Julian family, making Plautus distantly related to the emperor. And Plautus had married a granddaughter of the emperor Tiberius. So, Plautus could claim imperial credentials on both scores. And to add to his illustrious name, Plautus, young, charismatic and rich, was capable of charming the people and buying allegiance, should he set his sights on the throne.

Nero had originally been alerted to a potential threat from Plautus a year after he took the throne in AD 54. One of his mother's female friends had accused Agrippina of planning to marry Plautus, her cousin, and then take the throne from Nero and give it to Plautus. When defending herself against the charge, Agrippina had said that no one would testify against her, even "if Plautus or any other were to become master of the State and sit in judgment on me."[5] The charge had come to nothing, and neither Agrippina nor Plautus suffered on account of it. But Nero would not forget that Plautus had the credentials to replace him.

In AD 60, Nero had celebrated his first Neronian Games, which he had created as a festival of contests of both mind and body, along the lines of games conducted in Greece for centuries past and which Augustus had emulated at Rome and Actium with his Actiaca, Greek games held every four years during his reign. Not long after the last poet had spoken his last line in the Neronian Games and the last naked boxer had been crowned victor with a laurel wreath, a comet was seen to blaze across the night sky. According to Tacitus, to superstitious Romans the appearance of a comet was a portend of revolution.[6] It soon reached Nero's attention that many people were suggesting that should the emperor be dethroned in such a revolution, then Plautus would make the ideal successor.

Plautus, who lived austerely and discreetly, encouraged none of this talk. Guided still by Seneca at that time, Nero had written Plautus a letter in which he had suggested that for the sake of "the tranquility of Rome," Plautus "withdraw himself from mischievous gossip." Plautus had inherited large estates in the province of Asia Minor, and Nero said that there Plautus "might enjoy his youth safely and quietly."[7] Taking the hint, and taking his wife and a few close friends with him, Plautus had departed for Asia and a quiet life.

The second man feared by Nero was Faustus Cornelius Sulla Felix, brother of Messalina, who had been the late, unwise, and unlamented wife of the emperor Claudius. Though comparatively poor, Sulla was descended from the same Sulla who had ruled Rome as dictator during the youth of Julius Caesar and Pompey the Great. Well known and well liked, Sulla had in AD 47 married into the imperial family, wedding Nero's cousin Antonia, one of the daughters of the emperor Claudius. The couple had produced a son, who would have had a claim on Nero's throne in adulthood, as the next most senior male of the Julian line. But the sickly boy had died at the age of two.

Several years after Nero came to the throne, one of the imperial freedmen, the elderly Graptus, had invented a story that Sulla had planned to murder Nero one night as the emperor returned from his revels at the

Milvian Bridge, on the northern outskirts of the Campus Martius. The bridge was then a famous haunt of prostitutes, male and female, and Nero used to go there so that he could take his pleasures more freely outside the city. No proof was produced to support this accusation, but Sulla was ordered to depart Italy and confine himself within the walls of Massilia, modern-day Marseilles in the south of France. Sulla had been living at Massilia ever since.

In an AD 62 meeting with Nero, not long after Seneca's retirement, Tigellinus had made his move against the two men. With Sulla in southern Gaul in self-imposed exile, and Plautus in Asia, Tigellinus had used their very absence from Rome against the men, claiming that their distance from Italy actually exacerbated the threat they posed to Nero.

"I have no eye, like Burrus, to two conflicting aims," Tigellinus had said, implying that his Praetorian predecessor Burrus had divided his loyalty between Agrippina and Nero. His one thought, he said, was for Nero's safety, "which is at least secured against treachery at Rome by my presence. As for distant uprisings, how can they be checked?"[8]

He claimed that Sulla could lead an uprising of the Gauls against Nero, using his family connection with Sulla "the great dictator." At the same time, he said, he did not trust the nations of the East, which had fond remembrances of Drusus, Plautus' grandfather by marriage and cousin and adoptive brother of Nero's own grandfather, Germanicus Caesar. Drusus had won acclaim for his work as a statesman in the East. Plautus' familial connection with Drusus might be enough, said his accuser, for the people of the East to rise up to support him against Nero.[9]

Sulla had given no indication that he had ambitions to replace Nero. In fact, he showed complete apathy toward politics in general and had never made a single noteworthy speech. This was no defense, according to Tigellinus. That air of apathy displayed by Sulla, said Tigellinus, was a fabrication, designed to deflect suspicion, "while he is seeking an opening for his reckless ambition."[10]

Convincing Nero to authorize Sulla's execution, Tigellinus had acted without delay. Six days after the co-prefect's meeting with Nero, a Praetorian execution party landed at Massilia by ship. The executioners burst in on Sulla while he was reclining at the dinner table with friends. The

Praetorian centurion in charge promptly dragged Sulla across the table by the hair and lopped off his head while Sulla's companions watched in disbelief.

It was only necessary for a condemned man's head to be returned to Rome as proof of his execution. The head was displayed in public, usually on the Gemonian Stairs, which ran down the southern slope of the Capitoline Mount between the Tabularium and the Tullianum to the Forum Romanum. Sometimes, these heads were displayed on the Rostra in the Forum. When Nero saw the grisly object before it was put on public display, he nervously commented that the victim's hair was prematurely gray.

Plautus' removal was not as easy to accomplish. His wealth made him well placed in Roman society, with many influential men owing their loyalty to him—because they were his clients or were literally in his debt. So, it was necessary to fabricate a story about his "crime." Tigellinus had a rumor circulated that Plautus had attempted to bring Nero's famous general Corbulo, who was now governor of Syria and controlled a number of legions, into a plot against the emperor. According to another fabricated story that ran around the streets and bathhouses of Rome, troops had been sent to execute Plautus but the people of Asia had taken up arms in his defense, and the soldiers sent to be his executioners had gone over to his side, necessitating the dispatch of a larger execution force.

These rumors also reached the ears of Plautus' father-in-law, Lucius Antistius Vetus, in Rome. Vetus had shared the consulship with Nero several years back and had also served as governor of Asia—one of the most prestigious and sought-after of Rome's proconsular appointments. When Vetus learned that Tigellinus had received Nero's approval to execute Plautus and that a centurion was to lead a party of sixty Praetorians to Asia to carry out the act, the father-in-law sent one of the freedmen that Plautus had left behind at Rome hurrying to warn his master. With the benefit of good winds, the freedman's ship had landed him in Asia ahead of the Praetorians, and he was able to pass on Vetus' warning to Plautus.

Vetus' message cautioned Plautus to react not by taking his own life, as many a Roman would have done in the same circumstances, suicide being legal and considered a noble resort by the Romans. Instead, Vetus had said, Plautus should rally supporters around himself and seek every resource to repel the Praetorian detachment. Then, said Vetus, in the delay caused by a message being sent back to Tigellinus by his centurion seeking reinforcements to complete the mission, Plautus could raise an army and go to war against Nero.

Plautus ignored the warning from his father-in-law. Under the influence of two teachers of philosophy, who counseled that he "await death with firmness rather than lead a precarious and anxious life," Plautus went about his regular routine.[11] At noon one day shortly after, he was at the bathhouse. Stripped down to a tunic and an undergarment, he was exercising before entering the baths. The doors burst open, and in trooped the Praetorian centurion and his death squad. At their head was Pelago, a freedman on Nero's personal staff, who had been sent with the Praetorians to ensure the task was completed.

Without any ceremony, the centurion forced Plautus to kneel on the tiled bathhouse floor and ordered him to stretch out his neck. Unsheathing his gladius, the centurion hacked off Plautus' head, which Pelago promptly bore away. The dead man's distraught wife, Antistia Pollutia, came running to find her husband's headless body. Dropping to her knees, she clutched Plautus' corpse to her, ignoring the blood that covered her clothes. For the rest of her short life, Pollutia would retain the bloodstained garments worn by her husband at the time of his violent end.

The removal of Sulla and Plautus brought no outcry at Rome. This lack of public reaction, along with the very act of their removal, was a great relief to Nero, who heaped rewards on Tigellinus. These events cemented Tigellinus and the emperor's relationship and increased the distance between Faenius Rufus and Nero, as Tigellinus had hoped. By early AD 64, Tigellinus' power was increasing with each passing week.

That power was both financial and political. Nero had made Tigellinus a wealthy man with his gifts and rewards. One of those rewards was, apparently, either the entire Basilica Aemilia, or the basilica's portico fronting the Forum, which contained a number of shops. This massive building, 330 feet long and 100 feet wide, with two floors supported by columns and massive arches and topped by a third, attic floor, was one of Rome's major retailing precincts, the shopping mall of its day. At the intersection of the Via Sacra (Sacred Way) and the Argiletum, itself a street known for its cobblers' shops and booksellers at this time and fronting the Forum Romanum—the Fifth Avenue of ancient Rome— these Aemilian shops occupied prime retail real estate.

Five centuries earlier, there had been butchers' shops here. A century later, bankers had taken over the site. After a subsequent fire, the shops were renovated and became known as the *tabernae nova*, or new shops. In 179 BC, work began here on a basilica that was completed by Marcus Aemilius Lepidus. The Aemilian family had added to the building down through the decades. In 55 BC, a new, grander building, the one that now stood in AD 64, was erected on the site by Lucius Aemilius Pailus.

Early in the imperial era, the building had come into the possession of the imperial family. After another fire, in AD 14, the emperor Augustus had it restored. Another renovation eight years later was at the expense of Marcus Lepidus, of the Aemilian family. And now, the structure, or part of it, was Tigellinus' property. Indoors, rows of marble-floored shops lined a central nave. The basilica's restored portico, fronting the Forum, was similarly lined with shops and was dedicated by Augustus to his grandsons Gaius and Lucius.

Considered by some the most beautiful building in Rome, the Basilica Aemilia was certainly one of the most profitable, with the shops returning prime rents. To the Basilica Aemilia hurried slaves and freedmen each morning to shop on behalf of their masters and mistresses who lived in the mansions on the nearby Palatine, Capitoline, Caelian, and Aventine hills.

By a 59 BC edict of Julius Caesar, most wheeled traffic was banned from Rome's narrow streets during daylight. So, it was in the night that merchants' heavy four-wheeled wagons and farmers' two-wheeled carts streamed into the city from the outskirts and the Tiber River docks, laden with both manufactured goods and produce, fish and livestock. And dodging around them would be the carriages and litters of the "night livers," and parties of revelers out on the town, eating, drinking, and whoring. Rome was the original city that never slept. Provincials coming to

Rome for the first time would complain that they could not sleep for the din that filled the city from dusk till dawn.

The Basilica Aemilia was not the city's only shopping center. Rome possessed markets dedicated to the sale of livestock, produce, wine, clothing, footwear, and even markets specializing in the sale of herbs and flowers. Meanwhile, every winding street of old Rome was lined with businesses. Once their tall shutters were pushed back, all shops were open to the street, and a passerby could see the freedmen shopkeepers, their families, and their slave employees hard at work. Many shopkeepers slept on the premises, in cramped lofts above the store, with their families. In the ruins of Pompeii and Ostia today, a visitor might see four or five steps at the rear of typical Roman shops, leading nowhere. In Roman times, there would have been wooden ladders at the top of these steps, extending up to the lofts above the shops.

Countless grimy workshops operated in back streets: tanners and leather workers, with the smell of ammonia thick in the air; carpentry shops; iron foundries, with slaves toiling over hot, smoky forges. Brothels, which were legal in Rome, were usually in the back streets. Some taverns offered prostitutes on the second floor, as their wooden signs decorated with erect phalluses advertised. Brothels, called houses of seduction by some Romans and disorderly houses by others, only operated by night. Many fronted the street. A description exists of a first-century Roman brothel that had a quilt hanging in the doorway, to dampen noise but encourage entry. Inside, where customers and naked prostitutes nonchalantly roamed about, the premises were divided by wooden partitions into small bed cubicles, with a sign outside each chamber naming the prostitute working inside.

Surviving reliefs depicting shops at Rome show a butcher wielding a meat cleaver while various cuts of meat hang behind him; a green-grocer pointing out his fresh produce; a knife seller with his vast array of knives; and a pharmacist prescribing medicine for a patient, while an assistant pounds a pestle in a bowl. Another relief shows a store with fowl hanging by their feet; a woman hands fruit to a slave; wild birds occupy a closed wicker basket; cages contain live rabbits; a pair of chained monkeys sit forlornly on a counter. Wine bars occupied many city corners. More substantial taverns were also prevalent. Wine flagons were chained to columns outside, as advertisements. Large clay amphorae at the rear of the tavern were full of imported wine. When they were empty, these elegant amphorae, which look like giant cigars to modern eyes, were frequently smashed; there was no market for secondhand amphorae.

Hot-food establishments sent tantalizing aromas wafting on the air. Rome's bakeries and pastry shops offered everything from the standard Roman loaf—round, like a pie, and sliced the same way—to tempting pastry delicacies. In Pompeii, one of the towns that would be buried by the eruption of Mount Vesuvius in AD 79 and which had a population of roughly twenty thousand, more than one hundred wine bars, twenty taverns, and forty bakeries have been identified. Multiply these numbers by at least fifty for Rome, whose first-century population exceeded a million people.

In Rome, as elsewhere in the Roman world, shopkeepers displayed their goods outside their doors. Hairdressers and barbers sat their customers on stools on the pavement, working on them with razor and knife in full public gaze while exchanging gossip. A poet of the time would complain that Rome was one vast shop. The open doors of Rome's small, street-side schools revealed young students on stools, reciting the Twelve Tables, Rome's basic laws, or verses from Homer or Virgil. One of the students in one of the better schools, this winter of AD 64, was the nine-year-old Publius Cornelius Tacitus, the future historian.

Bankers, scribes, and up-market stores occupied the Basilica Aemilia: the best jewelers; importers of ridiculously expensive food delicacies; purveyors of the finest wines, including Italy's prized Falernian vintages. The brightly colored imported fabrics, particularly silks, of fabric merchants attracted Rome's wealthy ladies. A relief shows one such fabric store, with rich cushions hanging from the ceiling. Two staff members unravel a roll of cloth for several seated female customers. Fashion and fad drove the shopping impulses in Roman times, just as much as they do today. After he had ceased to be a man of power and of extravagance, Seneca wrote to a friend: "Look at the number of things we buy because others have bought them or because they're in most people's houses."[12]

All this shopping activity generated a hubbub that meant a visitor approaching Rome on the morning of any business day would hear the city before seeing it. The visitor might also see or smell evidence of it on the wind; according to Seneca, the air of Rome reeked of smoke and poisonous fumes from all the cookers of the metropolis, and ashes commonly floated on the breeze from the same source.[13] Here was Horace's famous "smoke, splendor and noise of the city," in this the commercial heart of the empire.[14] Tigellinus the Praetorian prefect had a tidy share of that commerce, but he would always be looking for more profit, more rewards, more real estate.

Greed was the driving force of Rome. More than one landlord of the city's forty-seven thousand *insulae*, or apartment blocks, had been guilty of setting fire to their own properties in the past. Not for insurance money; insurance was one innovation that escaped the otherwise business-savvy Romans. Landlords would then hastily build larger buildings on the ruined sites, providing smaller rooms and demanding larger rents. The landlords' profit in such instances was a long time coming. Tigellinus was interested in more immediate rewards.

THE POETS

Marcus Valerius Martialus, or Martial, as later generations would come to know him, rose before dawn as usual this winter morning. From his small apartment, three floors up in a nondescript apartment block sandwiched between countless others on Rome's Quirinal Hill, where once Cicero's good friend and correspondent Atticus had lived, and girding his cheap cloak around him, Martial made his way across the city though crowded, darkened streets to the house of Annaeus Mela, one of Rome's wealthiest men.

In his twenties, Martial had been born at Bilbilis in Spain. Although he boasted Celtic blood, Martial was a Roman citizen and the son of a Roman citizen. His parents had given him a good education, including tutoring in grammar and rhetoric. When Seneca was still Nero's chief secretary, the young Martial had come to Rome seeking to make his fortune. Martial rated earning above learning. "My parents were stupid enough to have me taught literature, a paltry subject," he would say, years later. "But what good were teachers of grammar and rhetoric to me?"[1] He had arrived from Spain with an introduction to Seneca, a fellow Spaniard. Their shared heritage paid dividends: The rich and hugely powerful chief secretary had taken Martial on as one of his many clients.

This promising start to Martial's career soon hit a major obstacle. Seneca retired from office not long after Martial arrived at Rome. Determined to melt into obscurity so as not to antagonize Nero, Seneca had divorced himself of most of his clients. Cast aside were men such as the wealthy and very social Gaius Piso, the noted author Fabius Rusticus, who, through Seneca's patronage, had risen to fame, and complete unknowns such as Martial. Only Seneca's physician, his in-laws, and one or two other useful people remained in the former chief secretary's now very limited circle. In divesting himself of clients, Seneca had passed Martial on to his younger brother Mela.

Mela had amassed an immense fortune as an astute businessman, but he did not mix in the same circles as Seneca, kept a low public profile, and had little or no political influence. Mela easily met the financial qualification for elevation to the Senatorial Order from the Equestrian Order—a personal net worth of 1.2 million sesterces. But Mela preferred to remain an Equestrian and keep well away from the Senate and from politics. He concentrated on making money. To Mela's mind, an Equestrian was the equal of even a former consul. So good was Mela at making money that after an introduction from Seneca, he had even been employed by the emperor to manage some of his private business affairs.

Martial was ushered into Mela's reception room. Numerous fellow clients milled about the room; they were here, like Martial, for the morning's levee with their patron. Some were of Equestrian rank; some were freedmen, former slaves. All had come to pay their respects to Mela, their patron. This was how the Roman social system worked. The only free man at Rome who did not have a patron or need one was the emperor.

As the system prescribed, Martial had several patrons, and after he departed Mela's house, he would hurry to the homes of other patrons and play the good client. Petilius, another of Martial's rich patrons, possessed, in addition to a city house, a regal country estate on the Janiculum, today's Gianicolo, a hill that overlooks Rome from the left bank of the Tiber. Julius Caesar had kept an estate and a villa on the Janiculum; Cleopatra had famously stayed in that villa when she came to Rome. Petilius' Janiculum estate boasted one of the finest vineyards in Italy; its product rivaled Falernian wine, the benchmark of fine Roman wine.

Martial would flatter each of his patrons and beg gifts and favors. And as he left each house, the master's steward would drop a small collection of coins into his hand. Between his patrons, Martial would return each day to his garret on the Quirinal Hill with a total of forty sesterces. It was, he himself considered, a wretched sum, and he detested the need of it. But without his daily dole, he would starve. As it was, Martial, whose greatest pleasures were to eat, drink, and converse with friends, lived beyond his means. Moreover, there were the duties of a client that Martial must perform. Just as a patron remunerated his clients and provided them with references, recommendations, and endorsements, so the client was expected to serve his patron and return the favors.

A good client would always rush to inform his patron of news that was to the patron's advantage. A client going on a journey would carry his patron's mail, for while Rome had a government courier service for official correspondence (the *cursus publicus velox*, or the state's very fast runner, which used coaches and dispatch riders), the Roman world had no mail service for private mail. In all things, a client would be expected to put his own needs after that of his patron, and a patron's most lowly clients—freedmen, as a rule—were expected to act as his *anteambulo*, preceding their patron when he passed along the street, clearing the way for him in the same way that lictors, official attendants provided by the state, did so for magistrates and commissioners.

At Mela's house, Martial communed with Mela's son Lucanus, or Lucan, as we know him. Of a similar age to Martial, Lucan was a talented poet. He had exhibited that talent in readings in private houses before appearing at the public theater and the Juvenile Games. He had gone on to win the garlands in AD 60 at the first Neronian Games, with a poem entitled *Laudes Neronis*, or In Praise of Nero. Back then, the young emperor had rewarded Lucan. But once Lucan's uncle Seneca had disappeared into obscure retirement, Nero, jealous of Lucan's gift and his works, "with the foolish vanity of a rival, had forbidden him to publish them," Tacitus notes.[2]

Martial, as a member of Lucan's circle of friends, would join private gatherings with Lucan and his wife Polla to hear the poet read his latest work aloud. As Martial knew, Lucan was currently working on an epic poem entitled the *Bellum Civile*. In it, Lucan described the Battle of Pharsalus in Macedonia between Julius Caesar and Pompey the Great.

It was Lucan's intention to take the work through the subsequent battles of the civil war, to culminate with Caesar's showdown with Pompey's sons in Spain, where Lucan himself was born.

Martial would applaud Lucan's latest reading and offer witty comments. In the opinion of a later friend and patron, Pliny the Younger, Martial was "a man of great gifts, with a mind both subtle and penetrating." Great fame and respect, but little money, came the way of Rome's best poets. Martial could not eat or drink fame or respect. He preferred money; in fact, his lifestyle demanded it. It would not be until AD 80 that he would publish poems of his own, poems "remarkable for their combination of sincerity, pungency, and wit," Pliny the Younger would say.[3] Martial's epigrams would subsequently make his name and give him fame that would last to the present day. But they would never make him rich.

Lucan, on the other hand, did not have to worry about money. His father's wealth permitted him to indulge his talent. Martial had no such family wealth to support him. Another Roman poet, Albiovanus Pedo, had likewise lived in a cramped Roman apartment. Pedo, a student of Ovid, was popular in the reign of Tiberius. This poet made his name, and a tidy sum, by publishing an epic poem about the German military campaigns of Nero's grandfather, Germanicus Caesar, against the German tribes led by Arminius. Pedo had been Germanicus' deputy cavalry commander and had written from rich personal experience. He found a ready audience, for Germanicus, who was murdered in his prime before he could succeed Tiberius as emperor, was revered by the Roman populace. Every year, they made sacrifices to his memory on June 23, Germanicus' birthday, a custom that would continue for several hundred years to come.

Seneca had known Pedo. When the chief secretary was still Martial's patron, Seneca told him a story that Pedo, a "delightful story-teller" in Seneca's opinion, had once related to him.[4] Pedo's apartment sat directly above that of Sextus Papinius, whose substantial residence occupied the entire ground floor of the building, a common choice of wealthy Romans who preferred not to go to the expense of a *domus*, or city house. Papinius, a former consul who took his own life in Tiberius' last days, had a reputation for being mean and grasping. He was also one of that fraternity at Rome who preferred to sleep by day and conduct their lives by night, the so-called night livers.

One night about nine o'clock, Pedo had heard the sound of cracking whips below. Curious, Pedo had gone downstairs and asked Papinius' night porter what was going on. Papinius was inspecting the household accounts, so Pedo was informed. Come midnight, Pedo heard the sounds of shouting. Again Pedo made a polite inquiry; this time, he was told that Papinius was conducting his daily voice exercises. About two o'clock in the morning, Pedo was again disturbed, as a horse-drawn carriage drew up in the street outside, then rumbled away again; Papinius was going for his nightly drive. As the sun was coming up, there were shouts from Papinius for servants and the sound of running feet, followed by much clatter in the kitchen; Papinius had emerged from his bath and was ready for a predinner appetizer. This was the type of neighbor that Martial would also have endured.

The monotony of city life was leavened for Martial by escapes during the summer holidays. In July and August, when the summer heat scorched Rome, a series of *ludi*, public games, were annually celebrated at Rome as part of the religious calendar. The public flocked to these games. And as plebeian visitors poured into the city for the games, the wealthy hurried out. The Senate did not sit; the courts were closed. So, unless a man of substance had official duties to perform related to the games, he fled the city's stifling heat to one of his country estates until after Sirius, the Dog Star, dimmed in late August.

The summer resorts of Rome's elite varied from villas on the west coast of Italy to estates in the hills of Rome. The coastal villas offered cooling sea breezes, but the air in the hills was humidity-free, and for many, this was a greater attraction than the seaside—Romans did not bathe in the sea. Seneca had a house at Alba Longa, in the Alban Hills, and when he was still chief secretary, he had hosted throngs of clients and retainers there in the summer. That resort was no longer available to Martial, but as a client of Mela and a friend of Lucan, he could expect an invitation to one of Mela's country houses in July.

And what a momentous July it would prove to be.

THE FORMER
CHIEF SECRETARY

As the mule arrived outside the hillside villa in the late evening, it was clear, by the closed doors, that the staff was not expecting the master. The handful of servants and retainers who had walked in the mule's wake clustered around the animal to help sixty-seven-year-old Lucius Seneca down to the ground. Bald and overweight, with double chin and paunch, he had at one time been a handsome man.

Once on his feet, Seneca stretched wearily, then groaned with the pain of aching bones. He had been worn out by the journey, "which was not so much long as thoroughly uncomfortable," he would soon be complaining to a friend. He had done away with the luxury and show of a carriage, a slave-borne litter, or a vast train of servants and was paying the price of his self-imposed austerity. But, as he himself said, "old age has made me better at putting up with a lot of things."[1]

Ever since he had withdrawn from public life two years before, Seneca had disposed of the obvious trappings of wealth and had frequently been on the move. Rarely visiting his mansion at the capital, he moved around his various country estates, only occasionally visiting friends. All his itineraries and the few friendships that he retained were, like his travel arrangements, calculated to make him politically invisible. Seneca knew that

Praetorian Prefect Tigellinus would have agents everywhere, reporting his movements, his meetings, perhaps even his conversations. How dramatically life had changed since his retirement. Once, Seneca had never hesitated to show off his riches and his power. Now, without power, his money was meaningless. In fact, to suspicious eyes, Seneca's wealth was a threat.

Seneca's elevation to power as Nero's chief adviser had been unparalleled in Roman history. He was a provincial, born at Corduba, capital of the province of Baetica in southwestern Spain. His father, also a Lucius Annaeus Seneca, the holder of Equestrian rank, had been a renowned teacher of logic in Rome before he and his wife Helvia returned to Corduba. There, the couple's three sons had been born—Novatus (the eldest) and Seneca and Mela. When Novatus was a young man, he had been adopted by a wealthy senator, Junius Gallio. It was common for childless Romans to adopt grown men as their sons, to prevent the forfeiture of their estates to the state after they died, as the law provided. An adopted man took the name of his adoptive father, so that Seneca's brother also became Junius Gallio. And when the elder Gallio died, his adopted son inherited much of his sizable estate.

The younger Gallio had gone on to become a consul and, in AD 50–51, Roman governor of Achaia. While Gallio was serving in Achaia, a Jew had been brought before him, accused of blasphemy by the leading Jews of the province. The accused man was Paulus of Tarsus—Paul the Christian apostle as he would become known in centuries to come. Paul had upset the Jewish authorities by preaching the teachings of Jesus of Nazareth. Finding that Paul had no case to answer under Roman law, Gallio had discharged him.

Younger brother Seneca had suffered from asthma while growing up in Rome and spent many years in Egypt, living with his uncle, the prefect of Egypt, where he outgrew the complaint. When Seneca was in his thirties, immediately after the execution of Praetorian Prefect Sejanus, he moved to Rome, becoming a client of the family of the late Germanicus Caesar. In AD 41, under the emperor Claudius, Seneca had been convicted of adultery with Germanicus' daughter Julia, for which crime he had been banished to the island of Corsica for eight years.

While living in frustrated exile on Corsica and supported in part from Rome by his elder brother Gallio, whom Seneca later described as his mentor, Seneca had produced some of his best literary and philosophical work, much of which he dedicated to Gallio. By AD 49, another of Germanicus' daughters, Agrippina the Younger, the mother of Nero, had married Claudius, her uncle. Agrippina was able to convince Claudius to recall Seneca from exile and to immediately make both Seneca and his brother Gallio praetors, placing them among the most senior of Rome's magistrates.

It was said that Seneca also had an affair with Agrippina and this was why she favored him so. Her trust in him extended also to his appointment as Nero's guardian and tutor. This had been the beginning of the fourteen-year relationship between man and boy, as Seneca guided Nero, first as his teacher and then, once Agrippina murdered Claudius and put Nero on the throne, as his most senior bureaucrat and adviser. Together with his partner in government, the Praetorian prefect Burrus, Seneca had kept a guiding and restraining hand on Nero's shoulder. But when Burrus' death brought the appointment of the detestable Tigellinus, Seneca began to see the writing on the wall.

Shortly after the death of Burrus, Seneca became aware of Tigellinus' desire for Seneca's neck—literally—when fellow senator Fabius Romanus brought both Seneca and his friend Gaius Piso before the Senate. The alleged crime was that Seneca and Piso were guilty of "stealthy calumnies," a charge that had the ring of Tigellinus' authorship about it.[2] Many years had passed since Seneca himself had last sat in the Senate, but this charge from Romanus had to be rebutted. So, Seneca had taken his seat among the former praetors and, once recognized by the presiding consul, had used his famous power of oratory to crush the charges against Piso and himself.

So expert was Seneca's speech, he made it appear that if anyone were guilty of stealthy calumnies, it was his accuser. Romanus dropped the charges. But both Seneca and his fellow accused Piso had been shaken by the episode. Piso would devise his own strategy to counter future threats from Tigellinus, but Seneca saw only one course open to him. Rather than fall victim to Tigellinus' continued plotting, Seneca had tendered his resignation.

"You have surrounded me with vast influence and boundless wealth," Seneca had told the young emperor the day he voluntarily ended his long period of imperial service. "So that I often think to myself, 'Am I, who am merely of an Equestrian and provincial family, numbered among the chief men of Rome?'"[3]

Seneca had told Nero that he could no longer bear the burden of his wealth and asked the emperor to order his agents to take over the management of Seneca's properties, and to include those properties in Nero's own estate. Nero had thanked Seneca for his offer, but said that people would think the worst of their emperor if he accepted it. He invited Seneca to speak up from retirement should his former teacher think that Nero had strayed from the righteous path that the older man had created for him. But both men knew that Seneca would never again dare to offer advice, just as Nero would never take it.

Now, as travel-weary Seneca stood in the portico of his Alban villa, one of his accompanying freedmen rapped on the door, and presently, there was a stirring inside. The doors were thrown back, and the doorman, with boat-shaped oil lamp in hand, looked with surprise and then panic upon the face of his master. "I find nothing ready for my arrival," Seneca would soon lament in a letter to a friend, "apart from myself."[4]

Seneca kept a baker and a cook on the permanent staff at the villa, as he did at all his properties. So now he called for bread and olive oil, for he was hungry after his journey. The doorman bustled away, calling to rouse the baker from his slumbers. Seneca sagged onto a couch in the dining room and waited. Soon the doorman returned, with the news that the baker was out of bread. Seneca strove not to let his irritation show.

"The farm manager will have some, or the steward, or a tenant," said Seneca, who was even prepared to eat stale bread.[5]

Again the doorman hurried away to awaken the farm manager, to alert the steward of the house, and to run to the homes of nearby tenants. Seneca's exhaustion now drove him to his bed. There, as he awaited his loaf of bread, he called in one of the secretaries and dictated a letter to his friend Lucilius, a native of Pompeii and the procurator of Sicily. By the time that Seneca was well into the letter, he had second thoughts about eating bad bread. "I shall wait then," he said, "and not eat until I either start getting good bread again or cease to be fussy about bad bread." And so he surrendered to his exhaustion and dropped off to sleep, without bread of any kind to satisfy his hunger.[6]

As the summer approached, Seneca would stay at various country villas. His vineyards at Mentana were considered among the best in Italy and begged regular attendance. Another of his favorite estates was at Nomentum, twelve miles northeast of Rome, which also boasted fine vines. The air there he considered favorable to his health, and once, when he came down with a fever at Rome, he had hurried to Nomentum, certain that the change of address would aid his recovery. His elder brother Gallio, Seneca wrote to a friend, had done something similar while proconsul of Achaia, sailing to an Aegean island in the belief that a change of air would be more beneficial to overcoming a fever than would any physician's prescription.

As the summer drew nearer, too, Seneca was taken aside by Cleonicus, the most trusted of his freedmen. Cleonicus had a confession to make. He had been approached by agents of Tigellinus—on Nero's command, he said. Through threat or bribe, those agents had cajoled Cleonicus to poison his master. Cleonicus had procured poison and had even prepared a deadly draught to administer to Seneca. But Cleonicus' conscience had got the better of him, and he had come forward to tell his master all.

This proximity to a violent death shook Seneca. He reasoned that while Cleonicus had proven loyal, another member of his staff might give in to bribe or threats and be prepared take his master's life. From this time forward, Seneca would not worry about bread or any other foodstuff produced or even handled by his servants. He would only eat wild fruit that he himself gathered, and he would only drink pure stream water that he collected personally. His life, Seneca was convinced, depended on such extreme precautions.

THE FLAME

March 1, the Kalends of March, was an important day on the Roman calendar. In times past, the Roman year had commenced on March 1. On that day, in a predawn ceremony presided over by the Pontifex Maximus, the vestal virgins renewed the Eternal Flame that burned year-round in the temple dedicated to Vesta, goddess of hearth and home. The March 1 date was too fixed in the routine of Rome for it to be altered. So now, Nero came to the small, circular Temple of Vesta in the Forum, for the Eternal Flame's renewal ceremony of AD 64.

The vestals, the priestesses who served Vesta, made up the most exclusive and most revered of Rome's religious orders. There were just six members of this, Rome's only all-female order. Priestesses joined the order between the age of eight and ten; Roman females were launched into adult life early, being legally eligible to become engaged at the age of twelve and to marry at thirteen. Most entrants would stay in the order all their lives. Down through the centuries, a number of vestals would be executed for breaking their vow of chastity—traditionally, buried alive. Many emperors overlooked the affairs of vestals, although within two decades, the emperor Domitian would crack down on unchaste members of the order. A small number of vestals left the order after many years' service, with some marrying, although that was traditionally considered unlucky for all involved.

It brought a Roman family great honor for a daughter to be chosen as a vestal. She was expected to observe chastity and lead a very regimented life, dressed in white headdresses and white robes. She lived in the expansive House of the Vestals on the Forum, beside the Temple of Vesta, although if she fell ill, she was expected to immediately move to the house of a relative until she recovered, so that she did not infect fellow vestals. The vestals' official carriage, a two-wheeled, enclosed *carpentum*, was the only vehicle, apart from builders' carts, permitted to traverse the streets of Rome in daylight. Preceded by a lictor, the carriage of the vestals had total right-of-way.

It was a capital crime should anyone harm a vestal, and the best seats were reserved for vestals in all theaters and amphitheaters; their front-row white marble seats can still be seen at the Colosseum to this day. On their rare public appearances, the women were heavily veiled. There was a legend that should a condemned Roman citizen see a vestal when on his way to his execution, he must be set free at once. The vestals were also entrusted with the safekeeping of important documents. Julius Caesar was one of numerous leading Romans who left his will with the vestals. Some of the vestals' most important duties occurred in June, leading up to and during the Vestalia, the Festival of Vesta. Critically, too, it was the responsibility of the vestals to ensure that the Eternal Flame was never extinguished. While the flame burned, it was believed, Rome would prosper. Should a vestal allow the flame to go out, she could be executed.

Now, in the predawn darkness, with the emperor watching and attendants holding torches high, the six women conducted the secret renewal ceremony, paying homage to Vesta and beseeching her blessing for the year ahead. Led by the chief vestal, the older priestesses guided their newest and youngest colleague. Just eighteen months before this, the vestal Laelia had died. She had been replaced by the prepubescent Cornelia, a member of the Cossi family. This child novice would rise to become chief vestal, only to be buried alive during the reign of Domitian for being unchaste, one of four vestals executed by Domitian. Now, the novice Cornelia, the elderly Domitia, the beautiful Rubria, and the three other vestals conducted the ceremonial that went back hundreds of years, under the watchful, and some say lecherous, eye of Nero—according to historian Suetonius, Nero once raped the vestal Rubria.[1]

With the ceremony completed and with Vesta's fire burning brightly in the center of the goddess's temple, Nero departed for his other early-morning duties before returning to his Palatium. March was a busy month on Rome's official calendar. As the name of the month reflects, it was devoted to Mars. And it was indeed a martial month, with various religious activities culminating late in March in the blessing of the implements of war—weapons, standards, and even military trumpets—prior to the year's military campaigning season. In Roman provinces bordering foreign states, the legions would similarly be preparing for campaigning. In western Britain, the legions would soon be countering the raids of the fierce Silure tribe. On the Rhine, there would be punitive Roman raids east against German tribes. In Syria, Corbulo would be consolidating his successes against the Parthians.

And as the legions went forth in spring, so Rome's latest crop of provincial officials would leave the capital to take up their appointments for the coming year. The proconsuls, the provincial governors appointed by the Senate, would set off for their one-year tenures, taking along gaggles of staff. Each governor was accompanied by a quaestor, the most junior of Rome's magistrates. Chosen by the emperor and rubber-stamped by a vote of the Senate, the quaestor was his governor's chief financial officer and was responsible for military recruiting in his province. A quaestor, on his return to Rome, could automatically take a seat in the Senate.

One such quaestor preparing to depart Rome this spring of AD 64 was Gnaeus Julius Agricola. In his twenties and a provincial (being a native of Massilia), Agricola had married Domitia Decidiana, a member of a leading Roman family. The couple had a sickly young son, and Julia was pregnant with their second child, but Agricola would have to leave mother and child in Rome while he served his year on the staff of Salvius Titianus, new proconsul of Asia. Agricola's chief would be taking his wife and elder children with him to Asia, as was the practice and the privilege of a provincial governor, but a humble quaestor had no such right. Still, Agricola and his wife "lived in rare accord, maintained by mutual affection and unselfishness," and both would bear the separation of the next year with good grace.[2]

As an officer cadet, Agricola had served on the staff of the governor of Britain, Suetonius Paulinus, during Boudicca's revolt and had lived through the bloody do-or-die AD 60 battle in which 10,000 Roman troops headed by the 14th Gemina Martia Victrix Legion had overcome 230,000 rampaging rebel Britons. The battle that destroyed Boudicca had made that legion the most feared unit in the Roman world. It would be some years before Agricola made his name, but when he did, it would be as a general, and back in Britain.

In a lottery-style process, candidates for provincial appointments put their names in an urn. Agricola's was one of a certain number drawn out to match the number of vacancies. Another draw was made to match names with vacant posts. This was how Agricola won his Asian appointment. Over the next year, he discovered that his proconsul Titianus was "an abject slave to greed." The proconsul's self-serving policy, to Agricola's mind, was one of "You wink at my offenses, and I'll wink at yours."[3] While Agricola was serving in Asia, his son would die, but during the same period, his wife Domitia would give birth to a healthy daughter. That daughter would one day marry the historian Tacitus.

As men such as Agricola and his superior Titianus were preparing that spring to leave Rome no later than July for appointments abroad, as the law required, others were returning after completing their yearly appointments. One such returnee to Rome that spring of AD 64 was Titus Flavius Vespasianus, better known to us as Vespasian, the future emperor. Fifty-four-year-old Vespasian, who had made a name for himself as commander of the 2nd Augusta Legion during the AD 43 invasion of Britain, returned to the capital after a torrid year-long posting as proconsul of the province of Africa, in North Africa. Vespasian was a no-nonsense soldier at heart, gruff, with no airs or graces. His soldierly style of government had been so unpopular in Africa that on one occasion, the locals had pelted him with turnips.

Along with Asia, Africa was the most sought-after of all the proconsular appointments, being the best paid, as it earned the appointee 400,000 sesterces for his year of service. A legionary in the ranks of

Rome's legions, meanwhile, earned 900 sesterces a year. As it happened, Vespasian had great need of those 400,000 sesterces. He had invested in mule farms. A mule farm with a contract to supply the military was a license to mint gold, but somehow, the farm managers had got it wrong. The farms had gone broke, and so had Vespasian. To escape his financial bind, Vespasian had been forced to sell his valuables and to mortgage his family home at Rome to his elder brother Flavius Sabinus, who was in his second term as Rome's city prefect, a combined city manager and chief of police. Vespasian's household silver had been among the first assets to go. His sons would remember the embarrassment of growing up without silver on the table and eating from wooden plates just like slaves.

Now Vespasian was back in that family home, which was on Pomegranate Street on the Quirinal Hill, in Rome's Regio VI, or Sixth Precinct. His brother Sabinus also had a house on the Quirinal. This was not one of Rome's best addresses. The private mansions clinging to the lower slopes of the Palatine and Capitoline hills claimed that distinction. The Aventine Hill, too, had become fashionable with Rome's elite in recent years after long being considered an ordinary address. But while the Quirinal was not fashionable, neither was it a dowdy address. It sat above the city, away from the industrial districts. One of the city's larger water reservoirs, the Fundanus Basin, called a lake by many Romans, sat at the foot of the Quirinal. The basin acted as a barrier between the Quirinal and the less salubrious valley suburbs such as the Subura, where Julius Caesar had a home before he came to power and which had a name for crime and unsavory characters.

Vespasian's eldest son, twenty-four-year-old Titus, was currently in Britain, serving as commander of an auxiliary cavalry *ala*, or wing, attached to his father's old legion, the 2nd Augusta. Vespasian's younger son, thirteen-year-old Domitian, was waiting at home for his father. Domitian would soon be studying rhetoric and declamation at a school conducted by one of Rome's leading teachers. Vespasian, a widower since his wife Flavia Domitilla died when he was in his twenties, would soon pay a visit to his longtime mistress, Caenis. A wealthy woman in her own right and a former slave, Caenis had in her youth been the most trusted servant of Antonia, daughter of Mark Antony and mother of the emperor

Claudius and his brother Germanicus. It had been Caenis who had carried a note from Antonia to her brother-in-law Tiberius to warn him of Sejanus' plot to topple him from his throne. When Vespasian became emperor, he would treat Caenis as his "wife in all but name," despite her lowly freedwoman status.[4]

Among Vespasian's first visitors now that he was back at the capital was one of his good friends, if one of his more eccentric friends, the forty-one-year-old Gaius Plinius, Pliny the Elder as we know him, uncle of Pliny the Younger, Martial's later patron. There had been a time when the elder Pliny was a devoted lawyer in Rome's courts, but by AD 64, he rarely left his house at the capital, where he studied and wrote relentlessly. A workaholic who slept little and wrote day and night, Pliny dreaded time-wasting. He was the noted author of many books, which ranged from his first literary work (a military handbook on throwing the javelin while mounted) to biographies, a textbook on oratory, and his thirty-seven-volume *Natural History*, which many considered his masterwork. His *German Wars*, a twenty-volume history of all Rome's wars with the tribes of Germany, would later be used as a reference by Tacitus for his greatest contribution to the written history of Rome, the *Annals*.

When he was in his late teens, Pliny was a "thin stripe" tribune, or officer cadet, serving in the Roman army on the Rhine. It was there that he befriended Vespasian, who was then the legate, or commander, of the 2nd Augusta Legion when it was still stationed at Argentoratum, modern Strasbourg, prior to participating in the invasion of Britain. A few years later, Pliny served as a prefect of auxiliary infantry and then commanded an auxiliary cavalry wing, also on the Rhine.

Now, when Pliny the scholar went visiting at Rome, he was carried from his house on the Esquiline Hill in a sedan chair, with a freedman secretary walking beside him taking notes in shorthand on wax tablets as his master dictated. At this time, Pliny was working on the eight-volume *Problems in Grammar*. Pliny's nephew, Pliny the Younger, who would himself become a noted writer, later commented that during this period in Nero's reign, "when the slavery of the times made it dangerous to write anything at all independent or inspired," his uncle deliberately chose to avoid political subjects and put his energies into this work on grammar, which could offend no one, least of all the emperor.[5] There was another reason that the elder Pliny was carried in a sedan chair. He was a stout man and suffered from a constitutional weakness of the throat, which was often inflamed, and as a consequence, he breathed with a pronounced wheeze. This meant that walking any distance was not an option.

Yet Pliny would not acknowledge a physical infirmity or use it as an excuse to be carried. To him, every moment that could be used for work should be used for work. "I remember how he scolded *me* for walking," Pliny the Younger related. "According to him, I need not have wasted those hours, for he thought that any time was wasted which was not devoted to work."[6] And so it was that the elder Pliny was carried along the dark city streets before dawn to see his friend Vespasian, preceded by a servant or a client bearing a flaming torch, at every step composing his grammatical thoughts.

Vespasian, meanwhile, now that he was back at Rome, appeared to rest on his laurels as a successful general and winner of the decorations of a Triumph. But, all the while, he was hoping for another lucrative appointment from Nero so that he could further improve his financial fortunes. To win another imperial post, Vespasian was prepared to join Nero's entourage when he traveled. The man under the emperor's nose was more likely to win the emperor's favor than another who failed to make the effort to flatter his lord and master. In short, Vespasian had no scruples about sycophancy if that fanned the flickering flame of prosperity.

THE WATER
COMMISSIONER

Well before the end of March, with the ceremonials devoted to
Mars continuing, Nero, impatient to escape the capital and begin
his planned performance tour, departed Rome. He did not go alone or
unnoticed. Carried in a litter, guarded by heavily accented German bodyguards from the German Cohorts and men from the Praetorian Cohorts,
accompanied by a train of litters bearing scores of leading Roman citizens, and followed by carts and wagons laden with baggage and thousands of slaves and freedmen on foot, the massive Neronian cavalcade
passed through the Porta Capena and proceeded down the Appian Way
to the south.

Praetorian prefect Tigellinus remained at the capital. Other serving
officials, too, would not be leaving Rome. The two consuls would remain,
as would the twenty praetors, who were the senior magistrates of Rome
and were required to preside at court hearings on all business days
through the year. Various other officials also had a reason, or an excuse,
not to accompany the emperor, among them the city prefect, Vespasian's
brother Flavius Sabinus, as well as the grain commissioner, the streets
commissioner, and water commissioner Publius Marius, who had just
begun his eighteen-month tenure in his new job.

Marius had been a consul two years earlier. As water commissioner, he was charged with keeping Rome's water supply flowing, and pure. So that he could achieve those goals, the water commissioner had control of two groups of slaves, the water gangs. Like so many Roman institutions and innovations, the state water gang had been established in the reign of Augustus. The other gang, Caesar's water gang, had been created by Claudius. The former, paid for by the state treasury, numbered some 240 men. The work of this gang was subsidized by water rights fees paid into the treasury by private individuals who piped water under imperial license from the aqueducts along their routes. The cost of maintaining the 460 slaves of Caesar's water gang was met by the emperor's private purse.

Between them, the 700 men of the water gangs were supposed to keep Rome's aqueducts in good repair. Some water gang members worked outside Rome, maintaining the underground and over-ground waterways of the vast and efficient water supply system that ran from the hills to the northeast, east, and southeast of Rome. The remaining water gang slaves worked on the water supply system within the city. The aqueducts were gravity-fed; not a single pump was employed. From many miles away, the aqueducts brought water coursing into Rome for government and private use. On the last stage of the water's journey, it traveled high in the air over massive arches that elevated the water channels up to 158 feet above the ground.

Once it reached the city, the water was distributed from the aqueducts into reservoirs throughout Rome—247 of them by the end of the first century—and from these in underground lead pipes running throughout the metropolis. Seventy-five of Rome's public buildings, including public baths and imperial palaces, received running water around the clock. A total of thirty-nine ornamental fountains and a dozen military and paramilitary barracks in the capital were likewise fed with water by the system. Water was also piped to 521 public water basins, from where the servants of apartment dwellers collected it for domestic use. Martial complained about the lack of running water in his tenement building, a shortcoming made all the more galling to him by the sight of an aqueduct close by.[1]

Private contractors accounted for about a third of Rome's total water consumption. They resold water to the owners of houses, apartment blocks, and businesses, including the many commercial bathhouses flourishing in the city. Accommodating both men and women, more than one hundred public bathhouses were scattered around Rome in AD 64; the number would increase to a thousand the following century. Every large house in Rome also had its own private bathhouse. To tap into the system, the private contractors were required, by decree of the Senate, to produce a license bearing the imperial seal, the Sardonychis.

The water commissioner was not responsible for the removal of wastewater via Rome's extensive underground sewer system, which emptied liquid waste into "Father Tiber," the Tiber River. This came under the control of another official of like rank, the commissioner of the "Bed and Banks of the Tiber and the Sewers of Rome." The vaulted stone and brick sewers of ancient Rome were so well constructed that some are still in use today. The largest was fifteen feet across; a wagon could be driven through it. Augustus' right-hand man Marcus Agrippa had taken such an interest in Rome's water supply and sewers, which he brought under his mantle, that he made an inspection tour through the sewers in a rowboat.

A total of nine aqueducts brought water to Rome in Nero's day. Under Nero, a single aqueduct, the Claudia, built by Claudius and modified by Nero, served both the Caelian and the Aventine hills. "The result," wrote Sextus Julius Frontinus, water commissioner under the emperor Nerva thirty years later, "was that whenever any repairs caused interruptions, these densely inhabited hills suffered a drought."[2] Storms, wear and tear, and shoddy workmanship made repairs to the water supply system by the two water gangs an ongoing task. Repairs were also necessary in country areas through which the system's subterranean tunnels passed, with damage caused by tree roots, illegal buildings, and even tombs built over the tunnels. Damage also occurred when greedy landowners bored into the tunnels to steal water. Because water consumption was at its height in summer, all but emergency repairs to aqueducts were carried out during the spring and autumn months, when disruption to the supply might not prove such an inconvenience to consumers.

The water commissioner of Rome was a very senior position; Frontinus had been a consul and governor of Britain prior to his appointment. Like the grain commissioner and streets commissioner, the water commissioner was paid to apply at least three months of his time every year to his official duties. But through laziness or graft, many water commissioners neglected the administration of the water gangs and failed to police the supply regulations. The business of stealing water was a profitable one for some. After Frontinus became water commissioner, he conducted a detailed survey of the water supply system one July: "There are extensive areas in various places where secret pipes run under the pavements all over the city. I discovered that these pipes were furnishing water by special branches to all those engaged in business in those localities, through which the pipes ran, being bored for that purpose here and there by the so-called 'puncturers.'"[3]

These puncturers were water contractors and corrupt water gang overseers who piped away large volumes of water without paying the state a license fee, selling it at great profit. Frontinus also discovered another cagey practice. Each new water licensee was entitled to insert a single outlet into the distribution pipe that passed his property. In the case of an existing license that had been surrendered because of the death or changed circumstances of the licensee, the outlet created by the previous licensee was supposed to be sealed. But this frequently did not happen, so that the new licensee retained the old outlet and created a new one as his license permitted, and took twice as much water as he was entitled to.

By prosecuting water thieves and plugging illegal pipes, Frontinus would stamp out the practice of puncturing. He would be so successful in restoring the overall volume of water reaching the legitimate outlets in Rome that he would divert one of the sources, at today's Frascati in the Roman Hills, to local consumption, while still delivering more water to the capital than before. Unfortunately for Rome, the water-theft industry flourished under the noses of water commissioners previous to Frontinus, including Publius Marius. Frontinus did not accuse his predecessors of being in the pay of the puncturers. But it was not impossible that some were corrupt. Frontinus did accuse his predecessors of laziness and indolence and for neglecting their duties while taking their salaries and using their state-assigned lictors, clerks, and other assistants for personal tasks.

The Senate produced page after page of regulations for water distribution, even specifying the size of nozzle by which water could be extracted from a pipe. But not a single bylaw was written to regulate the use of water to fight the fires that frequently broke out in the city. House fires were common, which is not surprising, considering that cooking and heating in Rome required the use of an open flame. But major blazes that ravaged significant buildings or entire regions of the city had occurred in almost every decade of the first century to date.

Fire had caused extensive damage at Rome in AD 6. An AD 12 fire had severely damaged the Basilica Julia on the Forum Romanum; the basilica was home to Rome's law courts. Two years later, the Basilica Aemilia, just across the Forum, also sustained serious fire damage. In AD 22, on the Campus Martius, the massive Theater of Pompey, site of Julius Caesar's assassination in 44 BC, had been totally gutted by fire. Tiberius, who paid for the theater's restoration, had commended his Praetorian prefect Sejanus for prompt action, which had confined the fire to the theater, and the Senate had subsequently installed a statue of Sejanus in the restored building. This was before Sejanus' spectacular fall from grace.

In AD 26, on the Caelian Hill, which had once been renowned for abundant oak trees but was subsequently covered with buildings, a massive fire destroyed every single closely packed structure. Sponsored by a donation of 100 million sesterces from the emperor Tiberius, new buildings were quickly erected to replace the old on the Caelian Hill that year. They were erected on top of the blackened rubble littering the hill, so that it was said the Caelian actually increased in height as a result of the fire.

In AD 36, a blaze erupted in the northeast corner of the Circus Maximus. Driven by a powerful wind, this fire quickly spread across the Triumphal Way to the Aventine Hill. There too, just as on the Caelian Hill a decade earlier, every single house, tenement building, bathhouse, and shop on the slopes was razed, although several temples appear to have been spared serious damage. And there on the Aventine, too, buildings swiftly rose anew in the wake of the disaster.

Until Augustus took the throne, Rome had no organized firefighting service. In those days, property owners throughout Rome had employed night watchmen who patrolled city blocks with a bell, and should they detect a fire, they rang their bell to warn sleeping residents so that people could at least escape with their lives. In AD 6, following the serious blaze that year, Augustus introduced the Cohortes Vigiles—literally, cohorts that stay awake, or the Night Watch as they would later be styled. Recruited from freedmen and commanded by their own prefect, these "vigiles" were paramilitaries who took over the guarding of Rome in the hours of darkness from the Cohortes Urbanus, or City Cohorts—called the City Guard by later authors.

The vigiles were lightly armed and served as night police. They had even carried out the arrest of Tiberius' overly ambitious Praetorian prefect Sejanus in AD 31. But their main role was that of firemen after dark, and like owls, they led a nocturnal life, sleeping during daylight. Augustus initially introduced the vigiles on a temporary, trial basis, but they had proved so popular that he retained them, paying them from his own purse. The vigiles were organized in seven cohorts, each of a thousand men. Every cohort was expected to guard two city precincts, and every cohort occupied a barrack house in its area of responsibility. The vigiles' firefighting equipment consisted of bronze or leather buckets, which they had to dip into the water basins and reservoirs in their vicinity, or into the Tiber. And there would have been an ax and a ladder or two at each vigile barrack house. But there were no fire hoses, no pumps, not even water wagons.

There was no provision for tapping into the water supply for firefighting purposes. Rome had no fire regulations and no building code. The city's fifty-five miles of streets were narrow and frequently winding. On only two streets in "old Rome," the part of the city enclosed by the Servian Walls, could two carts pass abreast: the Via Sacra and the Via Nova. Most other streets were only wide enough for a single cart. The back streets of Rome were merely pedestrian lanes—narrow, dark even at midday, and frequently unpaved, which made them muddy when it rained. On the urban hillsides, streets zigzagged seemingly without rhyme or reason.

Many landowners, to maximize rental space, built out over the street at second-floor level and higher. Four-story private residential buildings were the norm in Rome, with five and six stories not unknown. Several centuries after this, the city's tallest apartment block would rise an impressive seven floors and be spoken of with awe around the empire. As a result of this unbridled upper-floor construction, buildings on one side of narrow streets in some residential quarters almost touched buildings on the other. In these circumstances, the vigiles had little hope of dousing a major fire or preventing it from spreading once it took hold. Their one asset was their numbers; the seven thousand men of the Cohortes Vigiles had, between them, the ability to swiftly warn residents and help them evacuate fire-threatened buildings and areas.

In fact, the one common feature of all the fires in Rome since the introduction of the vigiles was the fact that Rome's historians of the time made no mention of lives lost in building fires. Those same historians would chronicle the great loss of life in other disasters around the empire during this period. As lifesavers, then, the vigiles had proven to be a successful innovation. As property savers, however, they were less successful.

Some would say that now, twenty-eight years since the last major fire in the city, Rome was overdue for a significant outbreak.

THE SINGING EMPEROR

Breaking the journey at the villas of court favorites en route, Nero and his massive entourage moved across the Campanian landscape like a creeping flood. So it was that the imperial caravan arrived at Neapolis on the Bay of Naples in time for the town's annual contests in poetry and song.

On the first day of the contests, local dignitaries flocked to the temporary wooden theater that had been erected in the town for the annual event, joining the throng of senators and Equestrians that had followed Nero down from Rome. Among these leading men who had joined the emperor's entourage was Gaius Petronius, who had only recently served as a consul. A wealthy, elegant, and cultured man who led an extravagant, stylish life, Petronius was so admired by Nero that the emperor had recently named him his official *arbiter elegantiae*, or director of good taste. Petronius subsequently became known as Gaius Petronius Arbiter. To him would be credited authorship of the hedonistic and satirical Roman novel *The Satyricon*. Petronius, one of the night livers—who Seneca thought defied nature by living their lives during the night hours and sleeping during the day—was astute enough to appear in the emperor's company when it mattered.

"A rabble of the townsfolk was brought together," Tacitus scornfully wrote of this day at the theater of Neapolis. They were joined by thousands more "whom the excitement of such an event attracted from the neighboring towns and [military] colonies."[1] The audience on the tiered seating of the half-moon–shaped theater was completed by men of the emperor's bodyguard, so that the venue, which was open to the sky, was packed.

The young Nero's singing voice had originally been, according to his biographer Suetonius, "feeble and husky." Once he had decided to take up singing seriously, said Suetonius, Nero "conscientiously undertook all the usual exercises for strengthening and developing the voice."[2] One such exercise involved lying on the back with a slab of lead on the chest, to develop and strengthen the diaphragm. Nero also used enemas and emetics (the latter to deliberately induce vomiting after eating). Both were recommended by Roman physicians for improving the voice and were regularly employed by orators. Julius Caesar had notably followed a prescribed course of emetics toward the end of his life. Certain foods, such as apples, considered harmful to the vocal chords, were banished from Nero's diet.

Nero suffered from severe nervousness prior to his stage appearances, and as his debut loomed, he would have been pacing back and forth behind the stage while two attendants attempted to steady his nerves with praise and assurances that all would be well. He had good reason to be nervous, for the rules of these contests were strict. A contestant must stand while performing, would lose points for clearing his throat, for spitting, for blowing his nose, or even for using his arm to wipe the sweat from his brow—contestants were not even permitted to take a handkerchief on stage. If a contestant made a major blunder while performing, he could be disqualified.

Like the other competitors, Nero had his name inscribed on a ticket of ivory, which the judges drew to decide the order of competition. Several competitors duly performed before, to the surprise of the audience, their emperor stepped out onto the stage wearing the long, ungirdled tunic of a lyre player and gave his preliminary oration.

Then, as he was handed his lyre by the senior officer of his bodyguard, the name of the song he would sing was announced by Cluvius Rufus, a former consul and a respected historian, who was a part of the imperial entourage and had volunteered to act as the emperor's herald. And then Nero played and sang. His performance was creditable and well received by the audience. After all the contestants had performed, there was a nerve-racking wait for Nero while the judges consulted and compared notes. Finally, the chief judge stepped out onto the stage. The winner, he announced, was Nero Caesar. A beaming Nero accepted the victor's laurel. The emperor was so pleased with his debut that he entered another of the Neapolitan contests scheduled for the following day.

In the interim, he gave his voice a rest, but the adulation of the crowd had been so seductive that he could not keep out of the public eye. So, that evening, after bathing in the town, he and the senior members of his entourage dined very publicly in the "orchestra" area at the front of the theater. As he passed through an applauding crowd on his way to dinner, people asked him what he would sing to them next.

"When I've downed a drink or two, I'll give you something to make your ears ring," he responded in Greek, the language of the song lyrics.[3]

The crowd applauded even more loudly.

The following day, Nero again took his chances in the draw for places. His fellow competitors, "whom he treated as equals," according to Suetonius, were put at ease by his grace and charm, although behind their backs, he disparaged them to his friends.[4] Not surprisingly, following the performances, the judges declared Nero again the winner. What judge would dare not give the prize to his emperor, to this emperor?

Come nightfall, the well-pleased crowd dispersed, the theater emptied, and in high spirits, Nero and his companions departed to the bath and the dinner table. The ordinary people of Neapolis and surrounding villages seemed excited and even flattered by the fact that Caesar had performed on their stage. The same could not be said for Rome's elite. Nero's appearance as a competitor on the public stage could be compared to a serving U.S. president competing on *American Idol* today. The general audience would no doubt be delighted, declaring it a refreshing departure for their country's leader to do such a thing, while the establishment would be horror-struck, claiming that it demeaned the office of president of the United States. Similarly, the members of the Roman aristocracy were appalled that their head of state could stoop to such a thing, but none expressed such a dangerous view to Nero himself.

The social mores of Roman society were tightly observed. Even the dress code was ridiculously emphatic. The tunic of a man of Equestrian or senatorial rank had to be a particular length; for formal occasions, it must be white, with a purple border, the border being thin for the Equestrian, thicker for a senator. It must be worn belted, and it must be short-sleeved. Pliny the Elder, as one of his eccentricities, wore a long-sleeved tunic, primarily to keep his arms and hands warm in winter so that he might keep writing. Within five years, a young Roman legion commander, Alienus Caecina, would scandalize society by wearing multicolored, long-sleeved tunics of the kind favored by the Gauls, while on duty. Julius Caesar had also defied custom and worn long-sleeved tunics, but he was Caesar. Nero's way of defying custom and social mores was by going on the stage.

That evening, as the populace of Neapolis bathed, strolled, and dined and as Nero celebrated his double victory, the city was shaken by an earthquake. Only minimal damage was done to the town, but the temporary wooden banks of seating at the theater, which, only hours before had been filled with thousands of spectators, came crashing down. Many people thought this an unlucky omen. Some would say it was proof that the gods were unhappy with Nero's stage debut. But Nero considered the message to be just the opposite. He reminded those around him that, had the earthquake taken place during the day, a massive death toll would have resulted, and he thanked the gods for sparing all loss of life. He immediately began work on an "elaborate ode," in the words of Tacitus, which praised the gods and celebrated the good luck that, he was convinced, the occasion represented.[5]

Within several days, the Neronian cavalcade was again on the move. Nero's success on the Neapolitan stage had convinced him that his original plan, that of competing in the famous contests in Greece, was a valid one. He was now on his way across Italy to the Adriatic coast. From there, he would take a ship to Greece. His first stop on his route to the Adriatic would be the crossroads town of Beneventum, thirty miles northeast of Neapolis, in the Apennine Mountains.

VIII

THE GLADIATORIAL CONTEST

It being the month dedicated to Mars, and with only very few Roman cities across the empire permitted to stage chariot races, other selected cities and towns honored the war god with a *munus*, a gladiatorial contest. Beneventum, modern Benevento, was one such town, and when the emperor and his cavalcade reached it en route from Neapolis to the Adriatic, it was in time for the town's gladiatorial show. Nero decided to pause a while at Beneventum to take in the show.

Beneventum's *munus* was staged and paid for by a local dignitary. There was a time when any Roman standing for elected office would stage gladiatorial shows to win popular support. The Republican Senate put a damper on this practice in 58 BC by declaring that no one could run for office who had staged a *munus* within the past two years. The emperor Augustus decreed that the praetors of Rome could stage two official gladiatorial shows a year, and the magistrates and priests of other cities once a year. But Augustus had also staged seven or eight "extraordinary" *muneri* annually, in the names of family members, and later emperors including Nero authorized private citizens to conduct "extraordinary" gladiatorial shows.

Claudius had decreed that only the quaestors, Rome's most junior judges, could stage the capital's official gladiatorial contests. Nero had made it optional for the quaestors. At the same time, Nero had banned provincial governors from putting on shows of gladiators, to prevent them from currying popularity with provincials, and, under cover of that popularity, getting away with "irregularities" in their province.

Nero had made *munus* staging mandatory for Celtic priests at the Temple of Claudius at Camulodunum, modern Colchester, capital of the province of Britannia. Prior to the AD 43 Roman conquest of much of southern Britain, the sons of British chiefs had been educated by the Druids, with many young men going on themselves to become Druid priests. Under Roman rule, Druidism was banned, and the sons of British chiefs had to serve in the Claudian Order at the Temple of Claudius. It came to be said that the staging of the *muneri* had so impoverished the British priests that they had conspired with rebel queen Boudicca to throw off Rome's then seventeen-year-old rule in Britain. It appears that in Boudicca's uprising of AD 60, these priests had given rebels access to the Temple of Claudius when thousands of Roman settlers took refuge there during the assault on Camulodunum and, in so doing, had brought about the refugees' capture and brutal deaths, and the fall of the city.

Beneventum's benefactor was the "deformed" Vatinius, who had been born and raised in the cobbler's shop of his freedman father. Vatinius suffered from dwarfism. During the reign of Nero's uncle Caligula, Vatinius had been brought into the imperial court, as a joke, to amuse the emperor. Vatinius had subsequently been a member of Caligula's entourage at the time of the short-lived emperor's assassination. Witty, sarcastic, and knowledgeable about the peccadilloes of courtiers, the "fool" Vatinius had become a permanent fixture of the court, on call to amuse the emperor and his guests with his "vulgar wit." In the opinion of historian Tacitus, little Vatinius, dressed garishly and frequently seen at Nero's side making fun of the Roman elite, was "one of the most conspicuously infamous sights in the imperial court."[1]

Vatinius' imperial patron had rewarded him with money and property, so that he was now an immensely rich man, even though only a freedman. And still he amused the emperor. Only recently, he had said to Nero, "I hate you Caesar, because you are a member of the Senatorial order."[2] Vatinius had, in keeping his ear close to the ground to glean tidbits about the unguarded and impolitic words and actions of leading men and women of Rome, become a valuable source of information for the emperor. "He grew so powerful by accusing all the best men," said Tacitus, "that in influence, wealth, and ability to cause injury, he was preeminent."[3]

For all the Roman public's enjoyment of blood sports, there had been little outcry when, for the previous years' Great Games, Nero had ended the practice of allowing victorious gladiators to take the lives of their defeated opponents. He had not even allowed criminals to be put to death in the arena. Nero did not take away the main attraction of gladiatorial contests: gambling. Under Roman law, it was legal to bet on contests of physical skill. Vast amounts would be wagered on every gladiatorial contest.

Vatinius' *munus* at Beneventum would have followed the usual pattern. Each day's show began at dawn and ended at dusk. Free tickets had been distributed to people in his favor by the man paying for the games, called its editor. Remaining spectators had to pay for admission. Well before sunrise, the crowd, consisting of both men and women, excitedly surged up the amphitheater's stone stairways to secure seats denoted by their numbered, clay tickets. Many had purchased the handwritten programs that had been on sale in Beneventum streets for days beforehand.

Once in their seats, the audience members excitedly perused the program, discussed the merits of this fighter and that, and laid their bets, every now and then glancing toward the enclosed tribunal, the official box, hoping to catch sight of the emperor. The most senior members of the emperor's sycophantic entourage, former consuls such as Titus Vespasian, Petronius Arbiter, and Cluvius Rufus, were seated with Nero. A vacant seat beside the emperor awaited the editor of the games.

As the sun rose, trumpets heralded a parade around the arena by all taking part, to the cheers and applause of the spectators. Competitors were led by the editor, Vatinius, who rode in a chariot. He was followed by uniformed *bestiari*, the animal fighters. All the staff of the amphitheater, slaves and freedmen alike—from those who raked the blood-soaked sand covering the arena's floor to medical attendants and arena musicians playing flute, lyre, trumpet, horn, and water organ—were uniformly dressed.

Next came the gladiators, the star attractions. Most were slaves and had ridden to the amphitheater in closed carriages. Now, wearing purple cloaks richly embroidered with gold, the gladiators paraded around the arena waving and gesturing to the crowd. Behind them came slaves bearing their armor and weapons. There were many types of gladiator, with varying types of weapons and tactics. The rebel gladiator Spartacus had fought in the Thracian style, for example. Spectators followed not only individual gladiators, but also particular fighting styles.

Perhaps two in ten of these gladiators were free men who had voluntarily taken to the gladiatorial life, for money, for thrills, for adulation. Even the occasional Equestrian or senator down on his financial luck took to the arena, to the horror of the Roman elite. Just months before this, female gladiators had appeared during the traditional ten days of gladiatorial contests held at Rome in December. Some had been ladies of distinction, from noble families. These volunteer female fighters had fought each other, not male combatants.

Now, the parading combatants halted in front of the arena's tribunal and faced the emperor. "Hail, *imperator!*" they chorused.[4]

Vatinius' program was a "crowded" one, according to Tacitus.[5] It would have seen gladiators or troops engage in carefully orchestrated mock combat during the morning, with wooden weapons and muffled shields, as a preliminary to the later, bloodier contests. Flavius Josephus, who would witness Rome's legions in training just three years from now, would describe legion drills as bloodless battles, and their battles as bloody drills. Vatinius may also have put on "acts"—panthers drawing chariots, lions releasing live hares from their jaws on command, tigers licking the hand of their trainer, elephants kneeling before the emperor's tribunal and tracing out Latin phrases in the sand with their trunks. Poet Martial and author Pliny the Elder witnessed such acts in the amphitheater and recorded their enjoyment of them.

The execution of criminals and beast hunts filled the middle of the day. Wild animals were released into the arena together with criminals condemned to death, with the audience enjoying what followed, as spectators ate their lunches. Once the prisoners had met their end, the beast-fighting *bestiari* then went against the larger animals, "hunting" and slaughtering them with javelin, fork, sword, knife, and bow and arrow. Frequently, some animals were permitted to live until the next spectacle, but occasionally, an editor would advertise that no animal would be spared at his games.

These beast hunts came to be the single most popular attraction of Roman spectacles. After Vespasian became emperor, five years after Nero's visit to the Beneventum *munus*, he would order a purpose-built amphitheater erected at Rome for beast hunts. He named it the Hunting Theater. Later generations called it the Flavian Theater. This was the Colosseum. Through its early history, the Colosseum would see many more beast hunts than gladiatorial contests.

Only in the afternoon did the best gladiators take to the sand. Many gladiators were made rich by the prize money on offer and by the gifts from admirers, including the emperor. Nero's favorite gladiator and the most famous of his day was Spiculus, who received houses at Rome and in the country from the emperor. It was the one-on-one contests that the crowd had come to see. Each pair slogged it out with their unarmed trainers standing right behind them and issuing instructions as the fight took place, even lashing them with whips to encourage more spirited displays. Despite this nearness to the fight, and to death, no trainer was apparently injured in a contest or was set on by his own fighter or an opponent. Such was the keenly observed etiquette of the arena.

During the afternoon, Nero was called away from the sport. A message had arrived from Tigellinus at Rome. The Praetorian prefect informed his emperor that he had received information that a leading senator, Marcus Junius Torquatus Silanus, had been lavishing gifts on noble friends. The talk was, Tigellinus said, that Silanus was winning support for a revolution against Nero. Silanus boasted imperial blood as a great-grandson of Augustus. In the eyes of some, this gave him a claim to the throne. Silanus' accusers also said that he used nobles as his secretaries and bookkeepers, when everyone else, the emperor included, used mere freedmen in these roles, with Seneca a notable exception. It was as if, the accusation went, Silanus were preparing his friends for loftier positions and preparing himself for the loftiest position of all, Nero's throne.

In light of these slim accusations, Tigellinus had dragged Silanus' most intimate freedmen off to the Praetorian barracks, where he would personally "examine" them, on the rack. Under Roman law, no Roman citizen could be tortured for information or a confession, but no such right extended to freedmen or slaves. Tigellinus personally conducted such interrogation sessions. Three years earlier, Tigellinus had racked the servants of Nero's divorced first wife, twenty-year-old Octavia Augusta, daughter of Claudius, trying to extract evidence that Octavia had committed adultery, a charge concocted by Nero's jealous second wife, Poppaea Sabina.

One of Octavia's women, Pythias, had bravely gasped from the rack, "My mistress's privy parts are cleaner, Tigellinus, than your mouth."[6]

By the third and last day of the Beneventum show, Nero received another communication from Tigellinus, this one telling him that Torquatus Silanus had taken his own life. Silanus, suspecting that his arrest was only a matter of time, had "divided the arteries in his arms" with a knife, taking his own life in the time-honored fashion favored by the Roman elite, rather than face trial and conviction in the Senate and a humiliating death at the hands of a Praetorian executioner.[7]

Nero seemed surprised by the news. "Though Silanus was guilty, and with good reason had put no trust in his defense," the emperor declared in a speech published soon after, "he would had lived had he awaited the clemency of the judge."[8] That judge was, of course, Nero.

Vatinius' gladiatorial show came to an end, and as Nero's party prepared to continue to the port of Brundisium, two hundred miles to the southeast, and a subsequent sea voyage to Greece, the emperor made a surprise announcement. He would, for the moment, not be going on to Achaia, he said, without giving any reason for his change of plan. He would instead be returning to Rome at once. Perhaps, just perhaps, Nero had been made uneasy by Tigellinus' preemptory action against Silanus. Was the emperor wondering what else the Praetorian prefect might get up to while he was away in Greece?

So, the entire cavalcade turned around and headed back down the road to Rome.

THE JEWS AND THE
CHRISTIANS

In Rome, twenty-seven-year-old Joseph bar Matthias was finishing his lunch, the main meal of the day for first-century Jews. To Romans, the main meal of the day was taken in the evening. Joseph was completing preparations for Pesach, the Jewish festival of the Passover, then only days away.

Just a decade later, Joseph would receive Roman citizenship as an author in the favor of Rome's Flavian emperors. He would take the Romanized name of Flavius Josephus. This spring of AD 64, Joseph, a native of Jerusalem, was in the early stages of a lengthy stay at Rome. He was on a special mission. Descended from Levi, who was the great-grandson of the biblical Abraham, Joseph had been entitled to enter the Jewish priesthood, as only the descendants of Levi, the Levites, could do. From age sixteen, he had spent three years studying the teachings of various Jewish sects, the Pharisees, the Sadducees, and the Essenes, also studying for a time under a Jewish ascetic in the desert. By nineteen, Joseph had returned to Jerusalem, where he became a priest of the Pharisee order. Eight years later, he had come on his mission to Rome.

Joseph himself explained: "When I was twenty-six, it happened that I took a voyage to Rome." That was in AD 63. "When [Antonius] Felix was Procurator of Judea, there were certain priests of my acquaintance, and very excellent persons they were, whom on a small and trifling accusation he put into chains, and sent to Rome to plead their cause before Caesar."[1] Felix's seven-year tenure as Roman governor of Judea had ended in AD 59, and these accused Jewish priests had been languishing at Rome, in prison or under house detention, ever since their arrest, existing on figs and nuts. It was Joseph's mission to orchestrate their discharge.

Like Joseph, these priests would have been Pharisees. To possess the right to have their appeals heard by Caesar, they might also have held Roman citizenship, which, for Jewish priests, was unusual. No classical text or inscription records this possibility, but some priests at Jerusalem might have been granted Roman citizenship during the reign of Caligula or that of Claudius. A vast number of foreigners are known to have been granted Roman citizenship during Claudius' reign in particular, via his wife Messalina, who took so many bribes for arranging the grants of citizenship that a joke went around Rome that it was possible to buy citizenship for just a handful of broken glass.

Claudius had been raised at the Palatium at Rome in the company of the Jew Marcus Julius Agrippa, grandson of Herod the Great. Agrippa, given a small tetrarchy by Caligula, had been at Rome at the time of Caligula's assassination and had been instrumental in Claudius' accession to the vacant throne. Claudius, in his gratitude, had crowned his friend, who became King Herod Agrippa I of Judea. To Agrippa had fallen charge of the Temple at Jerusalem and the appointment of the high priest. Under Agrippa's authority, the Great Sanhedrin, the seventy-member Jewish religious ruling council of priests at Jerusalem, was summoned. It is conceivable that Caligula or Claudius also granted Roman citizenship to priests who were at Jerusalem and were nominated by Agrippa, perhaps those who fulfilled their duties particularly zealously. Agrippa died of a heart attack in AD 44. Perhaps the custom of granting Roman citizenship to Jewish priests had died with him.

Another Jew had been dispatched to Rome by Felix's successor in AD 59, also to have his appeal heard by Nero. This was a Jew who certainly held Roman citizenship and who had also been a priest and a Pharisee. His Jewish name was Saul of Tarsus; his Roman name, Paulus. This was

Saint Paul the Apostle. Paul's Roman citizenship has never been questioned by historians or theologians. But no one has ever been able to explain how Paul came by that citizenship. Some scholars suggest that Paul's father held Roman citizenship; others that the entire population of the city of Tarsus, Paul's birthplace, might have been granted Roman citizenship. No evidence exists to support either theory. It is just as credible that Paul was granted Roman citizenship at the behest of Herod Agrippa I, ironically for his zealous hunting down of Christians. "Beyond measure I persecuted the church of God," Paul himself wrote, "and wasted it."[2]

It is likely that Joseph knew Paul, or knew of him. Saul, as he was then called, had trained as a Pharisee at Jerusalem under the renowned Jewish teacher Gamaliel I. When Joseph was a child, Paul had been a hard-line Pharisee at Jerusalem who led the persecution of Christians, during the late AD 30s and, possibly, into the early AD 40s, during the short reign of Caligula and at the beginning of Claudius' reign. It is entirely possible that Paul's grant of Roman citizenship came then, via King Agrippa, in the circumstances mentioned above. Only after this had Paul literally seen the light on the road to Damascus and become a follower of Christ.

In AD 59, Paul was sent to Rome in chains and under legionary guard. En route, the ship carrying the apostle and 275 other passengers had been caught in a massive storm in the Eastern Mediterranean and dashed on Malta's rocky shore. All aboard had survived, and the Roman centurion in charge of Paul's escort, Julius, had procured passage for prisoner and escort aboard another ship the following spring. Paul had arrived at Rome that spring of AD 60 and was handed over to the Praetorians.

Centurion Julius had put in a good word for Paul, and Praetorian Prefect Burrus, then in his second-last year of office, and of life, had ordered house arrest for the duration of Paul's long appeal process. Paul was able to rent accommodation in Rome; Christian tradition puts the house on the Triumphal Way, on a site where Nero would soon build a vast pond, the *stagnum Neronis*, and where the Colosseum would rise within another two decades. There, with a Praetorian soldier on his door, and wearing a chain, Paul waited for his case to be heard by Nero, or by the urban praetor, who was deputized to act for the emperor on occasion. According to the New Testament's Acts of the Apostles, Paul remained at Rome for two years. Theologians believe that Paul's case was ultimately dismissed and that in AD 62 he resumed his travels.

On his way to Jerusalem in AD 57, Paul had written to the Christians at Rome: "When I take my journey into Spain, I will come to you. For I trust to see you in my journey, and to be brought on my journey thitherward by you."[3] His arrest shortly after at Jerusalem put paid to that plan, but it is suggested that once Paul was released from custody in AD 62, he continued on to Spain as originally intended. The tradition in Spain is that Paul indeed founded the Spanish Church about this time, at Tarraco on the east coast. The late-first-century Epistle of Clement Romanus says, "he came to the borders of the West," which some interpret as confirming that Paul did reach Spain. Theodoret of Cyrrhus claimed in the fifth century that Paul preached in islands, which some have taken to mean Britain, others, Spain's Balearic Isles.[4]

During his two years of house arrest at Rome, Paul had communed with the small Christian community in the city and addressed representatives of the much larger Jewish community, Jews having flooded back once Nero had become emperor and tolerated their presence at Rome. Paul strove to increase the scope of the Christian congregation at the capital, preaching "those things which concern the Lord Jesus Christ, with all confidence, no man forbidding him."[5]

In a Pauline letter, 1 Corinthians, written from Rome during this period, Paul referred to Christians in Caesar's household. A Christian tradition holds that one was Torpes, "an officer of prime note in Nero's palace," while Dio Chrysostom claimed that Nero's cup-bearer and one of his concubines were also converts.[6] One tradition holds that this concubine was the emperor's mistress Acte. "This Acte," wrote Cassius Dio, "had been bought as a slave in Asia, but winning the affections of Nero, was adopted into the family of Attalus, and the emperor loved her much more than he did his wife Octavia."[7]

Nero had at one time thought about making Acte his wife, and her adoption by a Roman family was intended to make her more acceptable marriage material, but Nero's mother, Agrippina the Younger, put her foot down and refused to permit any such union. Acte would remain loyal to Nero for the rest of his life. The story of her conversion to Christianity seems to stem from a more recent source, the nineteenth-century novel *Quo Vadis*. Whether or not Paul did convert Torpe, Acte, and the cupbearer to Christianity, Acts reveals that Paul was less successful in converting the Jews of Rome.

When Joseph had traveled to Rome from Judea in AD 63, he too had survived a shipwreck; his overloaded vessel went down in the Adriatic at night. More than five hundred passengers and crew had drowned around him in the darkness. When dawn broke next day, Joseph was one of just eighty plucked from the water by another merchant ship. Joseph had come ashore when this merchantman docked at Puteoli on the bay of Naples, then Italy's largest commercial port. He quickly made contact with the local Jewish community, which put him in touch with a Jewish stage actor named Aliturius, who was, to Joseph's good fortune, "much beloved by Nero."[8] Through the good offices of Aliturius, Joseph would eventually receive an introduction to Nero's wife, the empress Poppaea Sabina.

Poppaea, a noted beauty who reputedly bathed in asses' milk, came from a noble bloodline including consuls and triumphant generals; although her father, a quaestor, had been executed by Tiberius as an adherent of Sejanus, and her mother had been punished for adultery. Poppaea, who was several years older than Nero, had been married twice before. Her first husband was Rufius Crispinus, an Equestrian, while the second had been Nero's best friend, Marcus Salvius Otho.

According to historian Plutarch, Poppaea had been seduced by Otho when she was still married to Crispinus, and Otho had convinced her to divorce Crispinus and marry him, after which he had offered to share her with Nero to further win Nero's favor.[9] Tacitus told a slightly different story: Poppaea, attracted by his "youth and fashionable elegance" and by his closeness to the boy emperor, had seduced Otho, then divorced Crispinus and married him. But, said Tacitus, her sights were on Nero, and she convinced Otho to allow Nero to share her bed, to add to his own influence with the emperor.[10]

There is a third version: According to Suetonius, Nero fell for Poppaea when she was married to Crispinus, and the emperor entrusted

Otho with the task of marrying Poppaea for the time being, until Nero could rid himself of his wife Octavia and overbearing mother Agrippina, who was determined that Nero and Octavia would produce an heir with pure Julian blood. All three, Plutarch, Tacitus, and Suetonius, agreed that Otho had fallen in love with Poppaea and soon began to begrudge sharing her. "He not only enjoyed Poppaea, but developed such a deep passion for her that he would not tolerate even Nero as a rival," said Suetonius. "We have every reason to believe the story that he rebuffed, first, the messengers sent by Nero to fetch Poppaea, and then Nero himself, who was left on the wrong side of the bedroom door, alternately threatening and pleading for the lady."[11]

According to Plutarch, Poppaea had enjoyed making both men jealous and even excluded Nero from her bedroom from time to time even when Otho was not around, to maintain his enthusiasm for her.[12] Tacitus said that she also wanted Nero to dispense with Acte, to whom he was extremely attached, deriding the relationship between emperor and former slave, as "low and degrading."[13] When Otho refused to continue sharing Poppaea and tried to keep her all to himself, Nero first cut him from his circle of intimates and then appointed him governor of the province of Lusitania, modern-day Portugal, well away from Rome. When, in AD 58, Otho set off to take up his appointment, his wife remained at Rome, to warm the emperor's bed. Otho had remained in Lusitania ever since, showing himself a capable governor.

For several subsequent years, Poppaea had been Nero's mistress, until she convinced him to divorce Octavia (whom he had married at the age of sixteen) for her inability to give him an heir. Divorce for Romans was an easy matter, with either party able to declare the marriage terminated, without formalities. Poppaea had divorced Otho, and just sixteen days after Nero divorced Octavia, he and Poppaea were married. It was not long before the new empress was able to orchestrate, with the help of Tigellinus, the accusations of adulterous behavior that led to young Octavia's execution.

Poppaea had promised Nero that she would bear him an heir, and sure enough, she was soon pregnant with his child. Early in AD 63, at Antium, where Nero himself had been born, Poppaea gave birth to a daughter, Claudia Augusta. Nero was ecstatic and seemed not to mind that Poppaea had failed to give him a son. Almost every senator flocked to Antium to congratulate Nero on the birth, and the Senate had decreed numerous celebrations and commemorations. Four months later, baby Claudia Augusta was dead, from illness, and Nero was devastated.

Charming, witty, and politically astute, never allowing her heart to rule her head, Poppaea was, according to Joseph, a deeply religious woman who looked favorably on Jews. She soon took a liking to the personable, bearded young priest from Jerusalem. For his part, Joseph kept from the empress the real purpose of his trip to Italy. He set about building a rapport with her during social occasions and, over time, would receive numerous gifts from her. At the appropriate moment, he would seek a favor, asking that she intercede with Nero on behalf of the Jewish priests awaiting their appeals, and procure their liberty.

For now, supported financially from Judea, Joseph continued to rent accommodations at Rome, mixing with the Jews of the capital, biding his time, and building his relationship with Nero's clever, domineering wife.

THE LAKE BANQUET

June 7. The days were lengthening, the sun strengthening; summer was just weeks away.

Nero, like his great-uncle Caligula before him, had developed a fascination with all things Egyptian. He had investigated the religion of the Egyptians and, for a time following the murder of his mother, had embraced the worship of the Egyptian mother goddess Isis and her consort Sarapis, even integrating feast days of the cult of Isis into the official Roman religious calendar. He longed to visit Egypt, and after terminating his trip to Achaia at Beneventum and returning to the capital, he had spent much time over the remaining weeks and months of the spring back at Rome "dwelling in his secret imaginations on the provinces of the East, especially Egypt," according to Tacitus.[1] Germanicus Caesar, grandfather of Nero and father of Caligula, had been equally fascinated with Egypt. When Roman commander in chief in the East, he had traveled up the Nile as an unescorted tourist on a private visit to the ruins from the age of the pharaohs, using a local priest as his guide.

As the spring passed, Nero had decided that this summer, instead of retiring to some rural or seaside villa as was his custom, he would sail to Alexandria and visit the antiquities of Egypt. Ordering preparations made for his departure, he issued a proclamation this first week of June. He announced his Egyptian trip, declaring that he would not be absent from

Rome long and that "all things in the State would remain unchanged and prosperous" while he was away.[2]

Now, early in the morning, prior to attending a ceremony at the Temple of Vesta, Nero visited the Temple of Jupiter on the Capitoline Mount. There, he made sacrifices and sought good omens and an indication of the most auspicious departure date. Nero then came down to the Forum and entered the Temple of Vesta. This was the first day of the seven-day Vestalia, the annual Festival of Vesta. The vestal virgins had been preparing for months, even personally baking countless salty wheat cakes for the banquets that formed part of the festivities. The festival, the holiest time of the year for the vestals, was to commence with a simple ceremony here at the circular temple that housed the eternal flame.

As the emperor entered the Temple of Vesta, where the vestals awaited him in their white vestments, his cloak became caught, holding him back, and then he felt a trembling sensation all over his body. As he was carried in a litter back to the Palatium, he decided these were signs that he should not leave Rome. He quickly released a new announcement, advising that he was canceling his trip to Egypt, because, he said, love of his country came before his personal plans. "I have seen the sad countenances of the citizens," his latest proclamation declared. "I heard their secret complaints at the prospect of my undertaking such a long journey, when they cannot bear even my briefest excursions, accustomed as they are to being cheered in their misfortunes by the sight of the emperor. Therefore, as in private relationships, the closest ties are the strongest, so the people of Rome have the most powerful claims and must be obeyed in their wish to retain me."[3]

This announcement was well received by the general public. The people felt more secure when the emperor was among them than when he was away, said Tacitus, not the least because they felt confident that while he was at Rome, he would never allow their grain supply to become scarce. As for the members of the Senate and other leading citizens, Tacitus wrote that they were not sure whether to regard Nero as more threatening while he was among them or while he was away.[4]

The Vestalia brought with it obligations for the state to provide public banquets during the week of June 7–14. While these free meals throughout the city were for the general populace, Praetorian Prefect Tigellinus had proposed to Nero that this year, he would personally finance a grand Vestalia banquet for the nobility. Tigellinus' sudden and uncharacteristic generosity might be put down to his nervousness about Nero's reluctance to leave him in charge at Rome while traveling outside Italy. Certainly, Nero's indication that he would have given clemency to Silanus had he not committed suicide strongly hinted at his displeasure over the way that affair had been handled. Tigellinus' offer, designed to cement his position as Nero's most trusted official, was approved.

Tigellinus' banquet was a novel and extravagant affair. There was a body of water on the Campus Martius known as Agrippa's Lake. Marcus Agrippa, Nero's maternal great-grandfather, had personally funded a large complex for the use and pleasure of the public, involving expansive gardens, a basilica, and this lake, which was linked to the Tiber River by a small canal. On this lake, Tigellinus had a large raft constructed. Small rowing craft that shone with gold and ivory were launched onto the lake and tethered to the raft like horses to a carriage.

In the late afternoon of the day of Tigellinus' banquet, the emperor and other official guests arrived and stepped onto the richly decorated raft. Among the guests, apart from Nero and his empress Poppaea, would have been all the usual dignitaries: the consuls Laecanius and Licinius, whose terms, which Nero limited to six months, would soon end; the twenty praetors for the year; Water Commissioner Marius and his fellow commissioners for grain, the streets, and the sewers; a score or more of former consuls, including Vespasian, Petronius Arbiter, and Cluvius Rufus; City Prefect Sabinus; numerous former praetors; other leading senators; the rival Praetorian prefects, Faenius Rufus and the day's host, Tigellinus. Probably, too, there were special guests in the party who had connections at the Palatium, men such as Joseph, the Jewish priest visiting from Judea.

Rowers in the small boats strained at their oars and dragged the raft around the lake. To the delight of some guests and the consternation of others, the lake had been populated with "sea monsters" such as crocodiles and birds from remote lands. On one shoreline, pavilions had been set up, where noble ladies crowded. The sign of the brothel, showing erect penises, hanging outside these pavilions and facing the lake would have made it perfectly clear to those on the raft what the pavilions were supposed to represent.

It is unclear whether the noble ladies knew about the signs. Had they not, and had they simply answered an invitation to assemble at the lakeside pavilions, this would have been a huge joke at their expense—a crude joke contrived by Tigellinus. Meanwhile, on the opposite shoreline, Tigellinus had installed genuine prostitutes, all quite naked, who made obscene gestures and movements as the raft passed slowly by. As the sun set west of the Tiber, the grove in the Gardens of Agrippa and the surrounding public buildings glowed with artificial light and resounded to the sounds of music and song. There at the gardens, the highly amused guests disembarked to dine.

Several days later, in a private ceremony witnessed by only his most intimate associates, Nero went through a mock wedding ceremony with a Greek freedman named Pythagoras, with Nero playing the part of the bride, complete with traditional orange marriage veil. That night, Nero and Pythagoras "honeymooned" together.

THE CHARIOTEER

The July heat beat down on the paving stones of Rome. The city streets were all but deserted. All public business had ceased. Downtown, shops were closed. Soldiers of the City Cohorts patrolled in squads, their helmets and armor shining in the sun and the hobnails of their military sandals crunching on the stone, as they kept a wary eye open for thieves and other wrongdoers trying to take advantage of the quiet. From the distance, beyond the Palatine Hill, a spine-chilling roar rose up on the morning air.

For weeks, the elite of the city had been flocking to the seaside, the countryside, and the hills to escape the summer heat. They were joined at their villas by family, friends, and clients. Only the members of the nobility whose official duties kept them in the city remained. The Roman commoners had no such ability to leave the city for a country seat in the summer or at any other time. To survive, they had no choice but to continue to earn a living at Rome. But at least the commoners had diversions to look forward to. The greatest diversions of all came during July, when there were two major *ludi*, or religious festivals. The first festival ran for seven days early in the month, the second for ten days at the end of the month, and each culminated in chariot races at the circus.

By July 13, the Ludi Apollinares had been running at the capital for a week. Dedicated to Apollo, god of music, song, and dance and protector of flocks, the festival had been celebrated at the Circus Maximus. There had been horse races and drama, mime, and song contests. How Nero had longed to take part, but he knew that it was too soon. First, he must win the laurels in Greece, as he had originally planned, before coming out in public at Rome as a singer.

Now, this last day of the games, Nero sat in the *tribunal judicum*, the judges' box, at the Circus Maximus, cheering for the Greens. Most Romans were lifelong supporters of one racing *factio*, or team, or another. There were four racing factions, the Greens, the Blues, the Whites, and the Reds, each controlled by a corporation. These corporations were vast business enterprises, operating stable complexes, training schools, stud farms, and even their own fleets of ships for transporting horses around the provinces. They owned hundreds of thousands of horses; their horse buyers even had preference over the army when it came to purchasing horseflesh. Racing corporation stock was frequently passed down from father to son.

Romans supported a particular faction all their lives, and on racing day, they turned up at the circus wearing flowers, ribbons, and scarves in the color of their teams. Around Nero this June day, a crowd of more than 200,000 people swelled, all sporting red and white and blue and green. Hundreds of years before, the long, thin, U-shaped Circus Maximus had been created, southwest of the Palatine Hill, its sides built of stone arcades atop which rose massive tiers of seating. Those tiers were built entirely of wood. The Circus Maximus was, and remains to this day, the largest wooden structure ever built. The following century, it would be enlarged even further, to accommodate an estimated 300,000-plus spectators, making it also the largest sporting stadium ever erected.

From dawn till dusk, the chariots raced. In Augustus' time, there were twelve races a day; Caligula, a huge fan of chariot racing, had increased the number to twenty-four. Just four chariots took part in each race, representing each of the factions. Some *ludi* featured two-horse teams. Occasionally, five-, six-, and even ten-horse teams raced. But the four-horse chariot, the *quadriga*, was the standard racing chariot. Of its four horses, the central pair were yoked, but the two outer horses were only in traces.

The left horse, the one that ran closest to the spine of the course, was the team's most important and most valuable, for this horse's cornering skill determined the course of the chariot, and of the race. The outside horse was the next most important, while the two central horses were there for their pulling power.

The Roman charioteer was the rock star of his age, even more cele-brated than the gladiator. Most charioteers came to the track as slaves, some as freedmen. Many became famous and rich. A number died on the track or later, from race injuries. The corporations split the race prize money equally with the winning drivers and paid them bonuses. Drivers also received gifts from their many admirers and won and lost vast amounts wagering on races—their own and others. Unlike dice throw-ing, but like gladiatorial fighting, chariot racing was considered a con-test of skill, and so betting on races was legal.

Fifty provincial cities were authorized by the emperor to erect hippo-dromes and conduct chariot races, but the races at the capital generated the most interest. Results from Circus Maximus races were eagerly sought throughout the empire, and Rome's handwritten daily newspaper, the *Acta diurna*—since its inception by Julius Caesar in 59 BC distributed to all corners of the Roman world—contained the latest race results.

The charioteer, who stood throughout, wound the ends of the reins of his horses around his waist to increase his leverage, leaving the right hand free for the whip and the left for the reins. As a consequence, if his chariot crashed or if he fell out, a driver would be dragged by his bolting team until circus attendants reined them in. Even if the drag did not seriously injure a driver, he was likely to be trampled by another passing team.

In Nero's day, every race consisted of seven laps of the circuit. At the drop of an officiating magistrate's napkin, the competing chariots charged from the starting gates at the flat end of the "U." They raced down the right side of the central spine, which was angled a little diagonally so that the track narrowed at the two turns, increasing the degree of difficulty for making the turn. If there was a false start, a white rope, the *alba linea*, which stretched across the track several feet above the ground halfway down the first lap, would force the teams to stop. If the start was fair, a judge let the *alba linea* drop to the sand before the teams reached it, and they passed over it.

As each lap was completed, high on the circus's spine one of seven large eggs was removed and one of seven gilded dolphins was reversed, to tell spectators and drivers alike how many laps remained. And then it was the last lap, and a champion might overtake his opponents to snatch victory in the last strides, accompanied by the roar of 200,000 spectators. This crescendo of voices meant that visitors approaching Rome on race days would hear the city before they saw it. To leaven the entertainment, there were novelty events and displays of trick riding during the middle of the day. This was when the traders in the arcades beneath the Circus Maximus did their best business, the hot-food shops and wine bars in particular. Here, too, beneath the arcades, prostitutes found ready customers.

Nero was more than just a spectator. Just as he had pretensions to be a stage performer, he also hankered for the circus sands. "Horses had been Nero's main interest since childhood," said Suetonius. "His chatter about the chariot races at the circus could not be stopped."[1] Nero's adherence to the Greens was formed during his school days. As a youth, he had diligently practiced horse management and had learned how to drive the chariot. He became a proficient charioteer and had wanted to show off his skill in public, but Seneca and Burrus had convinced him that it would not be politic.

Instead, the pair had encouraged the boy emperor to build a private chariot-racing circus where he could drive to his heart's content, behind high walls, and out of the public eye. Nero's circus was erected in the Vatican Valley, west of the Tiber. An Egyptian obelisk today stands in the center of St. Peter's Square; originally surmounted by a golden ball, the obelisk stood on the spine of Nero's Vatican circus, testimony to his fascination with all things Egyptian. The obelisk is linked with the pharaoh Ramses II and the Temple of Isis.

From the beginning of his reign, Nero "came up from the country to attend all the races, even minor ones," said Suetonius. "So, there was never any doubt that he would be at Rome on that particular day."[2] Still, Nero harbored ambitions of driving in competition in front of the roaring crowd, not just in his private circus in front of his servants, and of claiming the winner's golden palm trophy. But his confidence was not so great that he would venture out in front of the masses at the Circus Maximus. He could only watch, enviously, as each race unfolded and the teams thundered past his box, and he told himself that he could do as good as, or better than, any of these charioteers competing today.

It is likely that Vespasian was in the judges' box with the emperor this July 13. And accompanying Vespasian would have been his thirteen-year-old boy Domitian, a fan of the Blues and a fanatical follower of chariot racing, although he had no ambitions to be a driver. Once he became emperor, seventeen years hence, Domitian would add two more teams to the competition, Purple and Gold, so that six teams competed in every race, and would reduce the races to five laps so that one hundred races could be run in a day. He would also build a private circus within his Palatium complex on the Palatine, the *domus Domitiana*, so that he could stage and watch racing whenever he felt like it.

With the sun about to set, the last race of the Ludi Apollinares was run and won. Apollo's Games were over for the year. But the mass of people slowly departing the massive stadium in the twilight could look forward to more exciting racing before long. Just a week from now, on July 20, the Ludi Victoriae Caesaris were due to start at the Circus Maximus. Originally staged by Julius Caesar in 46 BC to celebrate his civil war victories and dedicated to his patron deity Venus, these games had been continued by his successor Augustus and by all the Caesars since. Like the Ludi Apollinares, the early days of the upcoming festival would feature drama, music, and other events such as gymnastics, but it would climax with three solid days of chariot racing.

Nero himself did not plan to attend the first week of the Ludi Victoriae Caesaris. He intended to almost immediately head for the seaside city of Antium, where he had an extensive villa. But Nero was not heading for Antium just for the sea air. The city would be staging a singing contest, and Nero intended following up on his success at Neapolis earlier in the year by also entering, and winning, the Antium contest.

At dawn on July 14, Nero and his typically enormous entourage of bodyguard troops, servants, and courtiers set off for Antium. On the emperor's last, dawdling visit to Campania at the beginning of the spring, he had traveled by road. But this trip was more hurried, for Nero wanted to be as rested as possible before he took the stage and competed for the victor's laurel at Antium.

A rider could accomplish the journey from Rome to Antium in a day. But for a party on foot to travel thirty-five miles in a day was virtually unheard-of. Even Rome's legions, composed of fit men accustomed to marching, marched only eighteen to twenty miles a day, and even then only in the mornings, before the heat of the day. To cover thirty-five miles in a day was considered, by legionaries, an extended forced march. Just five years from now, a thirty-three-mile forced march in a single day accomplished by a Roman army in northern Italy would be reckoned a remarkable feat.

For the sake of speed, Nero journeyed to Antium by sea. Tacitus noted that when the troops of Nero's bodyguard accompanied the emperor on his journeys to the lakes of Campania, which were near Antium, the trip was made by sea. A flotilla of small craft from the Misenum base of Rome's Tyrrhenian Fleet on the Bay of Naples would have come up the Tiber and been waiting to embark the emperor and his party at the Campus Martius. The ships would have rowed Nero and the imperial retinue down the river to the Tyrrhenian Sea. Then, turning south and setting their square sails, the ships would have sped them the short distance down the coast to the Cape of Antium and to the small and ancient city of Antium.

The imperial villa's rows of sweeping, gently curved colonnades hugged the shoreline, and the emperor's ships were able to dock right there. Nero and his party stepped ashore on the villa's doorstep in time for lunch, unaware that a disaster of unimaginable magnitude was just five days away.

THE FIRE

Activity was intense in and around the Circus Maximus on July 19. It was a baking hot day. This very morn, Sirius the Dog Star rose in the heavens, signaling the beginning of summer's hottest period. The following day, the Ludi Victoriae Caesaris were scheduled to begin, and in the circus, thousands of perspiring slaves were preparing the stadium for the first day's events.[1] Visitors were flooding into the city from country districts to attend the games. Some would stay at Rome's taverns and inns; others, with friends or relatives. Some would sleep beneath the arcades of the circus or the porticoes of city temples.

Come darkness, convoys of carts that always clogged the night brought the produce, fresh fish, game, and birds in from the countryside. In the arcades beneath the circus, the fires of bakers, pastry cooks, and hot-food stores blazed, so the crowd that descended on the stadium well before dawn could be supplied with their breakfast, their snacks for the day, their lunch. From hundreds of sources, smoke rose up from beneath the stadium and hung above it in a haze. That evening, a strong wind rose up from the north and began to buffet the city, clearing the haze.

At the circus and throughout the rest of the city, excitement mounted in anticipation of the next games on the Roman calendar commencing next day.

◔◍◔

This same day, Nero was at Antium. Since coming to the throne, Rome's fifth emperor had lavished money and honors on the town, his birth-place. Antium predated Rome, having been established by the Volsci people, who were later conquered by the Romans. The "beaks," or iron battering rams, from the prows of six captured warships of Volsci Antium decorated the speakers' rostra in the Forum Romanum at Rome, as trophies of Rome's victory four hundred years before.

Nero had built a new port to service Antium. The town had military colony status, which entailed numerous privileges and had brought retired legion veterans to settle, which meant status and wealth. To boost the former-soldier population, Nero had settled Praetorian veterans and wealthy retired centurions in the town. Here at Antium, too, Nero had leveled and rebuilt the seaside villa that Augustus had kept. It was here in this villa, set below the ancient walled town, that Nero had been born on December 15, AD 37.

Over the foundations of Augustus' Antium vacation house was raised a palatial complex that extended for eight hundred yards along the seafront. More like a small town, the villa included numerous gardens, pools, and temples and a drama theater. To the townspeople of Antium, Nero granted the right to conduct drama and music recitals and competitions in his new theater. And now he would grace the stage that he had built, by competing in Antium's singing competition.

On July 19, Nero spared his voice in preparation for his event that evening. Come nightfall, the emperor, dressed in a long, unbelted, Greek-style tunic, walked along one of the villa's long, marble-lined corridors to the theater, trailed by aides. Out front, beneath the twinkling stars, the stone tiers of the theater were lined with locals who had come to enjoy the night air and the competition. Many of the audience members were retired soldiers who had recently made Antium their home and who were still on the lists of the Evocati militia as their terms of retirement required. In one section of the theater sat unarmed serving troops from the emperor's German bodyguard; the duty cohort would have been stationed at the theater entrances. The half-moon theater's curving front rows, called, in all Roman theaters, Germanicus' Benches, in honor of Nero's famous grandfather, were occupied by the senators who accompanied the emperor and by An-tium's magistrates and members of the city's own elected senate.

Behind the scenes, Nero watched as the judges drew lots from an urn to decide the order of appearance of the competitors. After the lots were drawn, the first competitors took to the stage. As at Neapolis, Nero had been courteous and friendly to his opponents backstage. Finally, it was nervous Nero's turn to perform. First came his opening oration. He ad-dressed the judges with the utmost deference. "I will have done what I can. The issue will now be in Fortune's hands," Nero said, according to Suetonius. "Since you are men of judgment and experience, you will know how to eliminate the factor of chance."[2]

Then, introduced by Cluvius Rufus as he had been at Neapolis, and with lyre in hand, Nero sang his song. It was about the destruction of Troy by the Greeks during the Trojan War, after the cunning employ-ment of the Trojan Horse.

That same warm summer night, a blaze began in a shop beneath the Cir-cus Maximus. A cooking fire had got out of control, or a fire had been deliberately set—no one knew for certain. Tacitus later said that authors of the day gave both explanations. The fire began in the northeastern sec-tion of the circus, where it adjoined the Palatine and Caelian hills, said Tacitus.[3] Flames consumed the contents of the shop and then, via wooden rafters, spread to adjacent shops, which contained "inflammable wares" such as lamp oil.[4] From these shops, the flames rose into the wooden stands above. Soon, the strong northerly wind was driving the fire throughout the entire Circus Maximus complex, whose dry timbers burst into flame as if by magic. Never had anyone seen such a sight as the massive circus ablaze from end to end.

As the flames reached high into the night sky, the handheld fire bells of the vigiles responsible for Rome's Regio XI, which included the cir-cus, were jangling. Thousands who lived beneath the circus escaped with whatever they could carry. Tenement blocks adjoined the circus to the south. Driven by the wind, the flames engulfing the circus crossed the Via Triumphalis and attacked the residential buildings southwest of the circus.

Wooden window shutters and hanging drapes were soon alight. Flames rose up into the rafters, igniting the timbers of the floors above. Soon, entire gutted buildings collapsed in on themselves, crushing everything and everyone below.

"The blaze, in its fury, ran first through the level portions of the city," said Tacitus.[5] From Regio XI, driven by the strong wind, the fire quickly spread south into Regio XII and pushed toward Regio XIII. Before long, in the southeast, the flames jumped the four-hundred-year-old Servian Walls, once the protective boundary of Rome but beyond which the city had expanded over centuries of urban growth, and set alight buildings in Regio I, which adjoined Regio XII. The thousands of vigiles in service came from all the districts of the city to combat the blaze, as the prefect of the Cohortes Vigiles attempted to deal with the growing calamity. This prefect was not identified by Roman sources, but later events suggest he was Gaius Nymphidius Sabinus.

Fighting the raging, wind-driven blaze with buckets of water soon proved next to useless. All Prefect Nymphidius could do was order preventative measures such as the removal of inflammable materials from the path of the fire. Another measure, employed when desperation made it necessary, would entail knocking down buildings to create a fire break. But to maneuver the battering rams used in building demolition into position would take time. The speed of the windblown flames was threatening to defeat that measure before it could be attempted.

With the vigiles fully engaged and losing the battle, the ordinary people of Rome were left to fend for themselves. Cassius Dio described just how quickly the conflagration moved: "Here, men while assisting their neighbors, would learn that their own premises were on fire. There, others, before word reached them that their own houses had caught fire, would be told that they were destroyed."[6] Tacitus, too, wrote of how the fire seemed to come from several directions at once to confront the residents: "Often, while they looked behind them, they were intercepted by flames on their side or in their face."[7] Everywhere, collapsing masonry blocked the narrow streets.

Modern-day research on the behavior of wildfires has shown that no matter what the direction of the prevailing wind during a fire, embers will be carried in all directions and will ignite new blazes seemingly all around the source of the fire, almost as if someone were deliberately setting these new blazes. It is no wonder that many Romans came to believe that arsonists were at work, spreading the fire behind the backs of those trying to combat it.

The streets of the threatened areas were filled with people. "There was shouting and wailing without end," said Dio, "of children, women, men, and the aged, all together, so that no one could see anything or understand what was said because of the smoke and the shouting." While panic sent many running blindly, shock froze others in their tracks; some residents, said Dio, were seen "standing, speechless, as if they were dumb" at the sight of the conflagration devouring one narrow winding, irregular street after another.[8]

Most residents were able to escape with their lives, but very little else. "They crowded the streets or flung themselves down in the fields" outside the city, said Tacitus.[9] Others who rushed back into the burning areas in search of missing loved ones never returned. Sinister incidents were to follow. Looting became rife. Meanwhile, some people were seen hurling burning brands into untouched buildings. Were they pyromaniacs? Perhaps.

Reports would also emerge that when individuals attempted to fight the flames, they were warned away by unidentified men who claimed that they were under orders to prevent the fire from being extinguished. When challenged, these mystery men claimed, "There is one who gives us authority," although they would not name that person. These same people, too, were seen to plunder abandoned shops and houses.[10]

⁙

As dawn broke over the burning city and a pall of smoke hung over the southern regions, Flavius Sabinus, city prefect of Rome, took charge of the firefighting efforts, as responsibility for the security of the city transferred from the exhausted prefect of the vigiles at the start of the first daylight hour. The equally exhausted vigiles withdrew to find some place to sleep, handing the task of battling the conflagration over to three thousand men of the City Cohorts—just two of the City Guard cohorts were in the city—and imperial and state slaves such as the men of the water gangs. Prefect Sabinus' own house on the Quirinal Hill seemed safe from the fire. As for his family, it is likely that he had sent them, along with many of his household staff, to one of his country estates at the start of the summer.

Sabinus was a mature, pragmatic man in his late fifties or early sixties and not prone to panic. Once, when leading the 14th Gemina Legion during the invasion of Britain in AD 43, his unit and his younger brother Vespasian's 2nd Augusta Legion had been trapped by British tribes beside the River Medway. Sabinus, his brother, and their troops had endured a desperate night, fending off the Britons until another legion had fought its way across the river the next day to relieve them. Sabinus had not panicked then, and he would not panic now. He had served one term as city prefect early in Nero's reign, as the nominee of Seneca and Burrus, only accepting the post again in AD 61 after his successor as city prefect, Pedius Secundus, had been murdered by one of his own slaves. Future emperors would also entrust Sabinus with the post of city prefect, such was the respect he garnered for the way he executed his duties.

The task now faced by the city prefect was formidable. The fire was burning fiercely in the low-lying areas of several southern precincts, and it was advancing up the Aventine Hill, consuming the homes of the rich and the famous and the several temples that adorned the hill. But the wind that had driven the fire into the southern suburbs with such speed and ferocity had surprised everyone and had turned. Now it was blowing strongly from the south, fanning the glowing cauldron that was the Circus Maximus and sending flames from it toward the residences lining the southern slopes of the Palatine and Caelian hills. At the same time, the flames in Regio I were being driven north across the flat into Regio's II and V.

One of the first things that the prefect did was dictate a dispatch to the emperor at Antium to tell him of the disaster. Several grim-faced riders from the Praetorian Cavalry were soon galloping south along the Appian Way, bound for Antium. One of the cavalrymen bore a leather dispatch case over his shoulder containing the prefect's message. All along their route, foot traffic and riders alike would move aside for the Praetorians.

⟵∞⟶

Nero awoke early on the morning of July 20 in good spirits. He had won the singing contest the night before, and he intended to compete again on the Antium stage over the next day or two before returning to Rome in time for the Ludi Victoriae Caesaris' three days of chariot racing at the end of the month. By the middle of the day, the message arrived from Rome telling him of the fire. His first reaction was to ignore it. Singing came first. He would let the city prefect deal with the fire; that was his job.

Later in the day, a second message arrived; the fire was continuing to spread, it said. The flames were climbing the Palatine, Caelian, and Aventine hills and were pushing around the bases of the Caelian and the Palatine and driving north toward the Esquiline Hill, threatening the heart of Rome. This latest message won Nero's attention. The course of the fire was taking it both toward the old palaces on the Palatine and toward his latest construction, the *Domus transitoria*, a long, colonnaded building that ran from the Palatine all the way across the city to the Gardens of Maecenas, which occupied the Esquiline Hill.

Sending a message back to Rome with instructions that all steps must be taken to protect his property, Nero issued orders for a return to the capital the first thing next day.

⟵∞⟶

Up the Tiber came the emperor, with his flotilla of small boats. Smoke from the fire would have been visible for many miles before the party reached the city, while the sky over Rome would have been a dirty brown, with the sun an orange orb hanging in the firmament.

It was July 21, the third day of the fire, which was burning more fiercely than ever. Rome was in the grip of a firestorm, the likes of which would not be experienced in Europe again until the aerial bombing campaigns of the Second World War. It is likely that Nero landed downstream of the city, for the flames in the dock area of Regio XIII would have negated passage. There were other landing places further upstream, beside the Campus Martius, but the fire along the river's east bank would have made the river impassible. A shocked Nero would have traveled the last part of the journey by litter. Met outside the city by City Prefect Sabinus, he received a sober briefing: The city was at the mercy of the fire, which had "outstripped all preventative measures."[11]

Coming up the Via Prenestina, with the city burning away to their left, Nero and his party passed the intact barracks and stables complex of the Praetorian Cavalry, which sat at the foot of the eastern slope of the Esquiline Hill, outside and below the Servian Walls. In the stables, thousands of horses, smelling the smoke in the air, would have been whinnying with fear as their grooms attempted to calm them. The fields spreading east from the barracks, normally used by the cavalry for their training exercises, were filled with distraught refugees, who watched the imperial party pass, some wailing at the emperor in their distress, others gawking hollow-eyed at the long train of litters, soldiers, and servants tramping by.

Nero passed through the Esquiline Gate, where Praetorian troops stood uselessly on guard, then turned right and entered the Gardens of Maecenas. Up the paths and steps that, in better times, made these gardens reputedly the most attractive perambulation in all of Rome, Nero and his party climbed the Esquiline Hill. The gardens that covered this hill had been created late in the first century BC by Gaius Maecenas, who along with Agrippa had been the most senior of the emperor Augustus' lieutenants. Eccentric in dress and habits, Maecenas had been the patron of the poets Virgil and Horace and had himself some aspirations as a poet. Maecenas had a "passion for self-display," in the opinion of Seneca, a passion exemplified by his magnificent gardens.[12]

"Maecenas' greatest claim to glory is regarded as having been his clemency," said Seneca. "He spared the sword, refrained from bloodshed, and showed his power only in his defiance of convention."[13] But it was his gardens for which most Romans would continue to remember him. On his death, his mansion and the gardens on the Esquiline had been willed to Augustus, and they had been imperial property ever since. Maecenas' mansion, on the southwestern side of the hill, had been used by Tiberius for a time prior to his becoming emperor. When Philo Judaeus,

Jewish envoy from Alexandria, had met with the emperor Caligula one summer during his reign, three decades before this, it had been in the Gardens of Maecenas. Philo had noted that Caligula spent the previous three nights in the gardens, apparently staying in Maecenas' old mansion. Caligula had led the Jewish party on a tour of deserted buildings in the complex.

When Nero now topped the Esquiline Hill and looked down over the gardens spreading below, he could see that all the buildings fringing the gardens had been rapidly and deliberately demolished by the city and Praetorian cohorts and imperial slaves over the past twenty-four hours, to create a fire break and prevent the fire from spreading up the hill. Nero ascended a tower on the hilltop. The Tower of Maecenas was not a tall, narrow structure as might be imagined, but a solid, squat building of three stories. From the top, accompanied by senior members of his retinue, Nero gazed silently out over his burning capital.

Across the valley, the Palatine Hill, and all the imperial palaces of Augustus, Germanicus, Tiberius, and Caligula that occupied it, and the private mansions on the same slopes, were ablaze. The city prefect had managed to rescue most of the valuables and portable works of art from the various Palatiums and the Domus Transitoria, among them the solid gold chariot used by the emperor Augustus for his triumphal processions and by Nero's grandfather Germanicus in his Triumph of AD 17. This ceremonial quadriga was normally kept in the Temple of Apollo, which adjoined the Old Palatium, as Augustus' original, now gutted palace on the Palatine was colloquially called.

Suetonius indicates that many of the books held in Rome's libraries were destroyed in the fire, but a large number of the records held in the Tabularium, the state archives, a massive, 140-year-old building sitting on the lower slope of the Capitoline Mount overlooking the Forum, were removed to safety by the vigiles or City Cohorts. These rescued records, in handwritten scroll form, ranged from the *Acta Senatus*, the verbatim record of every word spoken in every single session of the Senate since the late Republic—made possible by the invention of shorthand by Cicero's secretary Tiro—to copies of every edition of the *Acta diurna*, the government's daily newspaper.

All these records Tacitus would consult, back to the reign of Augustus, when he came to write his *Annals*, three decades after the fire. The private, unpublished letters and memoirs of Augustus and the memoirs of Nero's mother, Agrippina the Younger, were among other records preserved, for Suetonius would be able to quote from them when he wrote his biographies of the twelve Caesars half a century after the conflagration.

The fire had reached the Forum Romanum at the foot of the Palatine, where it destroyed buildings, including the House of the Vestals, the Temple of Vesta, and the Regia—once the home of the kings of Rome and, later, of the pontifex maximus. Also being assaulted by the flames was Nero's Domus Transitoria, construction work on which had only recently been completed. It, too, burned before Nero's eyes. Rising high into the air, orange and red, turning, curling, dancing, across mile after square mile of the city, the flames were awesome in their destructive majesty. Nero was overheard to murmur that these mesmerizing flames possessed a certain beauty.[14]

Making the Gardens of Maecenas his base, Nero directed that more buildings below the Esquiline be leveled, to put a vast space in front of the fire. Having noted that the Servian Walls could and should prevent the fire from spreading north to the Campus Martius, he directed that the Gardens of Agrippa and all the public buildings associated with them on the campus be thrown open, to "receive the destitute multitude," along with all imperial gardens, which included the Gardens of Sallust on the Campus Martius and the Gardens of Caesar and the Servilian Gardens west of the Tiber. To provide shelter for those affected, Nero ordered that temporary structures be raised on the Campus Martius, which quickly became a vast and crowded refugee camp.[15]

Foodstuffs in the affected areas had been consumed by the fire, as had the grain warehouses on the Tiber docks in Regio XIII. Vast grain stocks were maintained at Ostia, the port at the mouth of the Tiber, so Nero ordered that supplies be brought upriver from Ostia and from all towns immediately surrounding the capital. For the time being, too, the price of grain to the city's remaining bakeries was substantially reduced. These disaster relief measures all won widespread approval for the emperor, said Tacitus.[16]

All the while, the fire continued to burn and to spread until the flames reached the cleared area at the foot of the Esquiline in Regio IV, where, said Tacitus, "the violence of the fire was met by clear ground and an open sky."[17] As dawn broke, five days after it had begun, the fire had apparently been brought under control. From their country resorts, Rome's wealthy and their houseguests hurried back to the city to survey the damage and ascertain their losses. Apart from their city homes, many of these people also owned apartment buildings in the city. They returned to find that much of their property had been lost.

That same day, as embers glowed and smoke continued to fill the air and attempts were made to calculate the scale of the damage, the fire sprang up anew. It began in the shops of the Aemilian Basilica, the property of Tigellinus the praetorian prefect.[18] From there, flames spread up onto the Capitoline Mount. The Capitol had been spared the ravages of the fire prior to this because the walls and colonnades on the sacred hill had proven a barrier to the flames, which had swept over the neighboring Palatine. In addition, the direction of the wind on the second day of the original fire had pushed the flames past the Capitol's ancient walls. But now the flames advanced up the Capitoline, too. Fire destroyed the sanctuary's wooden gates, then swept on, at terrifying speed.

The pace at which the fire had advanced uphill since the first outbreak on level ground had taken the Romans by surprise. Logic told them that flames would travel over the flat more rapidly than when they had to climb a hill. Even today, in modern times, we still have much to learn about the behavior of fires. New research in Australia on wildfires, or "bush fires," as they are known in Australia, where massive, death-dealing fires blacken thousands of acres every summer, has shown that a fire can travel up to eight times more quickly going up a hill than on flat ground. The greater the incline, the faster the burn.[19]

The soldiery of the capital had by now been thrown into the task of attempting to stem the flames and to remove the treasures kept in the Capitoline temples—an untold fortune in gold in trophies from wars waged and won hundreds of years past against the Carthaginians, the

Gauls, and the city-states of Italy. Then, too, there were priceless relics such as the Sibylline Books, three books of ancient prophesies from the time of the Roman king Tarquinus Superbus, or Tarquin the Proud, seventh and last king of Rome. These books were normally kept under lock and key in the Temple of Jupiter on the Capitol, to be consulted by the Senate in emergencies. Many treasures were only just rescued in time.

Soon, Rome's most sacred temples were tasting the flames. The historic Temple of Jupiter the Stayer, which had been vowed by Romulus, founder of Rome, was engulfed, as the fire reached the ancient timbers that supported the roof, burned them through, and brought the terracotta roof crashing down. The same fate was met by a six-hundred-year-old temple to Luna dedicated by Servius Tullus, sixth king of Rome, and the Temple of Hercules, another of the "historical monuments of men of genius," in the words of Tacitus, which was left a blackened ruin.[20] Priceless frescoes within these temples were likewise destroyed.

The fire continued on down the steep reverse slope of the Capitoline, leaping the Servian Walls at this point and setting alight several large public buildings at the foot of the Capitoline on the southern fringe of the Campus Martius, soon bringing rafters and roofs crashing down. One of the buildings gutted here was a basilica; another, the Theater of Taurus, was a medium-sized amphitheater of stone, brick, and timber erected only thirty-five years before by the immensely wealthy Sisena Statilius Taurus, a consul in AD 16, who had used the spoils of war to finance its erection. Here, too, the flames reached "the porticos which were dedicated to enjoyment," in the words of Tacitus.[21] It was only when the wind dropped, it seems, that a broad, protective expanse of stone colonnades beyond these buildings prevented the fire from spreading further across the Campus Martius, which was now home to hundreds of thousands of traumatized refugees.

Two days after the second outbreak and a week since the first flames had taken hold at the Circus Maximus, the Great Fire of Rome finally ended. The destruction across the city had been immense. Of the fourteen regios or districts of the city of Rome originally delineated by the emperor Augustus, three had been totally leveled by the fire and by firefighting measures. In another seven regios, "a few shattered, half-burnt" residences remained standing. Only four precincts had escaped the fire altogether.[22]

One of the latter was Regio XIV, on the west bank of the Tiber, for the waterway had held the fire back. The three other precincts where hearth and home had been preserved were mostly located north of the Servian Walls—Regios VII and IX, which between them covered the Campus Martius, and Regio VI, which included the Quirinal Hill residential district, home to Martial and Vespasian and his brother Sabinus. Regio VI was also the site, in the northeast of the city and beyond the walls, of the Castra Praetoria, barracks of the Praetorian and City Cohorts.

Now that the destruction and the dying had ended, the time had come for the recriminations.

THE BLAME

B y dawn on the morning of July 26, after the flames had consumed the city for six days and seven nights, the conflagration was at an end. Refugees from the disaster crowded the Campus Martius and the imperial gardens west of the Tiber. Other homeless Romans had taken shelter in the often massive tombs and monuments built for wealthy citizens of bygone days and which lined the numerous roads leading from the city.

A pall of smoke continued to hang over Rome, and the acrid stench of burnt matter and of death filled the nostrils. The destruction had been so complete that in the most devastated areas, only piles of ash and useless rubble remained, and most streets were impassible. The very marble and bricks of the city had seemed to melt in the flames. Modern experts would calculate that at its center, the Great Fire of Rome generated temperatures in the region of 1,100 degrees Fahrenheit.[1]

Many bodies had been entirely consumed. Nonetheless, corpses, often charred and beginning to rot in the summer heat, could be seen in the ruins. "Countless people perished," Cassius Dio would write.[2] There was no accurate way of calculating precisely how many people, free or slave, had died, although all chroniclers agreed that the old and infirm, who had been too slow to escape the flames or had remained in their lodgings and made no attempt to flee, accounted for the majority of the fatalities. It was also known that the number of deaths caused by the second eruption of the fire had been much less than that caused by the initial blaze. Compared with some of the afflictions experienced by Rome—in a single autumn one year during Nero's reign, thirty thousand deaths from plague were registered in the city—the death toll from the fire was negligible.[3]

To prevent looting, Nero issued an edict: "He offered to remove corpses and rubble free of charge, but allowed nobody to search among the ruins even of his own mansion," said Suetonius.[4] During daylight hours, the search for bodies and the cleanup became the task of the City and Praetorian Cohorts and the thousands of imperial slaves, and, after dark, of the vigiles. That task began at once. Nero decided to remove all the rubble from the city, rather than build over the top of it, as had been the practice after past fires. Once each of the many barges regularly bringing grain upriver from Ostia was unloaded, it was piled with rubble, which it then carried down the Tiber to the marshes at Ostia. This shuttle service proceeded day in, day out, and before long the Ostian marshes would be reclaimed by the blackened fill from Rome.

Even while the fire had still been burning, the same questions had been posed again and again by the shocked citizenry.

"How did it happen?" some asked, understandably.

"Who kindled it?" others pondered.[5] Why would they ask such a question? None of the larger fires that had singed Rome earlier in the century had been blamed on arson. Kitchen fires that got out of hand, careless workmen, even lightning could be pointed at as the source of previous blazes. Still, deliberate fires were not unknown. Roman landlords had frequently been suspected of fires that had gutted their own apartment blocks. Six years from now, two businessmen in Antioch, capital of the province of Syria, would be found guilty of deliberately setting a fire that destroyed 20 percent of their handsome city. That pair only intended to destroy the city archives, which contained records of their substantial debts, but the archives fire inevitably spread to other buildings.

Faster than the fire itself, stories spread about the men who had prevented others from dousing the fire on the first night. Who were they? No one knew. Under whose orders had they acted? Greedy landlords?

Possibly. But names were soon being suggested, and one name in particular: Nero. As fire breeds on oxygen, so rumor bred on these reports and took hold of the people. Tacitus, Suetonius, and Cassius Dio all chronicled these rumors and perhaps embellished them.

Like many rumors, the most persistent of them was based on fact. Tacitus reported: "A rumor had gone forth everywhere that, at the very time when the city was in flames, the emperor appeared on a private stage (that of his theater at Antium) and sang of the destruction of Troy, comparing present misfortunes with the calamities of antiquity."[6] Now the fact that the second outbreak had occurred on the property of Praetorian Prefect Tigellinus reflected not on the landlord, but on the landlord's imperial master. "It seemed that Nero was aiming at the glory of founding a new city and calling it by his name," said Tacitus, and this was the next rumor to do the rounds.[7]

In an instant, all the credit that Nero had received from the public for his prompt and humane disaster relief measures was negated by the accusation that now flew from mouth to mouth—that the fire had been ordered by Nero so that he could build a new city on the ruins of Rome and call it Neropolis. Some people, said Tacitus, observed that July 19, the day the fire broke out, was the anniversary of the fiery destruction of all of Rome except for the Capitoline Mount in 390 BC by an army of Gauls. The intimation was that the Great Fire had been deliberately ignited on this date with the same intent, the destruction of the city.[8]

By the time that Suetonius came to write his biography of Nero, fifty years after the Great Fire, the rumors and the innuendo had become part of folklore, and Suetonius happily repeated them as fact. He himself firmly believed that Nero had been behind the fire. "Pretending to be disgusted by the drab old buildings and narrow, winding streets of Rome, he brazenly set fire to the city," Suetonius wrote. The author added a claim that a group of former consuls had caught Nero's attendants armed with blazing torches and incendiary material trespassing on their property, implying that these attendants of Nero had gone on to set the fire. Suetonius also wrote that after the fire, Nero sang "The Sack of Ilium."[9] This was the sum total of Suetonius' evidence against Nero, his proof that the young emperor was behind the disaster.

In the third century, more than a century and a half after the event, Cassius Dio was equally convinced that Nero was behind the fire. On the basis of some assumptions and the claims of the likes of Suetonius, he wrote, "Nero had set his heart on accomplishing what had doubtless always been his desire, namely to make an end of the whole city and realm in his lifetime." He went on: "Accordingly, he secretly sent out men who pretended to be drunk or engaged in other kinds of mischief, and had them begin by setting fire to one or two or even several buildings in different parts of the city." He offered no source for this claim. Dio also stated, as Tacitus had done, that Nero sang of the capture of Troy. But to color his narrative, Dio made the additional claim that Nero sang the song from his palace roof while the city burned around him.[10] This was the source of the later myth that Nero fiddled while Rome burned.

Dio actually contradicted Tacitus, his primary source: "There was no curse that the populace did not invoke against Nero, although they did not mention his name, but simply cursed in general terms those who had set the city on fire." Dio wrote that during the reign of Tiberius, an oracle predicted that Rome would perish through internal strife in 900 years. The prediction, he said, was now "on everybody's lips."[11] According to the belief of the day, 864 years had by this time passed since the infant brothers Romulus and Remus, founders of Rome, had sheltered beneath a tree where the Comitium building now stood, putting the 900th anniversary of the city's origination little more than thirty years away. Nero, said Dio, quickly scotched this rumor by announcing that no record of any such prophesy could anywhere be found, after which those behind this story began singing new libelous tunes against the emperor.[12] Who the originators of these stories were, nobody knew.

Nero was, without doubt, deeply depressed by the disaster and by the loss of his own newly expanded palace in particular, and his depression could only have been exacerbated by the aspersions being cast against him by persistent but anonymous enemies. It is quite likely that he did, for a time at least, as Suetonius claimed, take up his lyre, close himself away, and sing sad songs. But he soon roused himself to action. He announced that the rebuilding of Rome would commence immediately and that for this purpose, he was establishing a relief fund, to which all the provinces of the empire would be expected to contribute. He also announced a range of imaginative measures to assist the rebuilding and to prevent a repeat of the disaster.

In formulating these measures, Nero took the advice of two men who were unlikely city planners. Only several months prior to the fire, Nero had launched a major construction project, a shipping canal from Lake Avernus in Campania to the mouth of the Tiber River. The canal would be 160 miles long and broad enough to permit two warships to pass each other, according to Suetonius. Nero had been inspired to undertake this project by Publius Egnatius Celer, a member of the Equestrian Order and a native of Berytus in Syria, modern-day Beirut in Lebanon, and by young senator Verulanus Severus. Celer was a philosopher of the Stoic School and, ultimately, a visionary of sorts. A favorite of Nero's mother, Celer had, for a time, been an administrator of the emperor's private estates in Asia. Severus, only in his thirties, had until very recently been commander of the 6th Ferrata Legion, in Syria, leading the unit during Corbulo's last Armenian campaign. It seems that Severus had been befriended by Celer the Syrian, who had come up with the idea of the Avernus canal.

According to Tacitus, Nero had "a love of the impossible."[13] But Nero saw lasting benefit in the grand project, to Rome and to his name. In times to come, he could imagine, people would say, "Nero Caesar did this," in the same way that people of his own time said, "Julius Caesar did this," or "Augustus Caesar did this," referring to the public works of the first Caesars. Nero had authorized the canal project, and teams of prisoners "from every part of the empire" had been shipped into Italy and had begun hacking into the dry, rocky hills south of Rome.[14] Now, those prisoners had to be diverted to clearing rubble in the city and working in stone quarries. The canal project was halted, never to begin again. Writing four decades later, Tacitus would scornfully refer to the scarred hillsides that evidenced Nero's abandoned canal project: "There still remain the traces of his disappointed hope."[15]

In the wake of Rome's great disaster, Severus and Celer, the pair behind the canal project, stepped forward to again offer the emperor their services and their advice. Under the influence of Severus and Celer, in the words of Suetonius, "Nero introduced his own new style of architecture to the city."[16] Nero announced that the reconstruction of the city would not go forward without planning or controls. Rome's affected precincts would be rebuilt, he said, with streets laid out with precision; they would be straight and measured. Here was the influence of Severus the general, for every legion camp was laid out with this measured precision, based on a grid pattern. Nero's new street design also provided for several broad thoroughfares where previously there had been narrow streets of one lane.

Now, too, Nero decreed a slew of building regulations, the first such regulations in Rome's long history. As a fire prevention measure, there would be restrictions on the height of private buildings. No new building could share a wall with adjoining structures. It would be mandatory for owners of new apartment blocks to provide courtyards at their properties and to erect colonnaded porches fronting the street—"to serve as fire-fighting platforms," noted Suetonius.[17] Nero undertook to personally meet the cost of these colonnades. All lower floors had to be "solidly constructed without wooden beams, of stone from Galbi or Alba, that material being impervious to fire."[18] The gray stone of Alba and Galbi famously resisted both fire and frost.

To encourage prompt rebuilding, Nero introduced an incentive scheme whereby each landowner was paid a bounty, in relation to his status and property, but only if and when he completed the construction of a certain number of houses or apartment blocks on his land within a prescribed period.

Nero had apparently received reports from City Prefect Sabinus and his Night Watch counterpart that their men had experienced difficulty finding sufficient water to fight the fire; either the supply had been meager at the water basins or the basins were inadequate in their distribution and location. Water Commissioner Marius was no doubt the one who now explained to the emperor that Rome had a water supply problem, because abuse of regulations had seen great quantities of water "illegally appropriated."[19] This was the problem of the "puncturers" that Julius Frontinus would chronicle and counter. Nero appointed several officers to ensure that this deficiency was overcome, and he also specified that water be delivered from the city's aqueducts to the courtyards of the new apartment blocks. "Everyone was to have, in the open courtyard, the means of stopping a fire," he announced.[20]

"These changes," Tacitus wrote, "were liked for their utility," and "also added beauty to the new city." Yet, Tacitus would note, there were those who were set in their ways and complained about Rome's new broad streets and open spaces. They were convinced that the old, narrow streets of Rome had been "more conducive to health," he said, because they had provided shade. Now, they complained, as clearance and reconstruction moved along at breakneck pace, the city's streets would be "scorched by a fiercer glow" of the sun.[21] Modern-day health experts and city planners would disagree; for the city's health, Nero's plan was the right one.

While Nero himself had been exploring Eastern religions over the past several years, he recognized that Romans were intensely superstitious and fearful of offending their pantheon of gods. There were major concerns among the populace that the gods must be propitiated to ensure that the new city did not suffer a disaster in the future. So, at Nero's direction, the Sibylline Books were consulted. A fifteen-member religious order, the Quindecimviri, was responsible for the safekeeping and reading of the ancient Sibylline Books, with the most senior of the quindecimvirs reporting their interpretation in accordance with the question put. In this case, the question was, Which deities was it necessary to appease to ensure Rome's future safety from disaster? The Sibylline Books were duly consulted, said Tacitus, "by the direction of which prayers were offered to Vulcanus, Ceres, and Proserpina. Juno, too, was entreated."[22]

Religious festivals devoted to each of these gods were in place on the Roman calendar during the months following the Great Fire, in the order that Tacitus set down above, and it is clear that the special prayers for the future of Rome were delivered on these occasions. The Vulcannia, the festival of Vulcan, god of fire, took place first, on August 23. The Fast of Ceres, goddess of agriculture, but more importantly also goddess of grain, on which Rome depended, was scheduled for October 4. A sacrifice was always offered to Ceres after a Roman funeral, to purify the house of the deceased; many funerals had taken place since the Great Fire. Meanwhile, prayers on the sacred day of Proserpina, daughter of Ceres and a deity associated with the underworld, would be offered on November 25.

Then there was Juno, goddess of homes and of protection, and the most powerful deity of the four. Several festivals were devoted to Juno through September and October. Juno, said Tacitus, "was entreated by the matrons" of Rome, "first, on the Capitol." There was a temple to Juno the Warner on the Capitoline Mount, and these prayers would have been offered there in the partly rebuilt temple. The prayers to Juno continued "on the nearest part of the coast, from where water was procured to sprinkle on the sanctuary and image of the goddess." The significance of the latter ritual is unknown. "And there were sacred banquets and nightly vigils celebrated by married women."[23]

Cassius Dio wrote that when it became known that Nero had ordered the Sibylline Books consulted, a new rumor took hold in the city. This rumor claimed that the sacred Sibylline Books had revealed a prophesy: "Last of the sons of Aeneas, a mother-slayer shall govern."[24] This, the rumor mongers said, referred to Nero and implied that he would be the last of his line. Nero had indeed had his mother killed, while his forebears of the Julian line claimed that they were descended from Trojan hero Aeneas, who, legend had it, had escaped to Italy after the fall of Troy and established the town of Lavinium.

Dio questioned the veracity of this supposed ancient prophesy and wondered whether it was not "for the first time inspired" by the present situation.[25] But to many Romans, it would have had a ring of truth about it. Through it, a seed was sown, casting doubt on Nero's future and the future of the Caesarian dynasty. For this rumor to take hold, its source had to be credible. Several years later, one of the Quindecimvirs responsible for the Sibylline Books, Thrasea Paetus, would come under suspicion as an enemy of Nero.

No matter what Nero did over the months following the fire, he could not escape the accusation that he was an incendiary prince. "All human efforts, all the lavish gifts of the emperor, and the propitiations of the gods, did not banish the sinister belief that the conflagration was the result of an order," said Tacitus. "Consequently, to rid himself of the report, Nero fastened the guilt on a class hated for their abominations."[26] This "class" was, it is now clear, made up of the numerous followers of the cult of Isis in Rome. Nero had interested himself in Isis, the Egyptian mother goddess, to such an extent that he had introduced Isean feasts to the official Roman religious calendar. But while he retained a fascination with all things Egyptian, his attitude to Isis had changed abruptly.

It is likely that Nero's disdain of Isis had been sponsored by the death of his infant daughter Augusta the previous year. Feeling let down by the goddess, he had grown contemptuous of her and her cult. Now he found in the followers of Isis, most of whom were slaves and freedmen, easy scapegoats for the Great Fire, even though one of the cult's own temples, on the Capitol, would have been destroyed by the blaze. The average Roman abhorred and execrated the cult's apparent worship of gods in animal form and would have applauded the cult members' persecution. At first, a few admitted followers of the cult of Isis, who were known as "Egyptians" by the general population, were arrested. Priests of Isis, with their shaven heads, were easy to spot. These men were put to the rack, and "on their information, an immense multitude was convicted, not so much of the crime of firing the city, as of hatred against mankind."[27]

As noncitizens, this "multitude" of guilty people had no right of appeal or to a clean execution in the form of decapitation. Theirs was to be a painful and humiliating death. For some, it was a slow demise nailed or tied to a cross. Others among the convicted were reserved for the arena, the usual destination for a slave convicted of a capital crime. They were kept behind bars until the next spectacle. In normal times, this event would have been the Ludi Romani, the Roman Games, also known as the Ludi Magni, or Great Games. Running for fifteen days from September 4, they were the longest games on the calendar. The Great Games were traditionally held at the Circus Maximus, but that fire-ravaged venue was of course now out of commission and in only the early stages of reconstruction.

One other circus remained intact at Rome, the Circus Flaminius, which had been established on the southwestern side of the Campus Martius in 220 BC. Apart from the marble Arch of Germanicus, dedicated to Nero's grandfather, which stood at the entrance, and an ancient temple dedicated to the sun god Sol, there were little in the way of permanent structures at the Circus Flaminius. Temporary wooden stands were erected around the race course each November for the Ludi Plebii, the Plebeian Games, and then dismantled again. This lack of incendiary material was no doubt why the Circus Flaminius escaped the Great Fire even though the nearby Theater of Taurus was severely damaged. Nonetheless, by sacred tradition, the Great Games had to be conducted in the Circus Maximus. No Circus Maximus, no Great Games; like the Ludi Victoriae Caesaris, they would not be celebrated this year.

As November approached and with the offerings to Vulcan, Ceres, and Juno made, the first opportunity to execute prisoners in the arena presented itself. The Plebeian Games of November 4–17 had, from their beginning, been held in the Circus Flaminius, and as that venue was intact, these games could go ahead. For the most part, the Plebeian Games program opened with stage performances and concluded with three days of athletics and horse races. Chariot races were not normally included.

It had been almost half a year since the last chariot races at Rome. Nero had missed them, and so, too, would have his fellow Romans. So, the emperor announced that he was sponsoring a day of chariot races at these Plebeian Games. The racecourse of the Circus Flaminius was smaller than that at the Circus Maximus, but it would still permit four two-horse teams to compete. Similarly, the seating capacity was no match for the Circus Maximus, but the members of the population without tickets would still wager on the races from afar. Perhaps, Nero would have been hoping, the announcement that within several days the Blues, Greens, Reds, and Whites would again be racing, courtesy of the emperor, would finally divert public attention away from the malicious gossip and rumors and put him in a good light.

So, members of the cult of Isis went to their deaths during the Plebeian Games. Many of the "Egyptians" were herded into the arena, where packs of savage dogs were let loose on them to tear them to pieces. "Mockery of every kind was added to their deaths," Tacitus later remarked. To anyone who knew anything about the worship of Isis and about ancient Egyptian religion in general, that mockery was quite apparent. Anubis, the ancient Egyptian god of death, had the head of a jackal, or dog, and these condemned "Egyptians" were executed by dogs. Even more poignantly, Tacitus noted that the Egyptians were sent to their deaths "covered in the skins of animals."[28] Priests of Isis traditionally eschewed animal products, wearing linen robes and sandals made from papyrus. To be covered in the skins of animals was a gross insult to the beliefs of the followers of Isis.

The Egyptians selected for crucifixion were affixed to crosses raised in one of the imperial gardens, which were likely to have been the Gardens of Sallust. Developed by one of Julius Caesar's deputies, Sallustius Crispus (Sallust the author), these gardens lay on the flat between the Quirinal and Pincian hills in Regio VI, close to the Salarian Gate, and had been imperial property since the reign of Tiberius. Like the Gardens of Maecenas, they had escaped the Great Fire. There, each evening for several nights, victims from among the Egyptian multitude were burned to death, "to serve as nightly illumination."[29] As Nero knew, fire played a key role in the worship of Isis, and the incineration of some of the prisoners was another deliberate insult. For sacred and symbolic reasons, November 13 is likely to have been the day set down for these "illuminations" to begin, for this was the combined festival day of Juno, Minerva, Jupiter, and Feronia—Roman goddess of fire.

Nero was "exhibiting a show in the circus" on the day the illuminations began, said Tacitus.[30] The young emperor had clearly been tempted to drive a chariot in the races at the circus himself, for although he just managed to resist that temptation, he drove into the imperial gardens that night in a chariot and dressed in the full racing garb of the charioteer: leather helmet, tight-fitting leather vest designed to protect the ribs, bottle-green tunic of the Green faction, his favorite, and leather arm-guards and leg-guards. Stepping down from his chariot once he arrived at the gardens for the spectacle, Nero "mingled with the people in the dress of a charioteer," as the public flocked to see the Egyptians incinerated.[31]

This lack of imperial dignity backfired on the emperor in charioteer dress. Sympathy grew in some quarters for the victims of his persecution. "Even for criminals who deserved extreme and exemplary punishment, there arose a feeling of compassion," said Tacitus. "For it was not, as it was portrayed, for the public good, that they were being destroyed." Not even fire could expunge the conviction among many Romans that their own emperor had set their city alight. If anything, his brutal punishments of the supposed culprits only damaged Nero's reputation all the more. The perception now was that the executions of the followers of Isis had merely been "to satisfy one man's cruelty."[32]

A little over a month later, on December 15, Nero celebrated his twenty-seventh birthday. At Rome and across the empire, most Romans celebrated with him, with prayers and offerings for their emperor's good health. Throughout that month of December, "never were lightning flashes more frequent" at Rome, and a comet was seen to streak across the night sky.[33] To the more superstitious Romans, who saw portents of the future in natural phenomena, this was "supposed to herald the death of some person of great importance," said Suetonius.[34] At the very least, said Tacitus, these were omens of "impending evils."[35]

THE CONSPIRACY

As AD 65 began, Nero, frustrated that his benevolent acts had failed to silence his critics and stung by the vitriol fueling the worst rumors and gossip about him, gave up all attempts to win public goodwill and became a recluse. He apparently decided that from now on, rather than continue to strive to please his subjects, he would please himself. The one person whom he trusted was his wife Poppaea Sabina, and they became closer during this period; by the spring, she would again be pregnant, giving Nero cause to be optimistic about fathering an heir and defying the supposed Sibylline prophesy that he would be last of the Julian line.

The emperor was not seen by the public on New Year's Day, nor on any other occasion as the winter passed. He had a new passion. Instead of simply rebuilding his gutted palaces on the Palatine and in the valley of the Forum, he had acceded to the suggestion of Severus and Celer that he use this opportunity to build the grandest palace that man had ever seen to replace the residence that the fire had taken from him. This pair, said Tacitus, "had the genius and the audacity to attempt by art even that which nature had rejected, and to fool away an emperor's money."[1] They were made directors of the project.

The new palace that they designed for Nero, to be called the *Domus aurea*, or Golden House, would cover two hundred acres. Like Tacitus,

Suetonius decried the expense and wastefulness of Nero's new palace: "The entrance hall was large enough to accommodate a huge statue of himself, 120 feet high."[2] This statue of Nero, which came to be called the Colossus, was several times life size and perched on a column. Combined, statue and column stood beneath the roof of the fantastic new palace's foyer. The foyer sat at the foot of the Palatine, beside the House of the Vestals, which, in its reconstructed form, was built on a slightly different axis from the building it replaced, to accommodate the Golden House's foyer next door.

From this lofty entrance hall, a pillared arcade, three stories high and called the Millaria, would run for an entire mile from the Forum valley, through the Carinae and Subura districts, to the Esquiline. Many of the palace's acres would be occupied by "an enormous pool, like a sea," said Suetonius.[3] Called the *stagnum Neronis*, or Nero's Pool, this sheet of water spread over the cleared site in the valley that, prior to the fire, had been occupied for the most part by houses, including the one in which the Apostle Paul is said to have lived for two years during his first stay at Rome.

Just seven years after it was created, this pool of Nero's would be drained by a future emperor to make way for a new structure on this site—Vespasian's Hunting Theater. Much later, the Hunting Theater would become known as the Colosseum. Many scholars believe that it took its unofficial name from Nero's statue, the Colossus, which would be re-erected in the Via Sacra outside the amphitheater, with Nero's head replaced, some say by that of the emperor Titus, others by a head representing the sun god Sol. Meanwhile, Nero's Pool, said Suetonius, "was surrounded by buildings made to resemble cities and by a landscaped garden consisting of ploughed fields, vineyards, pastures and woodlands, where every variety of domestic and wild animal roamed about."[4]

No extravagance was spared. Parts of the Golden House would be gilded and studded with precious stones and mother of pearl. The palace's main dining room was circular; its roof could revolve. The ceilings of all the dining rooms would be made of fretted ivory; they would open on command, with ceiling panels sliding back to allow a rain of flower petals to fall on diners below, or for perfume to waft down from hidden sprinklers. Seawater and sulfur water would be on tap in the palace's bath-house. The Golden House's lavish design pleased Nero beyond measure. "Good," he is reported to have said once it neared completion. "Now I can at last begin to live like a human being."[5]

To pay for the rebuilding of the capital and for the construction of the Golden House, all the donations from the cities and towns of Italy, the provinces, and the rulers of states allied to Rome—some donations voluntary, some compelled—were clearly not going to be enough. Much of the gold that had accumulated in the temples of Rome as votive offerings from triumphant generals and individual citizens, and rescued ahead of the flames the previous July, was now melted down into coinage, to the horror of traditionalists.

To advise him on other fund-raising methods, Nero had sent for his retired chief secretary, Seneca, who forwarded a message in response, requesting that he be permitted to remain in rural retirement. Tacitus thought that Seneca did this so that he would not have to contribute to the desecration of temples, but it is just as likely that Seneca, who never showed the least piety in either his deeds or his writings, feared that Nero would now accept his previous offer to hand over his properties; Seneca perhaps simply did not want to contribute to the rebuilding fund.

Nero would not take no for an answer and again demanded Seneca's presence. This time, Seneca claimed ill health, saying that he was suffering from a nervous disposition and was totally incapable of traveling, or of even leaving his bedchamber. After this second request, Nero left Seneca alone. In his quest for more funds, the emperor soon dispatched a commission composed of two men, one of them a freedman, to rove through the provinces of Achaia and Asia collecting votive gold from temples there and seizing gold and silver statues of gods for melting down to coin. In at least one town in Asia, locals attempted to resist the commissioners when the region's senior-most Roman official failed to support the imperial duo's mission.

Even as the new year began and Nero was poring over the plans for his growing new Golden House with designers Severus and Celer, several of the emperor's subjects became embroiled in a secret plot, which, if successful, would ensure that Nero did not long enjoy his extravagant new residence. In fact, it would emerge that more than one conspiracy was in the making and that before long, these various designs for Nero's demise would meld into a single plot to kill him.

"I could not easily narrate who first planned it," Tacitus wrote several decades later, "or whose prompting inspired a scheme into which so many entered."[6] But among the first to convert disquiet into a conspiracy to do away with the emperor were two officers of the Praetorian Guard, Subrius Flavus, a tribune commanding a Praetorian Cohort, and Sulpicius Asper, one of Flavus' centurions. At the same time, and quite separately, Lucan the poet, nephew of Seneca and close friend of his father's client Martial, began to conspire with Plautius Lateranus, whom Nero had selected to become a suffect consul from the beginning of July.

Lucan brought "an intensely keen resentment" to the plot, said Tacitus, because "Nero tried to disparage the fame of his poems."[7] As for Lateranus, the emperor had restored him to his senatorial rank, early in Nero's reign, after Claudius' Senate had condemned Lateranus for adultery with Claudius' infamous wife Messalina. Lateranus had originally been sentenced to death and only escaped with a loss of rank on the intercession of his uncle. Clearly, by approving his upcoming consular appointment, Nero considered Lateranus a man worthy of the highest honors. Tacitus admitted that Nero had done Lateranus no personal wrong, and the only motive that he could ascribe to Lateranus' desire to be rid of this emperor who favored him was "love of the State."

Two senators soon joined Lucan and Lateranus in the plot. Neither had previously showed any great interest in politics, and according to Tacitus, they were the last men that anyone would have given the credit of plotting a revolution. Both had personal reasons for wanting Nero dead. The "effeminate" Afranius Quintianus was well known and popularly disliked for his homosexuality; Nero had lampooned him for it in one of his published poems, and, said Tacitus, Quintianus was determined to have his revenge.

Quintianus' colleague in crime, Flavius Scaevinus, was best known as a spendthrift and heavy drinker whose life was widely viewed as one of "sleepy languor."[8] Scaevinus was, in fact, deeply in debt. It seems that his income had been heavily reliant on rents from city apartment blocks that had been destroyed in the Great Fire. With his income stream drastically reduced, yet with a continued dedication to his usual hedonistic lifestyle, Scaevinus, said Tacitus, was being pressed for payment by his creditors, and he did not have the funds to satisfy their demands.

Six months had passed since the fire. Despite the rumors and the gossip impugning Nero, just as no one had been identified as the source of the rumors, not a single soul had been indicted for conspiring against Nero since the death of Torquatus Silanus the previous spring. In these early days of AD 65, the four civilian conspirators, unaware that two Praetorian officers were having similar thoughts, carefully sounded out their friends and acquaintances, reviling "the emperor's crimes" and reminding their listeners of the portents the previous December of "the approaching end of empire." These conspirators agreed that more than just assassinate Nero, they must also select "someone to rescue the State in its distress."[9] A replacement emperor was needed. But who?

Decades of murders and executions going back to the poisoning of Nero's grandfather Germanicus in AD 19 had meant that there was no male member of the Caesar family's Julian line now living, apart from Nero. So, Nero's replacement, this "someone" who would save Rome, would have to be the first man to rule the Romans since Julius Caesar a hundred years earlier not to have the blood of the Caesars running through his veins. This thought was sufficiently daunting for the plotters to decide that it would be necessary to give Nero's successor legitimacy in the eyes of the Roman people.

To do this, they decided, they would marry their chosen candidate for the throne to the only other surviving member of the Julian family, the emperor Claudius' daughter Antonia. Through thirty-eight-year-old Antonia, widow of Sulla—the same Sulla executed in AD 62—a male heir with the blood of the Caesars would arise. It is conceivable that were Antonia not alive, this plot would never have been born. As for Antonia herself, she knew nothing of what was being plotted in her name.

The man on whom the mantle of potential emperor discreetly settled was Gaius Piso. This friend of Seneca, who, like Seneca, had escaped the accusations of an agent of Tigellinus in the Senate two years before, was a descendant of the eminent Calpurnian family, with a family tree dotted with consuls, generals, and governors. The only blot on the family record had been the AD 20 conviction of Gnaeus Calpurnius Piso for the murder of Germanicus Caesar. Gaius, the Piso chosen for Nero's throne, was tall, handsome, and an eloquent speaker and had earned "a splendid reputation with the people from his virtue." Or, his "semblance of virtue," Tacitus was quick to add.[10]

Piso, an accomplished legal advocate, had frequently employed his eloquence in the courts defending fellow Roman citizens. He was generous to his friends and showed courtesy and goodwill even to total strangers. On the other hand, in the opinion of Tacitus, Piso was not of solid character; "moderation in pleasure" was unknown to him.[11] Among those who were attracted to vice, Piso had a reputation of being of like mind, lowering his morals whenever it suited him, most conspicuously by stealing the beautiful wife of a fellow senator and by occasionally appearing on stage as an actor in Greek tragedies. He was also accused of showing off his wealth and sometimes eating and drinking to excess. In short, a Nero. But a Nero who did not lower himself to sing in public contests, or to race a chariot, or to "marry" a freedman. Above all, a Nero the conspirators could control.

Piso was actually on good terms with the emperor and had been for some years. So much so that when Nero's mother had taken up residence at the imperial seaside villa at Antium, Piso had offered the emperor the use of his own sumptuous villa at Baiae, on the Bay of Naples, as his coastal resort. Nero had not only taken up Piso's offer and used the Baiae villa for escapes from the city, but had made it his base for his second venture into murder, that of his mother.

Nero had an apprenticeship in murder in December AD 55, with the killing of his cousin and adoptive brother Britannicus, son of Claudius. Blame for that murder could be partly laid at his mother's feet. Agrippina had reacted spitefully after Nero had dismissed her favorite, Pallas, the Palatium secretary for finance under Claudius and initially also under Nero. Agrippina had threatened to take Britannicus to the Praetorians and declare him emperor in Nero's stead. That outburst had sealed young Britannicus' fate. Nero had procured poison from Locusta, a convicted "sorceress" then languishing in prison. Nero made Locusta the promise that she would receive her freedom if the poison worked.

Because slaves were employed as food tasters for the members of the imperial family to detect poison, Nero had conceived a novel way to rid himself of his cousin. In winter, Romans drank hot wine. At dinner one night, Nero had made sure that the wine served to Britannicus was much too hot, necessitating the addition of cold water to cool it. The wine was tested by Britannicus' food taster, but the cold water added to the wine was not. Shortly after drinking the now poison-laced wine, Britannicus was paralyzed and gasping for breath. As Britannicus was carried from the dining room by attendants, Nero had assured the other members of the family at the dinner that the epilepsy from which Britannicus had suffered as a child—a complaint he shared with another member of the Julian line, Julius Caesar—had no doubt returned. Britannicus, Nero's rival for the throne, had been dead before daylight. And the murderer had kept his word to Locusta the poison maker: "Nero rewarded Locusta for her services with a free pardon and extensive country estates," said Suetonius.[12]

Little more than three years later, Nero's mother was driving him to distraction, even attempting to draw him into her own bed to regain the control that she had exercised over him prior to his ascending the throne. Having succeeded in camouflaging one murder, Nero found the courage to plan another. Agrippina's servants were much too loyal to her, so that had ruled out employing one of them to administer poison to their mistress. Nero had been forced to be more creative than that. At the games in the circus one day, he had an inspiration. In front of him, a ship that formed part of a spectacle literally fell apart, on cue. On asking how this was done, the emperor was told that the ship had been constructed in such a way that it came apart when a single pin was pulled. This had set the boy emperor's mind to work.

From the naval city of Misenum on the Bay of Naples, Nero had summoned Anicetus, admiral of Rome's largest battle fleet, the Tyrrhenian Fleet. Anicetus, a freedman and a native of Pontus, had been Nero's tutor immediately prior to Seneca's taking on that role, so the pair knew each other well. After the emperor and the admiral had discussed the practicalities of building a ship that would float but which would fall apart on the pulling of a pin, Anicetus, aware of Nero's plan to murder his mother, undertook to have such a ship built by the following March and to provide a captain and a crew from his fleet who would perform the murderous deed with Agrippina aboard.

Relations between Nero and his mother had become so strained that the emperor had even withdrawn Agrippina's Praetorian and German Cohorts bodyguard. As March AD 59 approached, Nero had written a conciliatory letter to his mother, inviting her to join him on the Bay of Naples for the forthcoming Festival of Minerva. Agrippina owned an estate at Bauli on the Bay of Naples, where she could stay; Nero, meanwhile, would stay at the villa of his friend Gaius Piso. Agrippina, while wary, had accepted the invitation. A trireme from the Tyrrhenian Fleet had collected her from the imperial villa at Antium and brought her along the coast, landing her at the door to the Piso villa on March 19.

Nero had greeted his mother with kisses and embraces, then escorted her around the bay to her estate. There, drawn up on the sand, was a brand new little ship; it glittered with gold and jewels, and the single cabin in the stern was draped with silk. This, said Nero to his mother, was his special gift to her, to mark a renewal of their warm relations. Nero then invited her to join him for dinner at Piso's villa that night and departed. During the afternoon, Agrippina received a tip-off that there was a plot to kill her, a plot involving a ship. At that moment, the little ship gifted to her by her son was being prepared to convey her around the bay to Piso's villa. As a precaution, Agrippina traveled to dinner overland, carried in a litter.

The grand dinner at Piso's villa had been enjoyed by all present, who had included Seneca and then Praetorian commander Burrus. Agrippina, plied with much wine by her son, began to believe that Nero was genuine in his desire to reconcile with her. Around midnight, following the dinner, Nero had conducted his mother down to the jetty, where the brand new little ship, commanded by an officer from the Tyrrhenian Fleet, Volusius Proculus, sat waiting. Her fears allayed by wine and feigned affection, Agrippina had kissed Nero goodnight and boarded the vessel, accompanied by several retainers. Under a starry sky, with its oars rising and falling, the ship slid away across the flat waters of the bay.

When the ship was halfway to the Bauli villa, Proculus the captain had given a hushed order. A pin was pulled, and the stern of the ship, where Agrippina was reclining on a couch, had collapsed. But the ship failed to sink. When several crew members complicit in the plot with Proculus attempted to capsize the vessel, nonswimming crewmen had resisted them. The craft had eventually gone down, but Agrippina had swum toward the shore and been plucked from the water by fishermen. Once back at her Bauli estate, Agrippina had sent one of her freedmen to the Piso villa to inform the emperor that her ship had sunk, but that she was safe and well.

This news had sent Nero into a panic, and he had turned to Seneca and Burrus for help. Burrus had said that the admiral of the fleet, Anicetus, had promised to end Agrippina's life, so it was up to him to complete the deed. Anicetus was called in, and he agreed to do what had to be done. Leading a detachment of marines from the trireme that had brought Agrippina from Antium, Anicetus had marched around the bay to the Bauli villa. After the troops forced their way into the house, Anicetus and his officers had drawn their swords and bloodily ended the life of the emperor's mother as she lay on a couch. At Piso's villa, Nero had, with Seneca's aid, subsequently composed a letter to the Senate, claiming that Agrippina had been executed for plotting against him. Gaius Piso had been one of the many senators who had subsequently congratulated Nero in the House for terminating this maternal "threat" to his rule.

This, then, was the Piso whom the conspirators of AD 65 planned to put on the throne in Nero's place. Tacitus was convinced that Piso did not have the notion or the ambition to take the throne for himself until he was approached by others. The historian was even skeptical that Piso would be prepared to divorce his beautiful wife, Atria Galla, whom he had stolen from her previous husband and to whom he was famously devoted, to marry Antonia, the daughter of Claudius. Tacitus could only excuse Piso by suggesting that "the lust for dominion inflames the heart more than any other passion."[13]

Tacitus revealed that he obtained his account of the conspiracy from Pliny the Younger and did not know where Pliny came by his information. It is likely that Pliny's informant was his uncle's good friend Vespasian, who, while unconnected with the conspiracy, remained close enough to Nero to learn the facts of the matter in due course.

The initial revolutionary quartet soon attracted seven adherents from among clients, all of whom were members of the Equestrian Order, then cast about for supporters within the military. It was then that the feelings of the tribune Subrius and centurion Sulpicius became known to them, and through that pair, another two Praetorian tribunes and two centurions were also recruited into the plot. By February, one of the Equestrians had communicated with Piso and informed him of the conspiracy, its intentions, and its members. Piso said nothing to discourage the scheme, but he did not appear wholly enthusiastic, either.

The fact that four of the fourteen tribunes of the Praetorian Cohorts were party to the conspiracy would have been impressive to Piso, but not enough for him to sleep soundly, for the majority of tribunes might remain loyal to Nero. There could be no doubt that the success or failure of the planned coup would rest on the involvement of the capital's military. It had, after all, been the support of the Praetorians that had brought both Claudius and Nero to power. Piso soon heard that Faenius Rufus, Tigellinus' overshadowed co-prefect and a man of "esteemed life and character," was in sympathy with the revolutionaries.[14]

There was no doubting that Prefect Rufus was intimidated by his colleague Tigellinus, who, through "his brutality and shamelessness was held higher in the emperor's regard" than Rufus.[15] More than that, Tigellinus had more than once hinted that if Rufus stood in his way, he would tell the emperor that Rufus had once had an affair with Agrippina and had mourned her murder to the extent that he craved vengeance against Nero. For the past several years, Rufus had allowed Tigellinus to do much as he pleased, although since the Great Fire, Tigellinus had been maintaining an uncharacteristically low profile, as if on the outs with Nero, which would have encouraged the conspirators.

Because Rufus was seen to be such an upright man, no one had the courage to come straight out and ask him if he would support the assassination of the emperor, for fear that he would feel obliged to arrest them. Questions, while appearing to be casual, though carefully designed to gauge the man's position, were put to Rufus by the plotters, with the result that "the conspirators were assured by his own repeated language that the prefect of the Praetorian Cohorts had come over to their side."[16] This was communicated to Piso, and the plotters eagerly resumed their debate about a time and place for the fatal deed.

In one of these furtive discussions, Praetorian tribune Subrius Flavus suddenly offered to attack Nero when he was singing on the stage, or to set fire to his residence one night and then run him through in the ensuing chaos. But on thinking about it more deeply, Flavus came to the conclusion that in both cases, it would be next to impossible to escape following the crime—"that enemy of all great enterprises," according to Tacitus. Even if Flavus were successful, on the stage or in a burning palace, he feared that Nero's German bodyguards must surely catch him. For want of suicidal courage, the tribune withdrew his offer. So, the conspirators, still in quest of an idea and an opportunity for the perfect murder where no one would be apprehended, again hesitated to act, suspended as they were "between hope and fear."

By this time, a woman had become aware of the plot. Epicharis was a wealthy freedwoman—a widow, it seems. How she came to learn of the conspiracy is unclear, but she took it on herself to move it forward, even though, Tacitus would sarcastically remark, she had never before had a single noble thought in her head. Tired of the delays that had prevented the male plotters from going ahead with their plot, Epicharis came up with a plot of her own.

Epicharis decided that, while staying in Campania during the early spring, as was her habit, she would use her contacts within the Tyrrhenian Fleet to bring naval officers into the plot. She was acquainted with warship captain Volusius Proculus, who had commanded the collapsing vessel during the failed attempt to kill Nero's mother and later participated in dispatching her. Their friendship was intimate enough for Epicharis to be aware of Proculus' role in the murder of Agrippina and to know that the captain privately complained of not being well enough rewarded for that episode.

The admiral Anicetus had since left his post and left Italy, having in AD 62 volunteered to help Nero discredit his first wife, Octavia, by claiming that he'd had an affair with her. On Anicetus' evidence, Octavia had been banished to the prison island of Pandataria, where she was before long executed. Anicetus' "punishment" had been exile to the island of Sardinia, where he now lived on an estate, in the lap of luxury, at the emperor's expense. On Anicetus' departure, Proculus had expected his post as admiral of the fleet. But promotion had not come Proculus' way; hence his bitterness.

At the end of March, Epicharis dined with the disgruntled captain and discussed assassinating the emperor, hoping that Proculus would bring in other officers of the fleet. Proculus was receptive, telling Epicharis that he was determined to have his revenge on Nero and had been looking for the right opportunity. He said that he was not alone in despising Nero.

"No small help will be found in the fleet," the captain told Epicharis.[17]

Late the previous year, Nero had ordered the fleet, which had apparently been exercising in the Eastern Mediterranean and had lingered too long away from its home port, to return to its Misenum base, as it should for the winter, after the sailing season had closed in October and the weather had deteriorated. Hit by a gale from the southwest as it attempted to round the promontory at Misenum, a number of triremes and several other smaller warships had lost the battle with wind and wave. They ended up wrecked on the shore near the town of Cumae, modern Cuma, northwest of Neapolis on the Bay of Naples. Some officers of the fleet were said to blame the loss of friends in that disaster on the emperor.

"There will be numerous opportunities," the captain went on, "as Nero delights in frequently going sailing off Puteoli and Misenum." But, Proculus asked, what would be his reward?

"Gird yourself, Proculus," Epicharis responded, "to do your part and bring your bravest marines over to our side, and look for an adequate reward after."[18]

Encouraged by Proculus' reaction, the widow returned to Rome to tell her fellow conspirators of the conversation and of the possibility of murdering Nero at sea. Only days later, Epicharis was arrested by Praetorians; Proculus, certain of a greater reward from Nero than from Epicharis, had informed on her. Taken to the Praetorian barracks, Epicharis was confronted by Proculus, who, in front of the Praetorian tribune of the watch, repeated all that the freedwoman had told him. Fortunately for Epicharis, her accuser could produce no witnesses to their conversation. Nor had Epicharis given Proculus the names of any other conspirators, so there was no one else to arrest and question. After Epicharis denied every word, the matter was reported to Nero.

Suspecting that while there was no proof beyond Proculus' accusation, there might be some truth in it, the emperor ordered the widow detained until further notice.

THE UNRAVELING

The betrayal, questioning, and incarceration of Epicharis sent waves of panic through conspiratorial ranks. Thankful for Epicharis' plucky silence, her fellow conspirators decided to hurry forward the assassination, planning to carry it out at Piso's villa at Baiae. For that to transpire, Piso had to not only offer his villa to the emperor for a spring vacation, knowing that Nero was charmed by the place, but also encourage Nero both to immediately take advantage of the offer and to go to Baiae with only a minimal entourage, supposedly for the sake of peace and quiet. This latest plan fell in a heap when the plotters put it to Piso.

"The odium of such an act," Piso protested, "would stain with the blood of an emperor, no matter how bad he might be, the sanctity of my hospitable villa and the deities who preside over it."[1]

Piso proposed that the murder take place at Rome, so that the conspirators were seen to be acting on behalf of the state. To his mind, the murder should take place "in that hateful mansion piled up with the plunder of the citizens (the new palace now under construction). Or, in public." Piso was nervous about the whole affair, as well he should have been. Not only would discovery of the plot mean certain death for him, but Piso was concerned that many leading men of the state would "pity Nero as the victim of a crime" and, once Nero had been assassinated, would cast about for an occupant of the throne other than Piso.[2]

Piso's greatest fear was that these senators would offer the throne to Lucius Silanus, the descendant of a noble family with strong imperial connections. Some conspirators suggested that current consul Marcus Julius Vestinus Atticus be approached to become a party to the plot, because he and Nero had recently fallen out after Vestinus had married Statilia Messalina, Nero's latest mistress. Piso did not like this idea, fearing that the consul would either call for the return of the Roman republic once Nero was out of the way or, in his capacity as consul, appoint a new emperor of his own choosing. Piso told his colleagues that Vestinus was "reckless and dangerous."[3] Several conspirators were in fact engaged in long-standing feuds with the consul. So, at Piso's urging, Vestinus was left out of the conspiratorial ring.

At the same time, Piso was anxious to bring to his side men who would be respected, and daunted, by potential rivals such as Silanus and Vestinus. One man whom Piso badly wanted to involve was his old friend Lucius Seneca, a man whom Piso knew to be in fear of Nero and whom Nero had come to distrust. So, Piso sent word to Seneca, asking for a meeting as soon as possible to discuss a matter of great mutual importance. But Seneca responded with a refusal to meet.

So, Piso sent his client Antonius Natalis, one of the seven Equestrians who had joined the plot, to locate Seneca at one of his country retreats. The former chief secretary that Natalis found was looking emaciated now as a result of the strict diet that he had been following since discovering the scheme to poison him. Natalis complained bitterly to Seneca over his refusal to confer with Piso.

"Why are you excluding Piso from your presence," Natalis demanded, "when it would be better to keep up your friendship through regular intercourse?"[4]

Seneca disagreed. Through Natalis, he sent a fresh reply to Piso, excusing himself from any face-to-face contact with his friend, pleading failing health and the need to rest, the same excuse he had used to avoid meeting with the emperor. From one source or another, Seneca had become aware of the assassination plot. When Natalis returned to persist on Piso's behalf yet again, Seneca again rejected the idea of being seen in company with Piso.

"Mutual conversations and frequent interviews are to the advantage of neither of us," Seneca told Natalis. As Seneca sent the disappointed middle man on his way again, he told him to wish Piso well on his behalf, adding, cryptically, "My own life depends on Piso's safety."[5]

After receiving this latest message from Seneca, which led him to take comfort in the belief that his friend supported him, Piso turned to setting a place and time for Nero's destruction. Ever since the new year began, the emperor had seldom left either his residence or his gardens, so involved had he become in the minutiae of planning and approvals for the rebuilding of the city. One of the conspirators, Tullius Senecio, an Equestrian, was "especially intimate with Nero" and still pretended friendship with him, enabling him to keep the other plotters informed of Nero's plans and intentions.[6]

Some conspirators had expected that the emperor would venture forth come the spring to sing in competition at Neapolis, as he had the previous year, but the word from inside man Senecio was that Nero had made no mention of any such plan. Only one event, the plotters knew, was sure to bring Nero out in public—chariot races. The next race day on the calendar was set for April, during the Cerealia, a festival dedicated to the goddess Ceres. Running from April 12 to April 19, the seven-day festival was scheduled to include one culminating day of chariot racing at the Circus Flaminius. And, Senecio confirmed, Nero would be attending those races.

Access to the emperor would be relatively easy at the Circus Flaminius, and the plotters agreed that the consul-designate, Plautius Lateranus, one of the first members of the conspiracy, would approach Nero in the circus tribunal, the official box. Lateranus, a large, physically powerful man with plenty of nerve, would throw himself at Nero's knees, in the posture of a supplicant, seemingly to beg some favor. Lateranus would then grab Nero's legs and drag him from his chair, pressing him to the ground. The Praetorian tribunes and centurions who were party to the plot would then rush up and hold back Nero's bodyguards while the first lethal blow was struck.

The honor of that first blow was claimed by the senator Flavius Scae-vinus. Since the birth of the conspiracy, Scaevinus had been secretly wear-ing beneath his clothes a sacred dagger that he had taken from the Temple of Fortune in his Etrurian hometown of Ferentum, modern Fer-ento, in central Italy. Ferentum was also the hometown of Marcus Otho, the governor of Lusitania whose wife, Poppaea Sabina, Nero had stolen. No classical author could attribute a reason to Scaevinus' participation in the plot to kill Nero, but it is possible that he was a close friend and client of Otho and that he wanted to avenge his friend's humiliation and loss. Or, more likely, the heavily indebted Scaevinus was hopeful that Otho would handsomely reward him for the murder and relieve him of his fi-nancial problems. According to the plan now agreed on by the plotters, once Scaevinus had struck, the Praetorian officers and other conspirators would do the same.

This plan was put to Piso, who approved it. Pledging himself to marry Antonia, daughter of Claudius, and to accept the throne when it was of-fered, Piso said that on the day of the assassination, he would go to the Temple of Ceres and await word that Nero was dead. Praetorian Prefect Faenius Rufus could then summon Piso to the Praetorian barracks, at the same time sending an escort to bring Antonia to the barracks. In front of the assembled Praetorian Cohorts, Piso would be presented to the troops as their new emperor and be hailed by them.

The Temple of Ceres stood on the slopes of the Aventine Hill. Like every other structure on the hill, the temple had been seriously damaged during the previous year's fire, just as it had been in a 31 BC blaze. With the temples of Rome receiving first priority in the rebuilding process, and with Ceres being one of the four deities that the Sibylline reading had identified as requiring special attention, the almost six-hundred-year-old Temple of Ceres would have been quickly restored as part of Nero's re-construction program.

In going to the temple on the assassination day, Piso would be un-likely to arouse any unusual interest or suspicion from anyone who saw him. But Piso had an ulterior motive for choosing this place, of all places, to spend the time awaiting news of the murder of his emperor. The Tem-ple of Ceres was the headquarters of the plebeian aediles and was also

legally a place of sanctuary. No person claiming the protection of the goddess while in the precincts of her temple could be arrested. This was Piso's
insurance policy, for he was wracked with doubts and fears about the fate
of the plot. If all went awry, Piso at least could hope to escape arrest and
execution, by claiming the protection of the sanctuary.

Infected with this fear of failure, the plot to assassinate Nero Caesar
went forward.

⚬ᴜᴜᴜᴏ

Before dawn on April 18, Flavius Scaevinus, the conspirator who had
claimed the honor of striking the first blow against Nero, did the rounds
of his patrons, then called on Antonius Natalis, the conspiratorial ring's
principal go-between. After sending away the servants, the pair spent a
long time discussing the arrangements for the assassination they intended
carrying out the following day. Only when he was convinced that every
detail had been covered did Scaevinus go home to make his own final
preparations.

Methodically, Scaevinus tidied up his affairs. Taking out his last will
and testament, he read it, assured himself that it contained all that it
should, then closed it with his seal. After handing the sealed will to
Milichus, his chief freedman, for safekeeping, Scaevinus reached beneath
his tunic and brought into the light of day the sheathed dagger that had
been suspended around his neck for weeks. For the first time since he
had taken it from the Temple of Fortune, Scaevinus slid the ancient dagger from its sheath. A scowl came over his face, as he saw that the blade
was blunted by rust. This was the blade that he intended plunging into
the heart of Nero at the races next day, and he wanted it to enter the
tyrant's flesh with ease.

Handing the dagger to Milichus, he said, "Sharpen it on a whetstone,
to a keen and bright point."[7]

"Yes, master." Milichus took charge of the dagger.

Scaevinus ordered an extravagant banquet for the evening. His staff
noted that he was that day "depressed, and evidently in profound
thought" as he went about his usual bathhouse routine. That night, he
sat down for his grand meal as if it were to be his last. Over dinner, he

called in his favorite slaves and announced that he was manumitting them—granting their freedom. He gave money to several others. These were usually the acts of a dying man. Having astonished his staff, Scaevinus kept up an apparently merry conversation with those family members who reclined around the dining table with him. The last thing he did before retiring to bed was to instruct Milichus to prepare bandages for the next day, as if he were expecting to be wounded.

Milichus, Scaevinus' chief freedman, was troubled by all this. That night, as he lay in bed with his wife, Milichus told her all about the master's uncharacteristic behavior and demeanor that day. He showed her the knife from the Temple of Fortune that he was supposed to sharpen. Like Milichus, his wife suspected that Scaevinus was up to something. Both observed that the day was widely considered inauspicious for the sealing of wills. And they knew that their master was planning to attend the games the next day, even though he was not a particular fan of chariot racing. Both knew that their master planned to sit close to the emperor. And then there was this knife. Milichus' wife put two and two together.

Once Milichus' wife shared with him her suspicion that Scaevinus was planning to kill the emperor, his first reaction was to hold his tongue, to serve and protect his master, no matter what. His wife scolded him, pointing out that a number of others, both slaves and freedmen, had that day seen exactly what Milichus had seen, had heard what he had heard. She reminded her husband that his silence would be meaningless if others spoke up and warned the emperor; in fact, it would count against him. But if Milichus were the first to speak up, the rewards from the emperor for his information would be his and his alone.

Sunrise the next day, April 19, found Milichus and his wife outside the gates to the Servilian Gardens, west of the Tiber River, where the emperor was known to be residing while the construction work continued on his grand new palace. The tall wooden gates to the gardens were closed, so Milichus rapped on them, calling for the gatekeepers to let him in.

"I am the bearer of important and alarming news!" he yelled.[8]

The gatekeepers ignored him, so Milichus continued to bash on the doors and to shout the same message, with increasing desperation. Finally, his persistence paid dividends; the gates were opened, and the gatekeepers warily looked him up and down. After Milichus again repeated the same declaration, he and his wife were escorted to the sprawling villa in the gardens, which overlooked the river. They were brought before Epaphroditus, secretary *a libellis*, or secretary of petitions, whose job it was to receive and deal with approaches to the Palatium by Nero's subjects.

Across Epaphroditus' desk came everything from applications and recommendations for Roman citizenship to legal appeals from citizens convicted of a crime to approaches to the emperor from foreign envoys. With thousands of such applications to deal with, it was no wonder that the three Jewish priests that Joseph bar Matthias had been sent to Rome to free had been waiting now for four years for their cases to be heard. Tacitus would not have a good word to say about Epaphroditus, but Joseph, who came to know Epaphroditus well, would describe him as "a lover of all kinds of learning." In Joseph's estimation, Epaphroditus showed "a wonderful rigor and an excellent nature," and was above all a virtuous man.[9]

Now, the learned Epaphroditus listened as Milichus gushed out his story of an oddly behaving master, a knife, and that very day's circus games. Once Epaphroditus had learned of the suspicious behavior of Milichus' employer, he led the freedman and his wife to Nero himself. Milichus repeated his story for the twenty-seven-year-old emperor's benefit, warned him of the danger that he felt certain Nero was in, and handed him the dagger from the Temple of Fortune that he had been ordered to sharpen. As Nero turned over the dagger in his hands, Milichus urged him to summon Scaevinus to answer his charges against him.

Before long, a centurion-led party of armed Praetorian soldiers pushed roughly past Scaevinus' doormen, strode into his house, and placed Scaevinus under arrest. Surrounded by a grim-faced guard, Scaevinus was escorted through the city (which was now one giant building site) and across a Tiber River bridge to the Servilian Gardens and brought before the emperor. To Scaevinus' horror, Milichus and his wife were with Nero. The emperor held up the dagger, which would have carried an inscription relating to the goddess to whom it was dedicated, and asked Scaevinus to explain how he had come by it.

"That dagger has long been regarded by my ancestors with a religious sentiment," Scaevinus replied, appearing angry, not afraid. "It has been kept in my chamber, and was stolen by my freedman, using trickery." To accent his accusation, he glared at Milichus.[10]

Nero then asked Scaevinus why he had signed his will on an inauspicious day, and why he had given money and freedom to his slaves.

"I have often signed my will without taking into account the observance of specific days," Scaevinus replied. "I have previously made gifts of money and freedom to some of my slaves. On this occasion, I gave more freely because, as my means are now impoverished and my creditors are pressing me, I distrusted the validity of my will."[11]

Was Scaevinus truly in financial trouble? As far as the emperor knew, Scaevinus' table was always covered with the best silverware, and his lifestyle was and always had been a luxurious one. Scaevinus shrugged and said he could not doubt that his harsher critics would not approve of his expenditure in the financial circumstances in which he currently found himself.

The question about the preparation of bandages was not one that Scaevinus could be expected to answer easily. But instead of defending the accusation with some trifling excuse, Scaevinus went on the offensive. He claimed that no bandages had been prepared on his orders. "This, and all the man's other charges are absurd!" He added that if anyone was preparing to murder Caesar, it was Milichus. Turning on the freedman, Scaevinus fearlessly denounced him: "Infamous and depraved wretch!"[12]

Nero looked at the accused, at his accuser, and at Epaphroditus, unsure as to what to do. It appeared as if the accusations against Scaevinus, unsupported as they were by any evidence or corroborating testimony, were going to come to nothing. As Nero was about to dismiss the accused man, an outcome that would have given Scaevinus an opportunity to have Milichus charged with making false accusations, Milichus' wife spoke up. To this point, she had held her tongue, but now she reminded Milichus that Antonius Natalis had recently had a long conversation with Scaevinus, with all the servants told to leave the room. And, she added, Scaevinus and Natalis were both intimate friends of Gaius Piso.

Nero's ears pricked up. "Piso, you say?"

Nero had never forgotten the unproven charge against Piso and his friend Seneca three years earlier. Nero feared Seneca more than he feared Piso; that Piso might be embroiled in this case could also suggest that Seneca was involved and that he might even be orchestrating a plot against the emperor. Nero, with his suspicions heightened, ordered Antonius Natalis brought in for questioning, then asked Scaevinus what his furtive conversation with Natalis had been about.

The morning was still young when Natalis was hustled into the Servilian Gardens. Scaevinus had been taken into another room by the time that Natalis was brought before Nero. Natalis was asked what he had discussed with Scaevinus in their secret meeting. Natalis' version of what transpired turned out to be completely different from the one given by Scaevinus only minutes before. Nero, knowing that at least one of the men was lying, ordered the pair put in chains and questioned further.

Manacles were placed on the wrists of Scaevinus and Natalis, who were hustled away to the Praetorian barracks on the other side of the city. For the first time in almost a year, Praetorian Prefect Tigellinus once more took center stage. Sidelined by Nero since the Great Fire—perhaps because the fire's second stage had erupted on Tigellinus' property and Nero had subsequently kept the prefect at arm's length in an attempt to dispel the rumors that he had been responsible for the fire—Tigellinus was now called on by Nero to do what he did best and deal with traitors in his own inimitable style.

Taking charge of the prisoners Scaevinus and Natalis at the barracks, Tigellinus showed them his favorite toy, the rack. The very sight of the torture device was enough to unlock the lips of both men. First, Natalis, under separate questioning and promised immunity if he gave the names of other conspirators, confessed the details of the plot and named Piso as the head of it, also mentioning his meetings with Seneca on Piso's behalf. These names were put to Scaevinus. Believing that Natalis had revealed all, he confirmed these names, admitted his part in the conspiracy, and then proceeded to name all the other civilian conspirators. Yet neither he nor Natalis named any of the tribunes or centurions of the Praetorian Cohorts who were party to the plot. It is likely that in doing so, both men were hoping that the Praetorian officers would now act, lead a revolt of their troops against Nero, and free the accused men.

Word of the arrest of Scaevinus and Natalis had swept through the city that morning. Even as Scaevinus and Natalis were still being questioned at the Servilian Gardens, Gaius Piso received the news from several worried fellow conspirators. The plot was exposed, or soon would be, as Piso knew all too well, for neither Scaevinus nor Natalis had a reputation for courage, and both could be expected to reveal all through torture or the offer of reward. Piso's friends urged him to gather up his supporters and hurry to the Praetorian barracks, or mount the Rostra in the Forum and take the initiative.

"Test the feelings of the soldiers and of the people," said one conspirator. He believed that by making the movement against Nero public, Piso would attract many more followers. Nero had yet to call out his guards, he said, and there was still time to overwhelm the emperor before he realized the scope of the conspiracy.[13]

Another of Piso's friends felt that it was too late—troops would be on their way to arrest him at any moment. He counseled Piso to take his own life while he had the chance. "Justify your life to your ancestors and descendants," he urged.[14]

Piso, undecided as to which course to follow, went out into the street to gauge the public mood. Yet while the news of the arrests of Scaevinus and Natalis was now common knowledge, there was no sense of excitement or of panic in the streets, no talk of joining the movement against Nero, or of the military's coming out against the emperor. Daily life was continuing as normal. And Piso knew at once that the conspiracy was doomed to fail. Going back into his house, he closed his doors, ordered his servants to bring him wine, and sent for his secretary.

As Piso waited, he dictated a new will in which he heaped praise on Nero and left a portion of his estate to the emperor. This was designed to ensure that Nero would allow Piso's wife Atria to at least retain her dowry, as Roman law provided in the case of a normal death. Otherwise, the imperial treasury could confiscate Piso's entire estate, the usual outcome when a man was convicted of treason.

In quick succession, Praetorian detachments burst into one house and apartment after another across the city. Named conspirators were hauled in for questioning, as were their servants. Most of the arrested men confessed their part in the plot, sooner or later, but three of the accused steadfastly maintained their innocence—Lucan the young poet, Quintianus the senator, and Nero's erstwhile friend Senecio the Equestrian, the conspirators' "inside man." Their attitude changed when they were offered immunity from prosecution if they admitted their complicity and each gave the name of at least one co-conspirator. All three now confessed. Lucan named his mother Atilla as his co-conspirator. The other two men named their best friends. Lucan seemed to believe that if he named his mother, Nero would not stoop to arresting her, which in fact proved to be the case. Lucan and the other two were then set free and allowed to go home.

Nero now remembered, or was reminded, that the freedwoman Epicharis was still being held in custody, and he ordered that she be questioned a second time, this time on the rack. Tigellinus' men were quick to employ their skills as torturers. Epicharis was placed on the rack, face down, with her arms and legs stretched wide. She was "scourged"—whipped. Red-hot irons were applied to her skin. But she steadfastly denied the charge that she was involved with this conspiracy. So, she was stretched on the rack until her legs were dislocated. Still she denied any complicity and refused to implicate anyone else. By the end of the day, she was cast into a cell in agony, but without having given in to her torturers.

A detachment of Praetorians arrived outside Gaius Piso's closed doors. These troops were all men from outlying parts of southern Italy who had only joined the Praetorian Cohorts in the most recent draft. The older enlisted men, who had served under the Praetorian standard for many years, were "actually imbued with a liking" for Nero, according to Tacitus.[15] But Nero was worried that those older men might have grown some attachment to the popular Piso after living at the capital for so many years. Recent recruits, youngsters from outside the capital, would not know Piso. So, Nero had given specific instructions that new men be sent to arrest Piso.

The tribune in command of the detachment was informed by Piso's staff that their master had just this minute severed the arteries of his arms and would soon be dead. The officer decided to allow Piso the dignity of a self-inflicted death; his troops would remain at the house until it was confirmed that Piso was dead. The officer would then enter and view Piso's corpse. Drawing his sword, he would cleave off the dead senator's head. That head would be taken to the Servilian Gardens as proof of Piso's demise.

Nero, "more and more alarmed" as the plot unfolded before his eyes and more and more names were added to the list of conspirators, ordered the size of his bodyguard multiplied and the city brought under military control.[16] All cohorts of the German Guard stationed at their barracks west of the Tiber were called to arms. The fourteen Praetorian Cohorts were also summoned to duty. Praetorian detachments marched to the guard towers at all the city gates and occupied them, augmenting the small City Cohort detachments on duty at the gates. Armed with a list of suspects, the Praetorians stopped and questioned all persons leaving the capital. Other cohorts marched from the city to take up station along the bank of the Tiber River to prevent accused men from escaping by water.

Squadrons from the Praetorian Cavalry galloped from the city and down the Via Ostiensis to the coast, where, at Ostia, they joined the men of the 17th Cohort of the City Guard, which was then stationed at Ostia, to watch the docks for wanted men. To seek out suspects who were vacationing away from the capital, more cavalry pounded along the highways to outlying towns and villages, where they were joined by men from the German Cohorts, who were at that time stationed outside Rome. According to Tacitus, Nero trusted the German troops more than he did the citizen soldiers of the Praetorian Cohorts, and he now deliberately added squads of Germans to the Praetorian units, to ensure that the Praetorians did their duty and did not fail to round up members of the assassination conspiracy.[17]

Nero had historical reasons for doing this. Augustus had founded the German Cohorts with the conviction that these foreign troops, who did not hold Roman citizenship, would be unlikely to join any uprising against the throne, which proved to be the case. For the same reason, Tiberius had salted troops from the German Cohorts among Praetorian troops sent to put down a legion mutiny in Dalmatia early in his reign.

As Nero's troops now spread far and wide, Nero assigned a Praetorian tribune, Gavius Silvanus, the task of locating and questioning the former chief secretary, Lucius Seneca. In particular, Silvanus was under orders to put to Seneca the words of confessed conspirator Natalis who implied that Seneca had been aware of the assassination plot, and to demand to know if Natalis' claim was truthful. Silvanus strode away to fulfill his assignment. As had been the case for many months, Seneca was outside Rome. But unbeknownst to Nero, there was at least one Praetorian tribune who knew precisely where to find the former chief secretary. Either much of the day would pass before Silvanus obtained that information from his colleague, or he would stall for hours before acting on the information.

Unlike Seneca, the consul-designate Plautius Lateranus was close at hand and had no time to run before the Praetorians burst in on him. Several other well-placed conspirators had given Lateranus' name, and his fate was sealed. His arrest took place so quickly that Lateranus did not have time to take his own life or even to give his children a parting embrace. Tribune Statius Proximus was in charge of the troops who arrested Lateranus. The prisoner said nothing as he was hustled out the door with chains on his wrists, ankles, and neck and then dragged to a place outside the city customarily used for the execution of slaves. But Lateranus knew that Tribune Proximus was also a member of the conspiracy, and the prisoner was probably hoping that at the last moment, the tribune would save him.

Lateranus had no such luck. Tribune Proximus was only interested in saving his own skin and was in a hurry to silence the high-ranking conspirator. Pressed to his knees, Lateranus was told to straighten his neck. Proximus drew his sword and, with one solid, two-handed blow, took off the consul-elect's head.

NERO, emperor at sixteen, was overweight and just starting to express his artistic tendencies by the time of the Great Fire of Rome, ten years after he ascended the throne. (Capitoline Museum)

AGRIPPINA THE YOUNGER, Nero's ultra-ambitious mother, married the emperor Claudius then murdered him to put Nero on the throne, only for Nero to engineer her death. (Archaeological Museum of Istria, Pula)

POPPAEA SABINA, Nero's last manipulative wife, former wife of Nero's close friend Marcus Otho. (Archaeological Museum of Olympia, Greece)

LUCIUS SENECA, Nero's clever tutor and later powerful chief secretary. Depicted here at the height of his power, he would lose much weight after changing his diet subsequent to learning of a plot to poison him. (Antiquities Collection, Altes Museum, Berlin)

VITELLIUS, who as chief singing contest judge, called Nero back to perform on stage after the young emperor suffered stage fright. A lover of luxurious living, Vitellius would spend heavily during his brief reign as emperor. (Ny Carlsberg Glyptothek, Copenhagen; photograph by Wolfgang Sauber)

A MODEL OF ROME IN THE FOURTH CENTURY.
The city had grown along the lines sketched out by Nero following the Great Fire,
which leveled much of that part of the city seen here. The Circus Maximus, bottom left,
where the Great Fire began, continued to dominate Rome, while the palaces on the
Palatine Hill, immediately to the right of the circus, had risen from the ashes of the fire.
The circular Colosseum, Vespasian's Hunting Theater, at right, had been erected on the
site of Nero's Pond. (Museum of Roman Civilization, Rome)

THE CIRCUS MAXIMUS, where more than 200,000 spectators watched chariot races, and where, on July 19, AD 64, the Great Fire of Rome broke out. (Drawing by G. Gatteschi from Albert Kuhn, *Roma* 1913)

THE AQUA CLAUDIA, one of nine aqueducts serving Rome in AD 64, still cleaves through the Italian countryside on its way to Rome.

CORBULO,
Nero's tough general, who
reconquered Armenia for Rome,
only to be implicated by his son-
in-law in a plot to murder the
emperor. (Plaster cast of an
original portrait in the Centrale
Montemartini of the Capitoline
Museums, Rome, once indentified
as Gnaeus Domitius Corbulo)

OTHO, for a long time Nero's good friend,
turned against him after his wife Poppaea
Sabina set her sights on becoming empress.
Otho would briefly be emperor in AD 69.
(Capitoline Museum, Rome)

NERVA,
himself later a respected occupant of the throne,
served as one of Nero's four special investigators
who sought out sympathizers to the AD 65 Piso
Plot against the emperor's life. (Palazzo Massimo
alle Terme, National Museum of Rome, Rome)

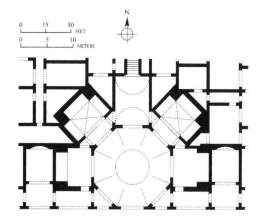

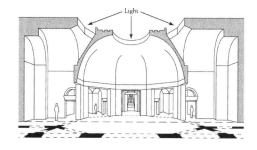

DOMUS AUREA PLANS showing a portion of Nero's vast Golden House.

DOMUS AUREA. Modern-day ruins of part Nero's extravagant Golden House palace at Rome.

GALBA
was an austere man of seventy
when the Senate declared him
emperor after deposing Nero.
(Antiques Museum in the
Royal Palace, Stockholm;
photo by Wolfgang Sauber)

VESPASIAN,
acquiescent senator and able general
under Nero, led the AD 67 Roman
counteroffensive in Judea designed to
put down the Jewish Revolt. He too
would become emperor of Rome.
(Ny Carlsberg Glyptotek, Copenhagen)

DOMITIAN,
youngest son of the cash-strapped senator
Vespasian, was a thirteen-year-old chariot-racing
fan in AD 64. He would live to see his father,
brother, and himself become emperor of Rome.
(Capitoline Museum, Rome)

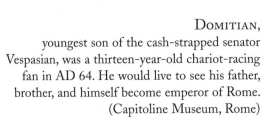

THE SUICIDE
OF SENECA

Early this same day, April 19, the day that the chariot racing was due
to take place in celebration of the Festival of Ceres, Lucius Seneca
and his wife Pompeia Paulina traveled in from a country estate in Campania and arrived at the villa of one of Seneca's friends—Novius Priscus,
apparently—just four miles south of Rome. Joined by Seneca's doctor,
Statius Annaeus, the party prepared to spend the night at the villa.

That evening, Seneca, his wife, his doctor, and his host had commenced
dinner when a large party of Praetorian soldiers came marching down the
road from Rome and surrounded the house, having tramped for upward
of an hour after leaving the capital. The detachment's senior officers were
on horseback. The officer in charge, the tribune Gavius Silvanus, dismounted and went inside the house to address the emperor's questions to
the former chief secretary. He found Seneca, his wife, and two friends in
a dining room, spread on couches around a low dining table. Seneca had
lost a great deal of weight since the tribune had last laid on eyes on him.
"His aged frame," said Tacitus, was "attenuated by frugal diet."[1] Standing
before the diners, Silvanus put his questions to the former chief secretary.

"Yes, tribune, Natalis was sent to me," the gaunt Seneca nonchalantly acknowledged in reply, leaning on one elbow with his wife reclining

beside him, "and he complained to me in Piso's name because I had refused to see Piso."[2]

The tribune asked why Seneca had refused to see Piso.

"I excused myself on the grounds of failing health and the desire to
rest," Seneca replied. "I had no reason for preferring the interests of any
private citizen to my own wellbeing. I have no natural aptitude for flattery; no one knows that better than Nero, who more often experienced
my outspokenness than my subservience."[3]

The tribune withdrew. Leaving his troops around the villa, Silvanus
rode back into the city to report to the emperor. He found Nero at the
Servilian Gardens, where the emperor was now accompanied by his wife
Poppaea and Praetorian Prefect Tigellinus. The empress and the prefect
had become, in this grave situation, "the emperor's most confidential advisers," said Tacitus.[4]

After the tribune repeated Seneca's answers to the questions put to
him, Nero asked, "Was Seneca considering suicide?"

"No, Caesar," Silvanus replied. "I saw no sign of fear, and perceived
no sadness in his words, or in his looks."[5]

Nero deliberated with Poppaea and Tigellinus on what course to follow.
Authors Tacitus and Suetonius were adamant that Nero wanted Seneca
dead, fearing both his influence and his ability. Tigellinus would have reminded Nero that Seneca's last words to Natalis incriminated him—the
comment that his safety depended on Piso's safety. This, the adviser would
have said, proved that Seneca was aware of the assassination plot and the
plan to install Piso in Nero's place once the emperor had been murdered,
but Seneca had not attempted to warn the emperor that his life was in grave
danger from Piso. Even if Seneca had not been an active member of the
conspiracy, his failure to disclose the plot to Nero represented treason.

"Inform Seneca that sentence of death has been passed on him," Nero
told Silvanus.[6]

"Yes, Caesar." The tribune hurried away to comply. But he did not return to the villa outside the city directly. Instead, in the summer twilight,
Silvanus went to the second Praetorian prefect, Faenius Rufus, whose association with the conspiracy was still a well-guarded secret. Tribune Silvanus was also a party to the plot, having joined it during its second surge

of recruitment, and was aware of Rufus' involvement. Silvanus informed Rufus of Nero's orders concerning Seneca and asked what he should do.

Rufus admonished the tribune for coming to him and instructed Silvanus to follow the emperor's orders without further delay. Silvanus took his leave and set off back to the villa outside Rome, where he had left Seneca. Tacitus said of Rufus, Silvanus, and other Praetorian officers involved in the assassination plot: "A fatal spell of cowardice was on them all."[7] Recording these happenings several decades later, Tacitus based his account, he revealed, on the writings of Fabius Rusticus, the historian who had been both a friend and a client of Seneca and who seems to have had particularly good contacts within the Praetorian Cohorts.

Tribune Silvanus was mightily troubled by the turn of events. It would transpire that his fellow Praetorian tribune Sabrius Flavus, one of the originators of the assassination plot, had not been happy with the other conspirators' choice of Gaius Piso as Nero's replacement. In Flavus' soldierly opinion, it was just as disgraceful to make a tragic actor emperor of Rome as it was to endure a harp player on the throne. Flavus had another candidate in line for the throne—Seneca. The tribune felt that Seneca was "a man singled out for his splendid virtues by all men of integrity" and would make a much better ruler than either Nero or Piso.[8] Seneca had experience in the job, after all, having been virtually a de facto emperor, ruling through Nero during the early years of the boy emperor's reign. Flavus' plan was to initially go along with the civilian conspirators, up to the point that Nero was slain. Flavus and several of his centurions, whom he had already brought into this subplot, would then murder Piso and hand the empire over to Seneca, who would take the throne as next emperor.

While this twist in the original plot had been inspired by Tribune Flavus, Seneca was apparently well aware of it. This was why he had come up to the house just outside Rome this day, to await news of Nero's death, and of Piso's death, and then to be conveyed to the Praetorian barracks and hailed as Rome's next emperor. Tribune Silvanus was also aware of this plan, but with Nero still alive and with Prefect Rufus unwilling to show his true colors, Silvanus did not have the courage to set the plot in motion himself. Nor did he have the courage to face Seneca. After riding back to the villa and arriving after dark, the weak-kneed tribune instructed one of his centurions to go into the villa and inform Seneca of the death sentence passed on him by Nero.

Inside the villa, Seneca, his wife, and his friends had waited tense hours for this verdict to be delivered from the emperor, although it is likely that Seneca had guessed that his time was up, and he was only living in hope that the Praetorian officers involved in the conspiracy would declare their hands and set the plot in motion and complete Nero's overthrow. The centurion who now delivered Seneca's death sentence was not involved in the conspiracy and was loyal to Nero, and as far as the messenger was concerned, the old man before him was a convicted traitor. As the centurion spoke, his hand would have rested on the hilt of his sheathed sword, to emphasize both his capital authority and his mission.

"Will you allow me to have [wax] tablets brought in so that I might write my will?" Seneca asked him.

"No," the centurion gruffly replied.

With a sigh, Seneca turned to his wife and friends. "As I'm forbidden to reward you, I bequeath you the only possession, but still the noblest possession, that I am still able to give—the pattern of my life."[9]

Seneca had made a name for himself as a philosopher, particularly with his writings during his exile on Corsica. Many of his sayings have passed down to present day. Yet, Seneca had frequently failed to live up to the high standards he set in his own philosophy. Far from living a simple life, he had amassed great wealth, had lived in luxury, and had charged exorbitant rates of interest on the money he had loaned out. It was said that in summarily calling in his massive loans to British tribes in AD 59–60, he had contributed to resentment in Britain that had led to Boudicca's bloody revolt. He had been convicted of committing adultery with one daughter of Germanicus Caesar, Julia, and was accused of being the lover of another, Nero's mother, Agrippina the Younger. A case can also be put that Seneca had even been involved in the murder of Germanicus, to win favor with Sejanus, Tiberius' powerful and ambitious Praetorian prefect. And there was no denying that Seneca had colluded with Nero in the final stage of the murder of the young emperor's mother and had orchestrated the subsequent cover-up. Blameless and virtuous his life had not been.

The pattern of Seneca's life, then, was far from worthy of emulation. Yet, Seneca had come to believe his own publicity, which had been propagated during his years in power, and believed himself to be a man of splendid virtues. Like many sinners, he felt that in being sinned against, he was the victim. He seems to have genuinely believed that he was ending his life as a martyr to tyranny, even though he had for many years been the tyrant's accomplice.

"If you remember it [the pattern of his life] after I am gone, you will win a name for your moral worth and steadfast friendship," he grandly added.[10]

Seneca's wife and his friends were in tears. Paulina was much younger than her husband, possibly less than half his age. Seneca's first wife and a young son, his only child, had died while he was in exile. Paulina, daughter of a former consul who was one of three men entrusted by Nero with the management of the public revenues, had been a loyal and loving wife to Seneca. Not long before this, Seneca had written as much to a friend: "She is forever urging me to take care of my health, and indeed as I come to realize the way her very being depends on mine, I am beginning, in my concern for her, to feel some concern for myself."[11]

Now, as tears flowed around him, Seneca urged his friends to dry their eyes and face what was to come with "manly resolution." And then he rebuked himself for allowing matters to come to this. "Where are your maxims of philosophy, Seneca, or the preparation of so many years' study against future evils? Who did not know of Nero's cruelty? After murdering his mother and his brother, all that remains is to add the destruction of his guardian and tutor."[12]

The centurion, watching and listening to all this, would have impatiently patted his sword. He was under orders from his tribune to permit Seneca to take his own life, but there was a limit to his patience. As Seneca embraced the sobbing Paulina, "he begged and implored her to spare herself the burden of perpetual sorrow." She should instead, he said, console herself with remembrances of the virtuous life they had spent together.[13]

It was clear that Seneca intended to commit suicide, despite the fact that he had recently written to a friend, "A good man should go on living as long as he ought to, not just as long as he likes. The man who does not value his wife or a friend highly enough to stay on a little longer in life, who persists in dying in spite of them, is a thoroughly self-indulgent character."[14] But the situation he now found himself in made a self-induced demise a more attractive prospect. Few Romans declined the opportunity to take their own lives rather than submit themselves to the executioner once they had been condemned to death. More than a fear of the pain of decapitation, these men took the option of suicide because their fate was still in their own hands to the end, whereas with execution as a bound prisoner, their fate was surrendered to another. This was why Romans considered suicide, far from being a crime, an honorable act.

Out of the blue, Seneca's wife announced, "I too have decided to die." She looked at the now startled Praetorian officer. "Take off my head, centurion."

The centurion responded that he had no orders regarding her execution and could not oblige her.

Said Seneca proudly to his wife, "Paulina, I have shown you ways of smoothing life. You prefer the glory of dying. I won't begrudge you such a noble statement. We will share the fortitude of so courageous an end, but there will be more in the manner of your death to earn fame."[15]

While waiting to hear Nero's verdict, Seneca had readied a dagger. Now, as the centurion, Priscus, and Statius all watched, the latter two and the servants in the room all bearing looks of horror, Seneca and his wife sat on the couch with his left arm and her right together, and Seneca slashed his arm and hers "by one and the same stroke," severing their arteries. Paulina's blood pumped freely from her wound, but Seneca's blood escaped only slowly. Seeing the centurion scowling impatiently, Seneca took up the knife once more and bent and cut the veins of his legs and knees. Seneca feared that his slow death might break his wife's determination to die with him—for he wanted Paulina to share his fate, as a dramatic statement that would find a place on history's pages. So, he bade his wife farewell, then had his servants carry her into another room, so that he and she could die separately.

The centurion now went outside and informed his tribune that Paulina sought "the glory of sharing her husband's death" and that both she and Seneca had opened their veins. Tribune Silvanus then mounted his horse and rode back to the capital.[16]

"I have nothing against Pompeia Paulina," said the emperor once Silvanus reported to him at the Servilian Gardens. "I forbid her to die."[17]

So Silvanus galloped back to the villa, where he instructed his centurion to stanch Paulina's bleeding. The centurion led several of his men into the house and found Paulina lying in a separate room, alive but weak, surrounded by her fretting servants. The centurion ordered Paulina's staff to bandage up her arm at once, which they did. Some reports would later claim that Paulina was unconscious by this time and knew nothing about the saving of her life. Tacitus wrote that others claimed that Paulina was still conscious when the troops reached her, and once she knew that Nero did not want her punished, "she yielded to the charms of life" and made no attempt to resist or to further harm herself.[18] Either way, Seneca was denied the dramatic statement he had envisioned with Paulina joining him in death. Paulina would recover.

In a nearby room, apparently unaware that he had been robbed of his double sacrifice, Seneca had been spending the time dictating to his two secretaries as he continued to slowly bleed to death. He did not write a new will as he previously intended; the will of Seneca which was later published had been written when he was still in power, some time prior to his retirement in AD 62. Instead, thinking his end near, Seneca thought of posterity and his reputation and dictated an account of his own end, giving his final words to his wife and friends for the edification of the public at large. It was from this account, published after Seneca's death by his friends, Tacitus said, that the historian was able to describe Seneca's last hours in such vivid detail and with verbatim quotations.

Well into the night, Seneca clung to life, even though he had chosen to part with it. His prolonged exit forced him to beg his physician, Statius, a friend of many years and whose medical skill he esteemed, to prepare poison for him. For at any moment, the centurion could stride in with a drawn sword and take matters into his own hands. Tacitus wrote that the drug that Seneca asked for "he had provided himself some time before," without explaining how Seneca had previously obtained the poison, nor for what purpose.

This lethal poison was, said Tacitus, "the same drug which extinguished the life of those who were condemned by a public sentence of the people of Athens."[19] The "public sentence" referred to the jury system practiced by the Athenians, and the drug in question was hemlock. Statius hurried to his baggage and his medical chest. Physicians in Roman times carried a variety of drugs with them. Administered in small quantities, some otherwise deadly drugs were used to treat a variety of ailments.

Statius mixed the poison, a powder ground from the leaf of the toxic hemlock plant when it was in flower, with water and wine, and this he brought to Seneca, who gulped it down. There are two types of hemlock, water hemlock and poison hemlock. The former, common throughout the temperate parts of Europe, produces vomiting and diarrhea among its symptoms. Poison hemlock, native to North Africa, produces muscular weakness, paralysis of the extremities, and blindness, followed by respiratory difficulties and heart failure. Seneca was not vomiting or producing diarrhea, but he did complain of feeling chilled throughout his limbs, indicating that it was poison hemlock he had taken. Despite the poison, still Seneca did not die.

His host, Priscus, ordered his staff to heat several baths in the villa's bathhouse, and as soon as he was informed that the fires had done their jobs, bloody Seneca was carried to the bathhouse and lowered into a warm pool. His words echoing around him, he sprinkled some water on his nearest slaves and recited the words normally uttered during a religious sacrifice: "I offer this liquid as a libation to Jupiter the Deliverer."[20]

The warm pool made little difference to his blood flow, so Seneca was carried to the hot bath. Steam filled the room as Seneca was lowered into this water. The slaves and Seneca's friends withdrew. Seneca died of suffocation in the steam-filled room. A little later, when the water cooled and Seneca's body was removed, the centurion appeared, drew his sword, and lopped off his head. While the head was sent to Rome to prove to Nero that the man who had guided him for more than half his life was dead, the corpse was placed on a pyre in the villa garden. In his will, Seneca, who had never been religious, had specified that he be burned without any religious rites. And so Lucius Annaeus Seneca passed from this world, the latest, but not the last victim of the plot to kill Nero.

XVII

THE PURGE

As the sun rose over the Praetorian barracks on April 20, the day following the discovery of the conspiracy to murder the emperor at Rome, the inquisitors of the prisoner Epicharis prepared to resume their questioning of the woman. After her unproductive torture the previous day, Epicharis had spent an agonizing night on a cell floor. Now, the guards came for her. Because her legs had been dislocated on the rack and she could not walk, she was tied to an ordinary chair, which was dragged from the cell and along a corridor toward the torture chamber.

In the night, Epicharis had managed to strip a strong length of ribbon from the bosom of her gown, and when the guards came for her, she kept the rolled-up ribbon concealed in one hand. As she was being dragged along on the chair by her careless jailers, Epicharis was able to loop the ribbon over the arched back of the chair, forming a noose. Into this noose she placed her neck. Then, straining against the noose with all her might, she strangled the breath from her body. It would be reported that, only after the guards had deposited Epicharis in the torture chamber, was it discovered that the prisoner was a corpse. Tacitus uncharacteristically praised the freedwoman for her courage; she had not given up the name of a single conspirator to save herself, "protecting strangers and those whom she hardly knew."[1] Freeborn men, including

Equestrians and senators, in the meantime, were giving up names galore, without even facing the torturers.

Outside the gates to the Servilian Gardens, west of the Tiber River in Regio XIV, long lines of accused men and their servants, all in chains, awaited interrogation. Some had been arrested in the city; others had been tracked down to country retreats and brought in for questioning. Seneca was dead, and so too were Piso and Lateranus. But many more conspirators and their sympathizers remained. Not the least of these were the officers of the Praetorian Cohorts who were party to the plot; not a single one of them had yet been exposed or, conversely, had taken a step to aid the accused.

In the gardens, Nero, with a massive bodyguard from the German Cohorts by the name of Cassius standing at his shoulder, was accompanied by both Praetorian prefects, Tigellinus and Faenius Rufus. Beside Rufus stood the military tribune and Praetorian cohort commander Subrius Flavus, who, unbeknownst to the emperor, was a committed conspirator and whose troops formed part of the guard of the prisoners. Both these men were armed. Conspirators had been convinced that this pair— Prefect Rufus and Tribune Flavus—would come out for them once the ringleaders launched their coup, but to this point, neither the prefect nor the tribune had made a move.

Palatium secretaries writing in wax and using shorthand were noting down every confession, every accusation, every hint of disloyalty from men desperate to shift blame to others. Tigellinus was now in his savage element. As each man who was named by confessed conspirators was brought forward and denied his complicity in the plot, the prefect was able to throw accusations at them—this man was seen entering a banquet or a show with one of the known conspirators; that man was known to have had an unexpected meeting with a conspirator; or, even, a man had once been seen to smile at a conspirator.

While this questioning was taking place, Prefect Rufus frowned fiercely at his accomplices, who did not name him as one of them, and he even threatened them if they failed to speak up when questioned. This was an extremely dangerous course for Rufus. Tribune Flavus, standing at Rufus' elbow and bemused by his superior's actions, thought that Rufus was simply playing for time. The tribune caught the prefect's eye and motioned as if to draw his sword and strike Nero then and there, while they had the opportunity—he was just feet away. Rufus, shaking his head, discreetly reached over and took Flavus' arm as the centurion's hand rested on the hilt of the sword sheathed on his left side and checked him. Had the tribune gone ahead with his intent to assassinate Nero at that moment, Roman history may have turned out very differently.

Prefect Rufus, meanwhile, was clearly hoping that none of the suspects would mention his name. It was a futile hope. Scaevinus had been brought back to confront the accused men. He may have been hoping that Rufus and the six other Praetorian officers who were complicit in the plot would take up arms to help him, and that was why he had not named them. But Scaevinus, seeing Rufus playing the hard man while he himself was being browbeaten by Tigellinus, who demanded more information and more names, produced a smile, looked directly at Rufus, and said, "No one knows more than he does."[2]

All eyes turned to Prefect Rufus, who paled.

"Show Nero Caesar how grateful you have been that he is a good prince, Rufus," said Scaevinus sarcastically.[3]

Rufus was visibly terror-stricken and could only respond haltingly and unconvincingly that he was Nero's loyal subject. There were several accused men in the room at the time, among them, Cervarius Proculus, one of the seven Equestrians who had embraced the plot from its early days. Proculus knew that Rufus had been involved, and he became angry that Rufus was trying to act the part of one of his judges. Now, in support of Scaevinus, Proculus also pointed his finger at the prefect. Others in the line of prisoners followed suit. Rufus was doomed.

"Seize him!" Nero commanded.[4]

For just a moment, a heartbeat, there was hesitation in the ranks of Rufus' Praetorians. But then Cassius, the emperor's massive German bodyguard, stepped forward and took hold of Rufus. As the prefect was being put in chains, Rufus looked ruefully but silently at the tribune Flavus. This was Flavus' last chance to change the course of history, but he lacked the courage to act. In a flash, he could have drawn his sword, slashed the throat of Cassius to free Rufus, and then, in almost the same movement, struck down Nero. But it could be argued that most tribunes of the Praetorian Guard were men of talk, not men of action. Unlike the soldiers serving in the legions on the empire's frontiers, the Praetorians had not seen action, real action, since two of their cohorts had fought under Nero's grandfather Germanicus when he led a Roman army in defeating German tribes deep inside Germany, fifty years back.

Besides, Piso, the man initially singled out to replace Nero, was now dead, and so too was Flavus' choice as emperor, Seneca. Flavus did not have the imagination to conceive of a third alternative. Either that, or perhaps, without an alternative leader waiting in the wings, Flavus was actually brighter than his action, or lack of it, makes him appear to modern eyes. Perhaps the centurion could see that without an obvious alternative to Nero on the spot, the only other option, with Nero's death, was chaos—of the kind that had befallen Rome after the death of Julius Caesar following the Ides of March a century earlier. If this was the case, then Flavus was remarkably perceptive, for this would indeed be Rome's fate once Nero was eventually removed, several years from now. But Flavus' actions suggest that he was nothing more than a coward.

With Rufus' arrest, the fate of Tribune Flavus and all the Praetorian officers implicated in the plot was sealed. Seeing that the Praetorians had failed to keep their part of the conspiratorial bargain, the embittered Scaevinus—whose own unguarded actions had been the catalyst for the discovery of the plot—now also pointed out the tribune as a fellow conspirator. Proculus the Equestrian backed him up. Tribune Flavus, too, was now arrested by his own men and disarmed.

"I am innocent, Caesar," the tribune protested. "I cannot be compared to my accusers. How can it be thought that I, a soldier, would combine with such traitors as these?"[5]

But Scaevinus and Proculus declared that Flavus had been the most ardent of the plotters, and one of the first. As Tigellinus pressed him and as Scaevinus and Proculus offered to testify about meetings that Flavus had conducted with them and Prefect Rufus, Flavus at last admitted his guilt.

"But why?" Nero asked, astonished that a Praetorian tribune could betray his emperor and his oath of allegiance. Nero, despite all his faults, believed totally in keeping his word once he gave his sacred oath. "What could have led you to forget your oath of allegiance to me?"[6]

"I hated you!" Flavus replied, flushed with honesty at last.

"You hated me?" said Nero, in disbelief.

"I did. Yet, not a soldier could have been more loyal to you, while you deserved to be loved. I began to hate you when you became the murderer of your mother and your wife, a charioteer, an actor, and an incendiary."[7]

Nero's eyes flashed with anger. Here were all the "crimes" that his worst critics had accused him of since the Great Fire, crimes stretching back years. It was likely that Flavus had been one of those behind the incessant rumors that put the blame for the fire at Nero's door. It was also possible that this tribune had sent men through the burning city on the first night of the fire to discourage firefighting, tossing burning brands into buildings and claiming that they were acting on the authority of a certain individual. Flavus may even have set the second fire on Tigellinus' property, so that the despised Tigellinus received blame and was removed from his post as Flavus' superior.

Nero turned to Veianius Niger, the tribune of another of the Praetorian Cohorts, and ordered him to take Flavus away and to personally deal with him at once. Flavus, in chains and stripped of his weapons, expensive armor, helmet, and white tribune's cloak, was left in just his white, purple-bordered tunic. He was hustled from the Servilian Gardens by a large body of men from Niger's cohort, to a field outside the garden walls. As Flavus watched, several of Niger's men dug a pit for his body. When they had finished digging and were clambering from the pit, Flavus shook his head. "It's too shallow, and too narrow," he scornfully declared. He looked at the soldiers all around him. "Even this is not according to military regulation."[8]

With his hands chained behind his back, he was pressed to his knees beside his grave. His fellow tribune drew his sword and stood over him.

"Present your neck, Flavus," said Niger, his trembling voice betraying his dread of what he must do.

"I pray that your blow is firm, Niger," said Flavus.[9]

Niger readied his aim, then brought down his blade. But it only penetrated Flavus' neck part of the way. As blood spurted, Niger, close to panic, raised his sword and struck again. This time, the prisoner's head flopped to the ground and his corpse toppled over. When Niger returned to Nero and held up Flavus' severed head by its bloodied fair hair as proof that the deed had been done, someone in Nero's entourage must have remarked that Flavus possessed a thick neck.

"Yes," said Niger, laughing now. "It took a blow-and-a-half to slay him."[10]

Sulpicius Asper, a centurion in Flavus' cohort who had initiated the assassination plot in company with Flavus earlier in the year, had also been identified by Scaevinus and Proculus, who were singing like birds by this time and no longer protecting any of the Praetorians involved in the plot. When Asper was brought before his emperor, Nero was still in shock to think that men who gave their sacred oath to serve and protect him had been planning to murder him. He also asked Asper, "Why did you want to kill me? When you swore to serve me?"

"I could not have rendered a better service to you than to end your infamous career," Asper spat back in answer.

"Let him suffer the prescribed penalty," said Nero with disgust.[11]

Asper was hauled away and, like Flavus, beheaded at once. Prefect Faenius Rufus, their superior, as a man of senior rank, was granted a little time to compose his last will and testament, and then he too lost his head. Rufus, full of self-pity, wrote in his will that he desperately lamented his foolishness in becoming involved with the conspirators. When he was taken to his execution, he broke down in tears and died bemoaning his misfortune. Information was also given by convicted men against four other Praetorian centurions. All were promptly dealt with; all received the blade soldier-like and composed.

Two more Praetorian tribunes were also accused of complicity in the plot. One, Gavius Silvanus, was acquitted for lack of evidence. But the charge had a factual basis, and apparently feeling dishonored in front of his military colleagues, this Silvanus took his own life soon after. The next Praetorian tribune to be accused was Statius Proximus. When brought before Nero, Proximus openly confessed to having been involved with some conspirators, although he made no mention of the plan to replace Piso with Seneca. To Proximus' surprise, because he had obeyed

Nero's orders and supervised Seneca's demise, the emperor gave him a full pardon, which he gratefully accepted. But Proximus was wracked with guilt, and he too also later committed suicide.

Three other Praetorian tribunes were said by conspirators to be known to hate Nero, although there was no evidence that any of them had been involved in the plot. To be on the safe side, Nero deprived all three of their tribuneships and removed them from his service. With the military purged of the murderous and the disloyal, Nero turned to completing the weeding out of the civilian conspirators.

Four men in particular proved industrious in pursuing lines of inquiry on the emperor's behalf. They set out to identify men who, if not undeniably in league with the convicted conspirators, at least had suspect loyalty to the emperor. One of these investigators was, of course, Tigellinus. Not only was he back in the emperor's favor, but he was now rid of his rival Faenius Rufus, through Rufus' own foolishness. Another who sought out the guilty was Nymphidius, prefect of the vigiles. The son of Nymphidia, a freedwoman seamstress who had been the lover of freedmen on the staff of the emperor Caligula, Nymphidius claimed to have been fathered by Caligula himself.

The other two investigators were entirely different men from the widely despised Tigellinus and Nymphidius. It was almost as if Nero relied on them to counter the excesses of the first pair. One was Petronius Turpilianus, an elderly, able, and renowned general who had resigned as a consul for the year in AD 61 to take over the governorship of Britain in the chaotic days following the quashing of Boudicca's revolt. Turpilianus gained a reputation for a wise and conciliatory administration, which enabled the province to regain its equilibrium in the wake of enormous bloodshed.

The fourth man who was active on the emperor's behalf was thirty-five-year-old praetor-designate Marcus Cocceius Nerva. He was the son of a former consul who had committed suicide during the reign of Tiberius by starving himself to death shortly after Nerva was born. Credited by all chroniclers with being a good and wise man, Nerva, who was soon due to take up office as a senior judge at Rome, was distantly related to Nero, by marriage. Twenty-nine years from now, Nerva would become Rome's twelfth emperor.

Through the agency of these four men, Nero was presented with a list of a dozen suspects who, it was thought, sympathized with the convicted conspirators and the conspiracy. At the top of this list was Seneca's friend Novius Priscus, at whose villa Seneca had died. Another on the list was Rufius Crispinus, the empress Poppaea's first husband. With no concrete evidence against them, all twelve suspects were, on Nero's command, exiled from Rome. Some were merely banished from Italy, to live where they chose, while others were sent to specific islands. Several took their wives with them.

One man whom Nero had been hoping would be caught in the conspiratorial net was Vestinus, the sitting consul. When Nero was younger, Vestinus had been one of his companions on his night revels, at a time when Nero, incognito, would pick fights with strangers in the street. Vestinus, a witty man, had been good company on these revels, but his wit had a sarcastic edge, and although Nero had not shown it at the time, the emperor had long remembered Vestinus' barbs, for many jests are exaggerated truths. Added to Nero's aggravation was the fact that Vestinus had only recently married Nero's latest mistress, Statilia Messalina.

Nero felt certain that Vestinus was deeply disaffected with him, and considering Vestinus an impetuous man, Nero was convinced that the consul must have been involved with the conspiracy. Yet, not a word against Vestinus had been uttered by any conspirator, and all inquiries by Nero's investigators failed to produce a single piece of evidence that incriminated the consul. Came the end of another day, and still no one had come forward with anything negative to say about Vestinus. It was reported to Nero that during that day, Vestinus had conducted his consular duties as usual and in the evening had welcomed a number of guests for dinner. Nero, fearful of waiting any longer in case Vestinus was about to act against him, decided to proceed with his arrest, despite the lack of evidence against him, to "forestall the plans of the consul."[12]

Vestinus' city house was a palatial mansion on the Palatine Hill, home to the palaces of the emperors. Like the old palaces on the Palatine, Vestinus' house, a structure "towering over the Forum," in the words of Tacitus, had been rapidly restored since the Great Fire.[13] In this mansion, Vestinus kept a staff of hundreds of male slaves, chosen deliberately by their master for their handsome appearance and youth. If Vestinus were to arm these men, he could effectively resist arrest or, worse, go on the offensive. So, Nero ordered an entire Praetorian Cohort to make the arrest. In the darkness, one thousand Praetorian soldiers commanded by the trustworthy Tribune Gerellanus marched from their barracks, crossed the city, climbed the Palatine, then surrounded the house, and sealed off the servants' quarters.

A party of troops led by a centurion burst into the house as the consul and his guests were reclining, unsuspecting, around the dinner table. The centurion announced that his tribune waited outside and asked the consul to accompany him. Vestinus knew exactly what this meant. Quickly coming to his feet, issuing orders to his staff, and asking his physician, who was one of his dinner guests, to join him, the consul withdrew into another room and closed and barred the doors. The physician sliced open the veins of Vestinus' arms. A warm bath was prepared on the master's orders, and as soon as it was ready, Vestinus was carried to it by servants and lowered in, as his life blood now colored the bathwater red. Not a word was uttered by the consul, who was resigned to his fate.

Back in the dining room, Praetorians had surrounded the diners, who were instructed to remain where they were. There they waited, for hours, half expecting to also face a fatal end to their banquet. Word of the state of affairs at Vestinus' house was regularly conveyed across the Tiber to the emperor, who was still residing at the Servilian Gardens. Even after it was reported that Vestinus had expired, Nero left the men in the dining room in suspense. According to Tacitus, he laughed at the thought of their terror. It was late at night when orders finally arrived for the troops to withdraw. Nero now had Vestinus' head, and that was all he required. The traumatized diners were permitted to go home.

Nero still considered four other men to pose continuing threats. The first was young poet Lucan. From the testimony of other conspirators, it became clear that Lucan had been one of the instigators of the plot against the emperor's life. What was more, Lucan was the nephew of Seneca, and that alone was sure to win him sympathy and followers from among Seneca's admirers. Lucan had been promised immunity if he named one other conspirator, and as if to poke out his tongue at Nero, he had named Atilla, his own mother.

Lucan's immunity offer had not come from Nero's own lips, but from Tigellinus. On the strength of that technicality and infuriated by Lucan's cheek, Nero sent the poet word that he had been condemned to death. Calling his friends around him, Lucan slit his veins. Remarking that he felt a chill creep through his hands and feet as the blood dripped from him, he lay reciting one of his poems, about a wounded soldier dying a similar kind of death. And so Lucan the poet died. His mother was never arrested or questioned.

Senecio, the "inside man" who had betrayed Nero's friendship as well as his trust, was the next to receive a visit from the Praetorians. He too was permitted to take his own life. Quintianus was next, and he followed the others' example, as did, finally, Scaevinus, the man who had claimed the right to plunge Fortune's dagger into the emperor's heart. Scaevinus' wife, Caedicia, was, on Nero's orders, exiled from Italy. Nero had the by-now-infamous dagger inscribed "To Jupiter the Avenger" and dedicated it in a temple at the capital.

In the wake of the wave of arrests and punishments, Nero called an assembly of the Praetorian Guard at their barracks. Thanking them for their loyal service, he distributed a reward of two thousand sesterces to every man and ordered that the corn the troops had previously been entitled to buy at market price should now be provided to them free of charge. Next, the emperor called a sitting of the Senate.

Delivering a speech to the packed benches of the Senate House, Nero read the confessions of the condemned men, which were also published by the Palatium in a proclamation. For their roles in putting down the conspiracy Nero presented three men with Triumphal Decorations. These were the crimson cloak, golden palm tunic, bay leaf crown, laurel branch, and statues in the Forum normally presented to a general celebrating a Triumph for a major victory over foreign enemies. The recipients were the Praetorian prefect Tigellinus, the general Turpilianus, and praetor-designate Nerva. So much had Nerva and Tigellinus distinguished themselves in his service, to Nero's mind, that he also had busts of both made and placed in his Golden House.

Tall, stern-looking Nymphidius, the freedwoman's son, was doubly rewarded. He received the decorations of a consul—the consular insignia, purple-fringed toga, and twelve lictors. More importantly, he was also awarded the post of prefect of the Praetorian Cohorts that had been vacated by the death of Faenius Rufus, becoming Tigellinus' colleague in power. Several past appointees to this post, including Rufus, had similarly held the post of prefect of the vigiles at the time of their promotion.

There were still enemies of Nero who would deny that a conspiracy to murder him ever existed, men who would claim that Nero had used this as a pretence to destroy innocent men through jealousy or fear. Tacitus, despite being no fan of the young emperor, said that those who "took pains to ascertain the truth" at this time "conclusively proved" that such a conspiracy genuinely existed, beginning and maturing before being discovered and terminated. The plot's existence, and people's complicity in it, was also admitted, said Tacitus, by men who were exiled by Nero and later returned to Rome; Tacitus seems to have, some years later, personally spoken with a number of them.[14]

All the participants at this sitting of the Senate "abased themselves in flattery" of Nero, said Tacitus, especially those who were mourning relatives and friends caught up in the purge, as they strove to prove their loyalty to the emperor.[15] Junius Gallio, who had been stricken with terror by the enforced deaths of his brother Seneca and nephew Lucan, had made a personal plea to Nero for his life. For days, Gallio and others had prostrated themselves at the emperor's feet and smothered his hand with kisses as they swore that they'd had no part in the plot and had known nothing of it.

Nero seemed content to hush up or ignore any evidence that implicated Gallio, said Tacitus, but now, the senator Salienus Clemens came to his feet and denounced Gallio, calling him an enemy and a traitor. But Clemens was shouted down by hundreds of fellow senators, for it was known that Clemens had a personal grudge against Gallio. Besides, the other senators wanted the bloody wound caused by the exposed conspiracy to heal as quickly as possible, so that no more leading men fell victim to it.

The Senate decreed offerings and thanksgivings to the gods because Nero's life had been preserved. Special honors were given to Sol, the sun god, because a temple to Sol formed part of the Circus Flaminius, where Nero was supposed to have been assassinated. The Senate also decreed that a temple dedicated to Safety be built at Ferentum, the town from which Scaevinus had taken the infamous dagger. One senator, Cerialis Anicius, even proposed that a temple be built at public expense and dedicated to "the Divine Nero," as if the emperor were a living god. No such temple would be erected.

Now, too, Nero rewarded the informant who had forestalled the plot and saved his life. Milichus, freedman of chief conspirator Scaevinus, was showered with gifts from the emperor and permitted to add to his name the Greek word for "savior." And, apparently because Nero had personally given his word that Natalis and Proculus, the first to identify Praetorian officers among the plotters, would receive immunity for identifying so many conspirators, both men went free.

"Rome all this time was thronged with funerals, the Capitol with sacrificial victims," said Tacitus.[16] Throughout the rebuilt city, houses were decked with funereal laurels. But this season of death, stemming from the foiled plot to kill the emperor, had yet to run its course.

THE NEW STAGE

That spring of AD 65, the Piso Plot, as it came to be known, had not long been quashed when the Neronian Games loomed. Also called the Quinquennial Games, this was the competition instituted by Nero, to be staged every five years and last run in AD 60, involving verse, song, gymnastics, and horse and chariot races.

It became clear to the members of the Senate that for the first time, Nero intended to appear on stage at Rome, to compete in these, his own games. Even though they had heaped praise on him for destroying the plot against his life, many senators dreaded the prospect of their emperor taking to the Roman stage, for they considered it shameful. As far as they were concerned, it was one thing to compete in rural or even in provincial competitions, but to appear on stage at the capital would be a scandal.

It was one of the great contradictions of Roman society that the upper classes flocked to the theater to see and applaud actors and singers, yet many snobbish nobles considered the theater profession contemptible. As recently as the twentieth century, acting was still considered a rather shameful profession by the upper classes. It is only in present day that the rewards of the cinema have made many actors rich and their profession acceptable, even desirable. So that "a veil might be thrown over a shameful exposure on the stage," the Senate, in advance, offered Nero the prizes for song and eloquence, to prevent him from taking the stage. But Nero "respectfully" responded that he could, and would, win the laurel crowns on merit.[1]

On the appointed day, the emperor joined the other competitors and took to the stage in the massive Theater of Pompey on the Campus Martius. Rome's first permanent all-stone theater, and for centuries the largest theater in the Roman world, Pompey's theater had escaped the ravages of the Great Fire. Opened in 55 BC, the theater had been paid for by Pompey the Great, Julius Caesar's onetime son-in-law and ally and later his adversary in the civil war that had brought Caesar to power. The theater's portico had also been the site of the fateful meeting of the Senate on the Ides of March, 44 BC, when more than sixty conspiratorial senators had executed the plot that saw the assassination of Julius Caesar. Ironically, the dictator had fallen at the foot of a statue of Pompey. That statue no longer stood in the theater; Augustus, Caesar's great-nephew, had removed it to another site on the Campus Martius.

Nero, nervous as always and announced by Cluvius Rufus as usual, recited one of his own poems to the vast audience. His performance was received ecstatically by the surprised general public. The judges were senators whose names had been drawn by lot, while the editor of the games and president of the judges was the senator Aulus Vitellius, another future emperor. Those judges now awarded Nero the winner's crown, to the great delight of the ordinary people in the crowd.

"Make all your accomplishments public property, Caesar!" called someone from the audience.[2]

Many others added their encouragement, for it had become well known that Nero also sang and played the lyre. To oblige them, Nero put his name down for the singing contest. The Theater of Pompey was full next evening as the lyre-playing singers prepared backstage to compete. Nero had joined the other competitors, while the audience out front clamored for him to make an appearance. But Nero's nerves got the better of him. Giving the excuse that he dare not compete without an express invitation to do so from the judges, he began to walk away.

On seeing this, Vitellius, editor of the games, hurried after him. Vitellius was grossly overweight from too much good living. And he walked with a limp as a result of a chariot crash during the reign of Caligula. This earlier emperor had challenged Vitellius and several other senators to a race, during which Vitellius' chariot had overturned. Nero liked Vitellius because the large man enjoyed the good things in life and was a chariot racing fan, even though he supported the Blues. Vitellius was also addicted to dice, which contributed to his growing debts. Nero himself was reputed to have wagered forty thousand sesterces on each dot of the dice in a single throw.

The limping Vitellius overtook the retreating emperor. "On behalf of the audience, Caesar," said Vitellius, so Suetonius would write, "I beg you to reconsider your decision."[3]

Persuaded by Vitellius, Nero turned back, regained his courage, again took up his lyre, and returned to his place among the contestants. Out front, the audience in the sprawling theater, numbering tens of thousands, waited excitedly for the popular song contest. Apart from the nobility, who occupied the front rows in the semicircular theater, the throng was made up of off-duty soldiers, city residents, visitors from towns in Italy, and businessmen and envoys from the provinces and allied states.[4] With word having spread quickly that the emperor would be competing, there was such a crush in the narrow approaches to the theater that it was rumored that two members of the Equestrian Order had been trampled to death.

Among the many senators present was Vespasian, who had managed to avoid any involvement with, or taint from, the Piso Plot. He knew that it would be dangerous to be absent from Nero's performance and that there were men in the crowd, informers probably in the pay of Tigellinus, who "secretly made it their business to scrutinize names and faces, and to note the delight or the disgust of the audience members." To even leave the theater before the performances ended was construed as an insult to Nero, whose games these were. So that they did not incite undue attention, leading men remained in their seats through both the day and the evening sessions. Gossip even has several men dying from heart attacks in their seats.[5]

As the evening session went late into the night, Vespasian nodded off. A freedman named Phoebus spotted the dozing senator, approached

Vespasian, and rudely prodded him awake, accusing him of discourtesy to the emperor. This would have been reported to Nero, but friends of Vespasian's and his brother the city prefect spoke up for him, and nothing came of the report.

When Nero's turn came, he took the stage, equipped with his lyre and in the proper costume. Again he performed creditably. He ended his number on one knee and with a sweep of the hand. Again the audience applauded loudly. Nero waited, obviously nervous, for the judges' verdict. Sure enough, he was again declared the winner. Once more, the enthusiastic city people in the audience "made the place ring" with "elaborate applause," which went on for some time. This reception to Nero's winning performance so went against the usual custom of polite applause that, says Tacitus, out-of-town visitors found their hands aching from the prolonged clapping. But when they left off the applause before it generally abated, these out-of-towners found themselves on the end of rough thumps from nearby soldiers, who jolted them into resuming clapping.[6]

Well received by the ordinary people of Rome, Nero now set his sights on winning the contests of Greece. But in the wake of his victories, immediately after the games, tragedy struck the Palatium. Nero's pregnant wife Poppaea Sabina died, along with Nero's unborn child. His critics would blame him for their deaths. According to Tacitus, "Poppaea died from a casual outburst of rage from her husband, who felled her with a kick."[7] Cassius Dio gave credit to the possibility that Poppaea's death could have been as the result of an accident: "Either accidentally or deliberately he had leapt on her with his feet."[8] Suetonius wrote that Poppaea was ill at the time and so had not been able to attend the games, and she had incited Nero's anger "because she complained that he came home late from the races."[9]

Tacitus added that several other authors claimed that Nero poisoned Poppaea, but he wrote that he could not bring himself to believe such a thing: "For the emperor wanted children, and was totally in love with his wife."[10] Suetonius agreed, saying that Nero "doted on his wife."[11] In fact, said Dio, Nero "missed her so much after her death that, on hearing of a woman who resembled her, he at first sent for her, and kept her."[12] Nero, still fascinated by all things Egyptian, ordained that his wife not be cremated, which was the normal Roman custom for the dead, but be embalmed in the Egyptian fashion.

Nero gave his beloved wife a public funeral, and in sympathy with their emperor, the ordinary Roman people came out to pay their respects. From the Rostra in the crowded Forum, Nero personally delivered Poppaea's funeral oration, eulogizing her beauty and other gifts. He then had her embalmed body laid to rest in the tomb of the Julian family. The Senate, at its next meeting, decreed divine honors to Poppaea, as if she were a goddess.

Meanwhile, the fate of Antonia, daughter of Claudius, who was to have been married to the rebel Piso to give his claim to the throne legitimacy, was never revealed by Tacitus. Suetonius, however, linked Antonia's fate to the death of Poppaea. He wrote that Antonia was executed by Nero "on a charge of attempted rebellion" after "she refused to take the late Poppaea's place" as the emperor's wife.[13] No other classical author commented on Antonia's fate, but she was never again mentioned subsequent to Nero's reign.

Poppaea's death was "a public grief," said Tacitus, but a delight to her enemies and to Nero's enemies.[14] Just before Poppaea's passing or perhaps in its wake, Nero acceded to her recommendation that he dismiss the legal cases against the three Jewish priests from Judea who had awaited a hearing for so long. Joseph, the rabbi who had worked so assiduously toward this end, was able to set off back to Jerusalem with his three colleagues. Joseph, or Josephus as he became, would give full credit for the release of the trio to the intercession of Poppaea. It seems that the Jewish party's departure came in the fall, once the sailing season had ended for the year, and that the party traveled back to Judea overland, for Joseph did not arrive home in Jerusalem until the beginning of the spring of the following year.

Nero, bitter about the loss of his wife and child, had forbidden leading senator Gaius Cassius Longinus to attend Poppaea's funeral. Cassius was a descendant of the man of the same name, Cassius the famous "Liberator," who with Marcus Brutus had masterminded the assassination of Julius Caesar and gone to war with Octavian and Nero's great-great-grandfather Mark Antony. A former consul and governor of Syria during Claudius' reign, the present Cassius was also considered the pre-eminent legal advocate of his day. His Senate speeches were legend, and no senator ever took the floor to argue against his opinions unless he knew he had the support of others. As the Piso affair unfolded, Cassius had remained uncharacteristically quiet. But now, something he said or did, quite probably in relation to Poppaea, seriously offended Nero and made the emperor suddenly loathe and fear the man.

"Nero, who was always timid, and now more frightened than ever by the lately discovered [Piso] conspiracy," said Tacitus, was "fearful of a sudden attack."[15] Out of the blue, Nero sent a speech to the Senate in which he called for Cassius and his young friend Junius Torquatus Silanus to be expelled from Rome. Silanus, also a senator, was the reckless nephew of the Silanus who had been forced to commit suicide by Tigellinus the previous year, when Nero was at Beneventum watching Vatinius' gladiatorial show.

Nero did not accuse Cassius of any specific crime, but mentioned that it had come to his attention that Cassius specially revered a bust of his ancestor Cassius the Liberator among the collection of busts of ancestors that decorated his house, a bust that was inscribed "To the party leader." According to Nero's letter, Cassius had intended to emulate his ancestor, sparking revolution by sowing the seeds of civil war against the House of the Caesars. In this scheme, said Nero, Cassius was associating himself with Silanus, to whom he was related by marriage.

While the shaken Senate debated what to do about this, Nero wrote to the consuls to specifically condemn Silanus, saying that he was guilty of the same crime as his uncle, that of preparing to take control at the Palatium. Silanus, said Tacitus, had in fact been terrified by his uncle's forced suicide and, ever since, had been extremely cautious not to do anything that could be deemed suspicious.[16] His fellow senators were aware of this, and there was no rush by the Senate to judge either Silanus or the much respected Cassius.

Just when the emperor's campaign against Cassius and Silanus appeared to be going nowhere, Nero's agents produced informants who swore that Cassius' wife Lepida had been sleeping with young Silanus, her nephew. Lepida was also charged with being involved in "some ghastly religious ceremony"—this may have referred to the now frowned-upon bestial worship of Isis.[17] Two senators and a member of the Equestrian Order were implicated by the informers with Lepida in the latter charge, but all three men were acquitted by Nero when they appealed to him directly. Cassius and Silanus were not so lucky.

The Senate now considered the old and the new charges, and sentences of exile were passed on both Cassius and Silanus, while a decision on Lepida's fate was referred to Nero. Cassius was sent to the island province of Sardinia, where he was left to live out the rest of his days in relative comfort. No action was taken against his wife, Lepida, who apparently accompanied Cassius to Sardinia. Silanus, informed that his exile was to be on the Greek island of Naxos, in the Cyclades group, was conveyed from Rome downriver to the port of Ostia, where he and his family expected that he would be placed aboard a ship that would convey him to the Aegean. Instead, Silanus' Praetorian escort hustled him away to the Italian village of Barium, in the Apulia district.

There at Barium, Silanus lived quietly until, sometime later, a centurion leading a Praetorian detachment arrived at his door. It was never revealed who sent these troops to Barium. A sentence of death had been passed on Silanus, said the centurion, and if Silanus did not take his own life, then the centurion would take it for him. Silanus, young, fit, and very powerfully built, exploded with rage.

"Although I have been resolved in my heart to losing my life," Silanus exclaimed, shaping up to resist even though he was unarmed, "I won't let a cutthroat have the glory of taking it!"[18]

"Seize him!" the centurion bellowed.

As the Praetorian soldiers advanced on Silanus with their swords still in their sheaths, the accused man swung powerful blows their way. Boxing with the hands bound with tape was one of the forms of "gymnastics" practiced in various *ludi*, including the Neronian Games. Many young Roman nobles were accomplished boxers, training and fighting at the gymnasium. Nero himself was known to box and wrestle. Silanus seems to have been particularly adept at the art. His blows floored several soldiers before he was finally overwhelmed by numbers and wrestled to the floor. As Silanus was being held down, the centurion drew his sword. Then, standing over the prisoner, the centurion plunged the blade into the prisoner's chest and into his heart. Silanus' head was soon on its way back to Rome.

A freedman of Lucius Antistius Vetus by the name of Fortunatus, which, as it happens, means "Lucky," now came forward and made accusations against his employer. This was the Vetus who was father-in-law of the late Rubellius Plautus, the cousin of Agrippina the Younger executed on Tigellinus' orders while living in self-imposed exile in Asia. Nero had never taken any action against Vetus for warning Plautus of his impending fate, but according to Tacitus, he hated Vetus and was reminded of Plautus' execution every time he saw the man's father-in-law.

Another man, Claudius Demianus, whom Vetus had imprisoned while governor of Asia, also offered evidence against Vetus and in return was released from prison on Nero's orders. Meanwhile, other freedmen on Vetus' staff tendered testimony on their employer's behalf, making the counteraccusation that Fortunatus had embezzled money from Vetus and had only come forward to accuse Vetus to cover up his own crime. When Vetus applied to the Palatium for an audience with the emperor to personally defend himself against the accusations, he was refused.

It was the month of May, and with the summer soon to arrive, Vetus collected his daughter Pollutia and his mother-in-law Sextia and withdrew from Rome to his seaside estate at Formiae, modern Formia, halfway between Rome and Neapolis on the west coast of Italy. Nero, who had also departed Rome for the season and was staying at Neapolis, ordered troops at Formiae to keep a secret watch on Vetus and his visitors. Formiae was probably one of the towns outside Rome, like Praeneste, where subunits of the German Cohorts were stationed when not on duty at the capital, and it was likely to have been German auxiliaries who now spied on Vetus.

Vetus' daughter Pollutia, the widow of Plautus, was furious at the accusations being leveled at her father. Ever since seeing Plautus' executioners depart with his head, Pollutia had wasted away in her sorrow, living on a near-starvation diet. Nero had acted gallantly toward women accused of crimes, so now the pale, slender Pollutia was sent by her father to Neapolis to implore Nero to give Vetus the opportunity to personally defend himself. Once Pollutia reached Neapolis, Nero's staff forbade her to approach the emperor. So, day after day, she stood outside the doors to the house where Nero was staying and called out to him.

"Caesar, hear an innocent man!" she cried. "Don't surrender one who has been your colleague in the consulship to the accusations of a freedman."[19]

When her pleas went unanswered, Pollutia became angry and yelled reproaches and threats directed at the emperor. These, too, were ignored. Pollutia, emotionally and physically exhausted, returned to her lodgings and sent her father a message to say that she had been unsuccessful and had cast hope aside, advising him to yield to necessity. Vetus had meanwhile received word from friendly senators at Rome, where the Senate was now in session and debating the charges against him. These friends firmly advised Vetus to take the honorable way out and to redraft his will, leaving the majority of his estate to the emperor so that at least some part of it remained for his grandchildren.

The defiant Vetus declared: "I am unwilling to disgrace a life which has adhered to freedom with a final act of servility."[20]

Vetus sent for Pollutia. Once she rejoined him at Formiae, in the last days of May, Vetus called in his slaves and distributed all his cash among them, then told each man and woman on his staff to take for themselves as much of his household goods as they could carry. Vetus, his daughter, and her grandmother were left with just the couches on which each of them reclined. Vetus had resolved to commit suicide, and Pollutia and the elderly Sextia chose to join him. After Vetus produced a dagger, he, Pollutia, and Sextia slit the veins of their arms. Each had previously put on a single outer garment, and now all three hurried to the villa's bathhouse, where a warm bath had been prepared for them. They slipped into the water and waited for death to claim them. Old Sextia was the first to die. Vetus followed her. Pollutia was the last to perish.

In early June, the Senate convened and heard treason charges against all three. They were found guilty, and despite the fact that Vetus, Pollutia, and Sextia were already dead and their bodies cremated, the Senate sentenced them to execution in "ancient fashion"—strangulation with a halter, with their bodies cast into the Tiber. Nero officially imposed his imperial veto on the sentence, so that their remains were left undisturbed. At this same session of the Senate, an Equestrian who had been an acquaintance of Vetus was found guilty of having been an intimate friend of executed Praetorian prefect Faenius Rufus and was sentenced to exile.

A final motion was approved: The names of the months of April, May, and June were changed by decree of the Senate to incorporate Nero's names. There had been precedents for this, with the month of Quintilis changed to Julius, our July, in honor of Julius Caesar, the previous century, and the month of Sextilis renamed Augustus, our August, in honor of the emperor Augustus. Nero's names, prior to his adoption by his uncle Claudius in AD 50, had been Lucius Domitius Ahenobarbus. On his taking the throne, he had changed his name to Nero Claudius Caesar Augustus Germanicus, honoring various imperial ancestors; apart from Julius Caesar, these were Nero's great-great-grandfather Augustus, his great-grandfather Tiberius (who was also a Nero), his grandfather Germanicus, and his uncle and adoptive father Claudius.

Now, the name of April, the month in which the Piso Plot had been thwarted, became Neroneus. The month of May, in which Vetus had died, became Claudius. And because both the latest Silanus to be executed and his previously condemned uncle were members of the Junius family, the name of the month of Junius, our June, was now declared inauspicious and renamed Germanicus.

⌇⌇⌇

In contrast to the tumultuous first half of AD 65, the second half of the year was quiet and undisturbed. No accusations were forthcoming, no plots unearthed, no arrests made, no sentences of death passed. Mourning deeply the loss of Poppaea and dreading more conspiracies against him, Nero was once more a recluse, with his expected departure for Greece to enter in the competitions there now on hold. Late in the year, the city of Lugdunum, modern-day Lyon, capital of the Gallic province of Gallia Lugdunensis, was severely damaged by a fire. Only several decades earlier, it had been leveled by an earthquake. After the Great Fire, Lugdunum had sent Rome a donation of four million sesterces. Now, Nero returned the compliment, sending four million sesterces as his contribution to Lugdunum's disaster fund.

Late that year, too, a plague erupted in Rome. "The houses were filled with lifeless forms and the streets with funerals," said Tacitus.[21] Slaves and the freeborn were equally affected by the disease, and a number of Equestrians and senators fell victim to it. This same year, Campania was devastated by a hurricane that destroyed houses and crops and swept as far north as the outskirts of Rome. Both calamities were considered heaven-sent, as a punishment, and there were those at Rome who would blame even these disasters on Nero.

THE INFORMERS

The new year, AD 66, was barely a month old when a fresh informant worried Nero with a tale of treason on his doorstep. Four years earlier, Lucius Antistius Sosianus, a headstrong praetor, (praetors being Rome's most senior judges), had been convicted of reading libelous verses that he had written about the emperor to a large gathering dining at the house of his friend Marius Ostorius Scapula, son of onetime governor of Britain Publius Ostorius Scapula.

The Senate was in favor of sentencing Sosianus to death, but outspoken former consul and renowned Stoic philosopher Publius Thrasea Paetus proposed a sentence of exile, saying that he wanted Sosianus to be a living example of official clemency. The consuls referred the sentence to Nero, who, far from being thin-skinned or wishing to suppress criticism, wrote back to say that while Sosianus had uttered "outrageous insults against the sovereign" unprovoked, he would not stand in the way of leniency.[1]

"It was strange how amazingly tolerant Nero seemed to be of insults that everyone cast at him, in the form of jokes and lampoons," Suetonius wrote. "He never attempted to trace the authors, and, when an informer handed the Senate a short list of their names, he gave instructions that they should be let off lightly."[2] Following Nero's lenient lead, the Senate had supported Thrasea's motion, setting aside the death sentence and sending Sosianus into exile.

Of late, the banished Sosianus had heard from contacts at Rome how informers had been well rewarded the previous year for exposing threats against the emperor. From his place of exile across the sea, this man who had once lampooned Nero now wrote to him to say that he would "communicate important news which would contribute to his [Nero's] safety if he could obtain a brief respite from his exile."[3] Several Liburnian warships were dispatched by the Palatium to collect Sosianus and bring him to Italy. Light and fast, Liburnian ships relied more on oar power than wind power, so that the ships sent to fetch Sosianus were able to do so in the face of the inclement winds that prevented the sailing of sail-powered cargo vessels at this time of year.

Before long, Sosianus was being led into Nero's Golden House, which was still under construction. With Nero listening intently, Sosianus informed the emperor that he had learned that a Greek freedman by the name of Pammenes, who had been exiled to the same place that Sosianus had for practicing astrology at Rome, had regularly been in communication with leading men at Rome who had previously employed his services. Among these men, said Sosianus, was the wealthy former consul Publius Anteius.

Just as Sosianus had hoped, Nero pricked his ears at the mention of Anteius, a onetime favorite of his mother Agrippina. Anteius had been regularly sending money to the exiled astrologer, said Sosianus. The accuser had also succeeded in stealing a letter to Pammenes from Anteius. What was more, he had also pilfered the astrologer's notes on Anteius' horoscope, which included his forecast for Anteius' future career.

Sosianus had also discovered the astrologer's secret predictions for the life and career of Sosianus' friend Marius Ostorius Scapula. It had been at Scapula's house that Sosianus had read his libelous lampoons about the emperor. Scapula had subsequently testified in Sosianus' favor during his trial in the Senate, claiming he had not heard the lampoons in question, to no avail. Despite Scapula's support for him, Sosianus the opportunistic informer was not going to let friendship or a debt of honor stand in the way of a permanent end to his exile.

Nero eagerly read the two men's horoscopes handed over by Sosianus, who implied that both documents had been prepared at the request of

Anteius and Scapula. The zodiac was important to Romans. Every legion, for example, in addition to its unit emblem, carried the star sign representative of the time of the legion's founding, or "birth"—frequently the sea goat of Capricorn. But the practice of astrology, forecasting of the future using the stars, had been banned by one emperor after another, and its practitioners branded charlatans. Despite this, interpretation of the zodiac had long been attractive to ambitious Romans who were prepared to flout the ban in order to see whether they were destined for great things. Anteius and Scapula had been prying into their destinies and Nero's destiny, said Sosianus, who accused the pair of "grasping at empire."[4] Nero sent all this information to the Senate for its consideration.

Tigellinus was acquainted with Anteius, and when the matter first raised its head in the Senate, he advised Anteius not to delay preparing and sealing his will. Anteius had thought the charge so trifling and ridiculous, coming as it did from a man who had been convicted of libeling the emperor, that he ignored Tigellinus' advice. But Anteius soon found that he was being treated as a guilty man even though the matter was still being debated in the House. Only then did he realize the wisdom of preparing his will. Once he had done so, he had become such a pariah that no one he approached was prepared to put his name on the document as a witness. In the end, Tigellinus personally attested the will. The shocked Anteius, realizing that a sentence of death was imminent, attempted to commit suicide by taking poison. Like Seneca, Anteius found that the poison he downed was too slow-acting. Emulating many before and after him, he finally resorted to slitting his veins and died at his own hands.

Ostorius Scapula, on the other hand, seems to have felt that the Senate would not convict him. While serving as a prefect of auxiliaries in Britain over the winter of AD 47–48, when his father was governor there, Scapula had won the Civic Crown for saving the life of a Roman citizen in battle. The Civic Crown was the most prestigious bravery decoration that a Roman officer could be awarded, the forerunner of today's Medal of Honor in the United States and the Victoria Cross in the United Kingdom and British Commonwealth countries. The Civic Crown was rarely awarded and was greatly prized. Julius Caesar had won it as a young officer. Recipients were treated as VIPs by fellow Romans throughout the remainder of their lives. On the strength of his Civic Crown, Scapula apparently felt that he was safe from a death sentence. Just the same, to keep a low profile and not invite further criticism, he left Rome and withdrew to a remote country estate in Liguria, a coastal region in northwestern Italy that today borders France.

Scapula had judged wrongly. Before long, a detachment of Praetorian soldiers came marching along the road to his villa. The centurion in charge ordered every exit barred to prevent escape. He then confronted Scapula and informed him that he had orders to return to Rome with Scapula's head, one way or another. Scapula was famous for his courage and his skill with a variety of arms. A broad-shouldered, physically powerful man like his father, he had a fearsome reputation as a soldier. Yet Scapula did not fight. To avoid the indignity of decapitation while he still lived, he withdrew to his chamber and slit his veins. But the blood flowed too slowly, and in dread of the centurion's sword, the decorated fighter called one of his slaves to him and handed him a dagger. Making the man hold the dagger firmly as he stood before him, Scapula took hold of the slave's hands, steadying the knife in front of his throat, then pushed forward, impaling himself on the blade. So died Scapula, decorated Roman hero.

In the late days of winter, both the news of these two deaths and the reports of Sosianus' reward in the form of a pardon sparked a rash of informers. Many informants came forward in search of rewards, accusing a number of leading men of having links with the previous year's Piso Plot. At the top of the list was Nero's close friend Gaius Petronius, the emperor's famous arbiter of good taste. One of Petronius' slaves accused his master of having been the intimate friend of Scaevinus, the man through whose agency the Piso Plot had unraveled, implying that Petronius had been aware of the plot. According to Tacitus, this slave was paid handsomely by Tigellinus the Praetorian prefect to invent his accusation. Tigellinus had long been jealous of Petronius and of his influence with the emperor. In Tacitus' view, Tigellinus "looked on him as a rival, and even his superior in the science of pleasure."[5]

Nero was on the road, heading down through Campania to spend time at Neapolis, which he liked for its Greek heritage and as the site of his first stage victory, when Tigellinus produced this slave, who told the invented tale to the emperor. The imperial cavalcade, of which Petronius was customarily a member, had reached the coastal town of Cumae on the way to Neapolis when Nero received this information. As the cavalcade prepared to move on, Praetorian troops arrived at Petronius' quarters, and when the imperial party departed Cumae, Petronius remained behind, under guard.

The arbiter had seen enough other men perish around him to know what he must do. At least Nero did not hurry his end. Petronius' friends remained with him as he sliced open his veins. Then he bound them up again and called for dinner. As Petronius and his friends dined, he encouraged them to recite light poetry and playful verses. Summoning those of his slaves accompanying him, he rewarded the good with generous gifts and punished the bad by ordering them to be flogged.

Dictating his will, not only did Petronius fail to leave any part of his fortune to Nero or to Tigellinus, but he also included an elaborate account of the nightly revels he and Nero had enjoyed when the emperor was younger, naming Nero's many female and male sexual partners in that period. After adding his seal to the will, Petronius dispatched it to Nero himself and then destroyed his signet ring so that his seal could not be used to change his will or forge further documents in his name, documents that might incriminate others. Late in the evening, Petronius unbound his wounds and let the blood flow once more, then lay down his head as if he were turning in for the night as usual. Petronius Arbiter died in his sleep, from loss of blood.

When Nero read Petronius' will, he was furious at the disclosures that his former friend had made. And he was perplexed at how Petronius had known the identity of all his sexual partners, for Petronius had not always been in Nero's company. But there was one person who had; this was a senator's wife, a woman named Silia. She had shared almost every one of the young emperor's teenage nights on the town and was also close to Petronius. Convinced that Silia must have revealed all to Petronius at some time, Nero ordered that she be sent into exile for revealing imperial secrets.

Now that Tigellinus had rid himself of his rival Petronius, the prefect followed up his success by fabricating an accusation against Minucius

Thermus, a former praetor. One of Thermus' freedmen had possessed the audacity—and the stupidity, to Tigellinus' mind—to bring criminal charges against the Praetorian prefect. Tigellinus now punished both the freedman and his employer, felling two birds with the one stone. Putting the freedman on the rack with the excuse that he suspected Thermus of treason, Tigellinus forced the man to concoct charges against Thermus. The freedman's original temerity cost him considerable pain and cost Thermus his life.

The informers came thick and fast now, offering accusations of treason about elderly senator Cerialis Anicius and also Rufius Crispinus. The latter had been prefect of the Praetorian Cohorts during the reign of Claudius and had been rewarded for his service with consular decorations even though he was only a member of the Equestrian Order. Crispinus had been exiled to Sardinia in AD 65 for his connections with members of the Piso Plot and a suspicion that he might have been involved in the conspiracy, but the latest accusation placed him at the center of the plot. Informed that he had now been sentenced to death, Crispinus took the usual "noble" way out.

Mela, father of Lucan the poet and brother of Seneca and Gallio, was next to fall victim to the informers, accused by one of his late son's closest friends, Fabius Romanus, of sharing in the Piso conspiracy with Lucan. It turned out that following Lucan's death, his tight-fisted father had called in money owed to the young man. Romanus had been one of Lucan's debtors. When Romanus had failed to pay, Mela had resorted to legal action. This accusation of treason was Romanus' revenge and probably his way of avoiding paying up.

As proof of his accusation, Romanus even produced a letter that he said Lucan had written to his father about the conspiracy. Nero, not convinced of the letter's authenticity, sent it to Mela and demanded a reaction. Mela, believing that, whatever he said, his fate was sealed, quickly wrote a new will. He left a large part of his immense estate to Tigellinus and Tigellinus' son-in-law, Cossutianus Capito, to ensure that the remainder went to family members. He also wrote bitterly that he felt it unjust that he was forced to end his life while two other accused, Crispinus and Cerialis, men whom Mela knew despised Nero, were still permitted to live. It seems that Mela was unaware that Crispinus was already dead. Mela then slit his veins and died. Cerialis, a man who was both disliked and distrusted by his fellow senators ever since he had exposed a plot against the life of the emperor Caligula many years before, soon followed suit.

Tigellinus' son-in-law Capito now saw an opportunity to settle an old score and stood up in the Senate and leveled accusations against Publius Thrasea Paetus, the dour, serious Stoic who had for many years been one of the most highly influential members of the House. Early in Nero's reign, Thrasea had impeached Capito in the Senate for extortion while serving in Cilicia. Thrasea had succeeded in having Capito convicted, after which the Stoic had him removed from the Senatorial Order as punishment. Several years later, Capito had been restored to the Senate through Tigellinus' influence, but Capito had never forgotten that Thrasea had been responsible for his conviction.

Capito knew that Thrasea had never liked Nero and that the feeling was mutual. Thrasea had walked out of the Senate when it was debating Nero's treason charges against Agrippina the Younger in AD 59, after Agrippina's murder at Baiae, refusing to participate in her condemnation. Nor had Thrasea ever sponsored the Juvenile Games, long a passion of Nero's, which was expected of former consuls. Thrasea had led the Senate in reducing the sentence of Nero's slanderer Sosianus. Moreover, the senator had failed to attend the House session that had decreed divine honors to the empress Poppaea, and neither had he attended her funeral. Even though he was one of the fifteen priests, the Quindecimviri, in recent times Thrasea had failed to attend the January 1 recitation of the oath of allegiance and public prayers for the emperor on the Capitol, and never had he offered a public sacrifice for the safety of the emperor as other priests made a habit of doing.

Thrasea's feelings toward the emperor could not have been more plain, just as Nero could not be blamed for disliking this man who disrespected him so obviously and so publicly, and to whom so many other senators looked for their lead. Capito, then, was tilling fertile ground at the Palatium when he began his campaign against Thrasea by writing a letter to the emperor, condemning the man.

By AD 66, Thrasea had not appeared in the Senate for three years. Throughout that time, he had kept out of the limelight and out of all political affairs, only concerning himself with his personal business and that of his clients. No longer going to the theater, attending the games, or officiating at temples, Thrasea had been receiving visitors in his famously beautiful gardens at Rome. After listing the numerous examples of Thrasea's brazenly insulting behavior toward the emperor, Capito was able to turn Thrasea's recent absence from public life against him. Capito pointed out that while Thrasea had refrained from taking his seat in the House to vote down the convicted traitors Vetus and Silanus, in times past he had made a point of voting on even the most ordinary of motions.

Tigellinus' son-in-law likened the schism between Thrasea and the emperor to a state of war. Capito told Nero, "He is the only man who doesn't care for your safety or doesn't honor your accomplishments." He accused Thrasea of being the leader and the adviser of a group that wanted to change Rome's system of government. "They make a show of freedom," Capito said, "to overturn the empire. Should they destroy it, they will assault freedom itself." Capito urged the emperor not to write to the Senate to express his views on Thrasea, but to let the House debate his conduct and settle his fate.[6]

At this same time, another prosecution was about to be launched in the Senate, against yet another leading man. This was directed against the former consul Barea Soranus. As governor of Asia in AD 64, Soranus had made himself unpopular with the Palatium that year by not punishing locals who had resisted the efforts of the emperor's commissioners sent to remove gold and silver statues and valuable paintings from temples at the city of Pergamos for Rome's Great Fire relief fund. Soranus, apparently a native of Asia, now stood accused of secretly supporting Rubellius Plautus when Plautus was living in self-imposed exile in the province, and with having been involved in intrigues designed to lure the people of Asia into revolt in support of Plautus and against Nero.

As Nero was considering the contents of Capito's letter at Neapolis, word reached him that King Tiridates I of Armenia and his entourage had entered Italy from the northeast. For close to nine months, Tiridates and his party, which included numerous members of the Parthian royal family, had been making their way overland from Armenia. The king's personal escort included three thousand Parthian cavalry—the Parthian army was primarily made up of mounted troops, both horse archers and heavily armored *cataphracts*. They were accompanied by numerous Roman mounted troops, among them Mazacian cavalry from Mauritania in northwest Africa. Tiridates was now on the last leg of his journey to Rome, to take part in the planned ceremony during which he would swear allegiance to Nero, and when Nero would officially bestow the kingship of Armenia on Tiridates. Arrangements had long been in the works for this event.

Nero now issued instructions for a two-horse carriage and Praetorian cavalry to be sent to convey to Neapolis the king and his wife, who had ridden all the way from Armenia on horseback. And, as he ensured that every detail of the official welcome for the king was being finalized, Nero also set down a date in April for a meeting of the Senate to debate the fates of Thrasea and Soranus. The hearing of charges against the pair would coincide with King Tiridates' arrival at Rome.

THE CROWNING
OF A KING

Down the highway from the Picenum district in eastern Italy came the vast cavalcade of King Tiridates I of Armenia and its Roman escort. "Their progress all the way from the Euphrates [River] was like a triumphal procession," Cassius Dio would write, likening the royal cavalcade to the parade that followed a Roman general when he celebrated a Triumph through the streets of Rome. All along its route from Parthia, the vast caravan of horses, carts, and pedestrians had been welcomed at every Roman city through which it passed. There were bright decorations, garlands of flowers decking official buildings, and crowds "who shouted many compliments" to the passing king.[1]

Parthian-born Tiridates was the brother of Pacorus, king of Media, the northern neighbor of Parthia. More importantly, Tiridates was also the brother of Vologases, king of Parthia, that eastern empire that had been Rome's most implacable enemy for centuries. One of Rome's greatest defeats had been suffered at the hands of the Parthians, when the triumvir Marcus Crassus had in 53 BC perished and forty thousand of his legionaries had been killed or captured in a running battle at Carrhae, in today's Turkey. For a Parthian prince to travel to Rome to bow down to the emperor of Rome was unheard-of, but here was Tiridates embarking on just such an exercise.

The credit was due to Roman general Corbulo and Roman force of arms, which had twice humiliated Parthian forces since AD 62. The very presence of Corbulo in the east threatened Roman invasion of Parthia, and the Parthians clearly dreaded such a prospect. Yet, while the Parthians considered Corbulo a great general, their respect was chiefly reserved for the man who had appointed him and sent him to the east, his sovereign lord Nero Caesar.

Tiridates arrived at Neapolis with his wife, who all through their journey had worn a golden helmet with a visor that covered her face in place of a veil, "so as not to defy the traditions of her country by letting her face be seen," said Dio.[2] The king was met by Palatium freedmen who, noticing that he wore a dagger on his belt, informed him that he could not wear that when he met the emperor—no armed man apart from his bodyguards was allowed to approach Nero. When Tiridates refused to remove his dagger, a compromise was struck; the king had the dagger nailed into its sheath, so that it could be worn but not drawn.

The day for the meeting between emperor and king arrived. Tiridates was a middle-aged man, tall and slim with a mustache and bushy beard. He wore a loose, long-sleeved tunic, trousers, sandals, and a turban. A rich cloak, pinned at his right shoulder, hung down his back, almost reaching the ground. A belt circled his waist, and slung on his left hip was his dagger, nailed into its scabbard as agreed. He walked with the aid of a long staff. Nero, garbed in the outfit of a triumphant Roman general, sat on his curule chair of ivory and gold and beckoned Tiridates forward. Along an avenue of fully armed Praetorian troops standing stiffly at attention, the king approached. Just several feet from Nero, the king stopped. Laying aside his staff, he dropped to his knees. Crossing his arms across his chest, he bowed low, paying obeisance to the emperor of Rome. "Nero admired him for this action," said Dio.[3]

An entertainment had been arranged for the king and senior members of his party, which also included his sons and several nephews. It being the month of March, the port city of Puteoli, farther around the Bay of Naples, was staging its annual *munus* in honor of war god Mars. Nero's party and the king's party combined to move up to Puteoli, which was on the route to Rome, and halted there to enjoy the Puteoli *munus*.

The editor of the Puteoli games was Nero's freedman Patrobius, and it was "a most brilliant and costly affair."[4]

Patrobius' Puetoli *munus* was a pageant of diverse people and 'pleasures.' On one day of the games, for example, in addition to the usual gladiatorial contests, only dark-skinned Ethiopians—men, women, and children—were sent into the arena to face wild beasts. Two tribunals had been set up in the stands of the Puteoli amphitheater for the king's visit, one for Nero and his imperial party, the other, across the arena, for Tiridates and his party. By way of paying honor to the editor of the games, Tiridates shot at animals from his tribunal, using the traditional Parthian bow.

Parthians were famed for their skills as archers. Their horse archers had perfected a technique, called the Parthian shot, whereby a horseman would turn and fire back over the rump of his horse with devastating accuracy as he rode away from his opponents, just when they thought he was retreating. This, some claim, was the origin of the term that we use today: *a parting shot*. All Parthian nobles were taught how to ride and shoot from an early age, and it turned out that Tiridates had been an excellent student and was a crack shot with the bow. "If one can believe it," Cassius Dio wrote, Tiridates was said to have "transfixed and killed two bulls with a single arrow" there in the Puteoli arena.[5]

Following the Puteoli games, the massive combined cavalcade continued up the Appian way, with reportedly no less than a thousand vehicles in the train. Around Nero himself rode the Mazacian cavalry, their outriders jingling with bracelets and medallions. Word had been sent to Rome that the cavalcade was nearing the capital, and "all Rome rushed out to welcome the emperor and see the king."[6] Among the throng were all those members of the Senate who were not traveling in Nero's entourage, with one exception—Thrasea Paetus, the leading senator under threat of prosecution at the forthcoming Senate session, for, on Nero's orders, he was banned from leaving the city.

The procession came up the Via Appia, passing the tombs of noble Romans and entering Rome through the Capena Gate. Moving along city streets lined with a cheering multitude held back by the troops of the Praetorian, City, and German Cohorts, who all hailed their emperor as he passed by, a smiling, waving Nero acknowledged the reception as the king took in all the splendor of the city at the center of the world. They made their way to the Golden House, Nero's vast, near-completed new palace.

In the twenty months since the Great Fire, the palace and its astonishing gardens had risen where blackened rubble had once lain. The Circus Maximus had been rebuilt in timber, at the expense of numerous forests in distant provinces, while two-thirds of the city of Rome had been entirely rebuilt in stone. The temples and public buildings were restored. New, wider streets replaced the former rabbit warrens of streets that had characterized old Rome. Colonnades and public squares equipped with water basins had appeared in the rebuilt residential areas. It was a new city and a more beautiful one than the old, Tacitus observed.[7] There were still large numbers of workers, slave and free, employed in construction and restoration work, which would continue for a time yet, but the majority of the work had been done. To the eyes of the easterners, new Rome must have been breathtaking.

Numerous buildings had been decorated with garlands, incidentally to welcome the emperor and the king, but also in preparation for the Megalesia, the annual seven-day festival dedicated to the Magna Mater, or Great Mother, the goddess Cybele. Running from April 4, just a few days away, the festival would this year showcase the greatness of Rome for the benefit of King Tiridates and his party.

That night, oil-fired lights glowed throughout the city, illuminating the shining marble, gold, and precious stones adorning the temples and palaces. Teams of slaves worked through the night, completing temporary wooden grandstands erected along two sides of the Forum Romanum. Yet, Suetonius wrote, the day fixed by Neronian edict for the ceremony in which Tiridates would swear allegiance to Nero—that is, the day before the commencement of the Megalesia Festival—dawned overcast and gray. The omens were not good. The ceremony was postponed for a day.

The sky that night was clear, presaging a fine day next morning. Well before dawn, vast crowds flooded to the Forum and its surrounds. The lucky ones had invitations; the spectators were arranged according to their rank, from Equestrians at the front to freedmen at the back. Clad in white and each holding a laurel branch, symbol of victory, they occupied the stands in the Forum. The ordinary people had clambered onto rooftops all around to obtain a view of the proceedings. The spectators were so thick on the roofs, said Dio, that "the very roof tiles of all the buildings in the vicinity were completely hidden from sight."[8]

As the sun rose, thousands of Praetorians could be seen lining the Forum in front of the stands; the soldiers stood "fully armed" with shields and javelins, in neat ranks. The troops were equipped "in shining armor," said Dio, "their weapons and standards flashing like lightning," bolts of lightning being the motif that the Praetorian Cohorts sported on their shields.[9] The standard-bearers of each cohort and of each maniple—the Roman military subunit equivalent to a modern-day company—gathered on the raised Rostra at the northern end of the Forum.

Their standards varied from the Praetorians' golden statuette of Victoria to the raised silver hand of each Praetorian maniple. The animal figures of the German Cohort standards, too, were represented. A small forest of close to a hundred standards would have been arrayed on the Rostra in the hands of their proud standard-bearers, the Praetorian standard-bearers wearing lion-skin capes, with lions' heads perched atop their helmets.

As the sun rose into the clear morning sky, trumpets sounded. The people in the stands came to their feet and waited in expectant silence. From the vestibule of the Golden House, Nero emerged. He again wore the garb of a triumphant—tunic, cloak, and mural crown. He was accompanied by the consuls for the year, one of whom was Suetonius Paulinus, who, as governor of Britain, had put down Boudicca's Revolt six years previously. Next came the prefects, including the Praetorian prefects Tigellinus and Nymphidius and the city prefect Flavius Sabinus. Then came all the magistrates for the year, the praetors and the quaestors, followed by all the commissioners, including the new water commissioner, Fonteius Agrippa, who had been a consul at the time of the murder of Agrippina the Younger in AD 59. Hundreds of senators fell in behind, notable exceptions being the accused men Thrasea and Soranus.

Thrasea had written to Nero, demanding to know the charges against him and asserting that he would be able to clear himself if he were informed of the supposed crimes of which he was accused and given an opportunity to refute the charges. "Nero eagerly received this note," hoping that Thrasea had incriminated himself in it or even perhaps confessed his crime. But the emperor was disappointed to find that Thrasea's carefully composed request for a meeting contained neither incrimination nor confession. Afraid of both the glower and "the defiant independence" of Thrasea—in the opinion of Tacitus—Nero refused to grant the senator the requested audience; he would let the Senate decide the matter.[10]

Through the Forum strode the young ruler of the Roman world, the single most powerful man on earth, before climbing the curved stairs at the rear of the Rostra and taking his seat on a chair of state. Flanking him were his senior officials, with the military standards and their bearers forming a glittering backdrop. The senators massed below the Rostra. A signal was now given for King Tiridates to make his appearance. From the Golden House, where he and his party had been staying, Tiridates, his wife, and his sons and nephews entered the Forum and walked between the silent ranks of Praetorians, with the eyes of the spectators following their every step.

Tiridates and his family members halted in front of the Rostra. This was the same Rostra from which Mark Antony had given his famous speech on the day of Julius Caesar's funeral. For today's ceremony, a temporary ramp had been built fronting the Rostra. On Tiridates' cue, he and his wife, sons, and nephews dropped to their knees and repeated the same form of obeisance that Tiridates had observed on his first meeting with the Roman emperor, crossing their arms and bowing low.

A great approving roar rose up from the surrounding crowd. Tiridates was seen to look fearfully around the crowd, which was now abuzz with conversation. It was as if the king suddenly feared the fate of so many enemy leaders who had been led through the streets of Rome in years past in the Triumph of one conquering general or another—execution with the halter. Such a fate was contrary to the treaty that Tiridates had agreed to with Nero's general Corbulo, the treaty that had terminated the war for Armenia and guaranteed Tiridates the Armenian throne in return for his pledge of allegiance to Nero.

Tiridates would have been told that Corbulo's son-in-law Annius Vinicianus had been sent by the general to Rome to make the arrangements for this ceremony. Vinicianus was, Tiridates knew, well liked by Nero, who had approved the young man's appointment as a *legatus legionis* prior to his reaching senatorial age, a rare honor. That appointment had permitted Vinicianus to join his father-in-law's army and take command of the 5th Macedonica Legion during Corbulo's last campaign in Armenia, against Tiridates and his Parthian and Armenian troops. But now, Tiridates was literally in the lion's den, and his fate was entirely in Nero's hands.

The duty tribune of the Praetorian Cohorts, the day's *narrator*, called for quiet. The audience obediently fell silent. Nero beckoned the king. Tiridates came to his feet and, alone, climbed the ramp to the Rostra, where he again prostrated himself, this time at Nero's feet. Nero now reached out a hand and "drew him to his feet, and kissed him."[11]

Tiridates then addressed a speech to Nero in his native tongue, which was translated aloud into Latin by a former praetor. "Master, I am the descendant of Arsaces, brother of the kings Vologases and Pacorus, and your slave. I have come to you, my god, to worship you as I worship Mithras. The destiny that you spin for me shall be mine, for you are my Fortune and my Fate."[12]

Nero replied, with his words translated for Tiridates' benefit, "You have done well to come here in person, so that in meeting me face to face you might enjoy my grace. For what neither your father left you nor your brothers gave and preserved for you, this I do grant to you. King of Armenia I now declare you, that both you, and they . . ." he cast his hand around the crowd, "may understand that I have the power to take away kingdoms and to bestow them."[13]

With that, as Tiridates bowed his head, Nero took the turban from the king's head and replaced it with a crown held out to him by an aide. The crowd erupted into cheers and applause. To the minds of many ordinary Romans, this was Nero Caesar's finest hour.

This was the first day of the Megalesia Festival. At dawn that morning, the priests of Magna Mater had offered herbs to the goddess at her temple and flailed themselves until they bled. Now, they bore a statue of

Cybele through the streets of the city, accompanied by tambourine and cymbal players. The statue was set up in the Theater of Pompey, and once Nero and the king had departed the Forum, the people left their vantage points and hurried across the city and out the northern gates onto the Campus Martius, to find seats in the theater.

By special imperial decree, today's theatrical performances were to honor the emperor and his crowning of the king, and for this event, the theater's already impressive stage had been gilded, as had much of the interior of the theater. All the furniture and fittings on the imperial tribunal likewise shone with gold. Over the heads of those in the imperial box hung a sunscreen of purple cloth embroidered in gold with the figure of Nero driving a chariot and with golden stars gleaming all around him. The bedazzled people who attended the theater on this day would forever after refer to it as a "golden day."[14]

A little later, first Nero and then Tiridates arrived at the theater. On gaining the tribunal, Tiridates again prostrated himself at Nero's feet. Then, at the emperor's bidding, he occupied the seat immediately on the emperor's right. Together, they watched the day's performances of mime, tragedy, and music, every now and then indulging in chitchat. At one point, the name of Corbulo, Nero's conquering general, came up. "Master, you have in Corbulo a good slave," Tiridates remarked.[15]

That evening, Nero and Tiridates sat down to an expensive official banquet attended by Rome's leading citizens. Following the banquet, for the king's entertainment, Nero took up the lyre and sang. And later, apparently at his private Vatican circus, Nero showed off his chariot-driving expertise to Tiridates, wearing the racing tunic of the Greens and the full outfit of a circus charioteer. According to Dio, Tiridates was privately disgusted by the emperor's singing and chariot driving, reportedly commenting that the only fault he found in Nero's general Corbulo was that the general could put up with such a master.[16]

Yet, if these genuinely were Tiridates' sentiments, they seem not to have reached the ears of his brother, Vologases, the Parthian king. As later events would demonstrate, Vologases' respect for Nero, and even his awe of him, would not diminish over the next few years. Nero had several times issued an invitation for Vologases to similarly bring himself to

Rome. Vologases, no doubt suspicious of entrapment on Italian soil, had excused himself by saying that, unlike Nero, he did not possess mighty fleets of warships via which he might traverse the oceans. The Parthian king had suggested that both rulers leave their respective capitals and meet halfway, in Asia Minor. But this did not interest Nero.

The entertainment that Tiridates witnessed during the Megalesian Games included the pancratium, a contest of ancient Greek origin and an Olympic Games event, combining boxing and wrestling. Contestants stripped naked. After anointing their bodies with oil as part of their religious observances, they cast sand over their bare, oiled skin, to allow their opponents to literally come to grips with them. No holds were barred. The clenched fist could be used, although the hands were not strapped as in straight boxing contests and so were less lethal. Feet could also be used. The ultimate offensive move was the stranglehold, and if the man on the receiving end did not give up, he could and would die from strangulation. Locked in a hold or seriously injured, a competitor could surrender the contest by raising one finger.

It was perfectly legitimate for a standing competitor to strike a fallen opponent. Tiridates, on seeing this, was horrified. He exclaimed, "It's not fair that a man who has fallen should be struck."[17]

This greatly amused his hosts. It was the Roman way. In life, as in the pancratium, a fallen adversary was fair game. Many who had been implicated in the plots against Nero over the past two years had found this to be the case. Thrasea and Soranus were about to learn the very same lesson. The Megalesia Festival ended with a day of chariot racing in the rebuilt Circus Maximus, with Nero and Tiridates among the excited spectators.

Nero had enjoyed showing off to his new royal vassal and was amenable to granting Tiridates a favor. During Corbulo's first campaign in Armenia, his legions had leveled the Armenian capital, Artaxata, in the northeast of the country. Corbulo had taken the city without a fight, but, deciding that it was too remote to successfully defend, had ordered the city's population to evacuate to the southwest, then had his troops destroy the riverside metropolis stone by stone. Tiridates now asked Nero for permission to rebuild the city, sugaring his request with the promise that he would give the restored capital of Armenia the name of Neronia, in honor of Nero. Not surprisingly, Nero agreed to the request. The city would indeed be rebuilt and named Neronia.

More than that, Nero also offered Tiridates the services of a number of artisans who had been working on the rebuilding of Rome following the Great Fire. Stonemasons, carpenters, artists who painted the wall frescoes—these craftsmen were not slaves but paid freedmen or peregrines, noncitizens, very often of Greek background, who had come to Rome specifically to work on the city's restoration. While Nero was generous with his offer of artisans, he retained those men who were needed for the remaining work in Rome. Tiridates not only accepted the men offered by Nero, but also secretly sent his agents around the artisans' camps at Rome and recruited more, offering them higher pay than they were receiving from Nero. But Tiridates would be outwitted. When these workmen reached Cappadocia on their way to Armenia with Tiridates, Nero's general Corbulo would only permit those men authorized by Nero to work in Armenia to enter the country.

Nero also provided Tiridates with sea transport for part of the king's return journey. When he left Rome within days of the conclusion of the Megalesia, Tiridates traveled down the Appian Way all the way to Brundisium, where he and his party would board ships of Rome's Adriatic Fleet to cross the Straits of Otranto to Dyrrhachium, modern-day Durres, in Albania. From there, Tiridates' cavalcade would continue overland along the Agnatian Way through Macedonia. After crossing the Dardanelles, Tiridates progressed through the grand cities of Asia Minor, which would serve, said Cassius Dio, "to increase his amazement at the strength and beauty of the Roman Empire."[18]

As soon as the Megalesia Festival was over, even before Tiridates departed Rome in the middle of April, the consuls' lictors were on the city streets, conveying a message that called on members of the Senate to sit the next day. At the top of the senators' agenda were the charges against Thrasea and Soranus. In the wake of this summons, worried friends of Thrasea rushed to his residence to offer conflicting advice. Some urged him to appear in the House and defend himself, even though the consensus was that Nero was determined to see a guilty verdict returned.

"Posterity would at least distinguish between the memory of an honorable death and the cowardice of those who perished in silence," said the pessimists.[19]

Others among Thrasea's friends recommended that he stay at home, to maintain his proud record and avoid the insults and mockeries that would be thrown at him by his accusers. There was even a suggestion that some people might resort to violence against Thrasea, or for him, if he put in an appearance, and they begged him to spare the Senate such a scene. These men feared that if violence did break out, Thrasea would be blamed, and Nero would also punish his wife and family.

One of Thrasea's clients, an enthusiastic but impetuous young tribune of the Plebeians by the name of Rusticus Arulenus, offered to make an official protest against any sentence imposed on Thrasea by the Senate. Thrasea felt this would be futile, as he was convinced that the majority of senators would fall into line with what they believed Nero wanted and would convict their fellow senator. Arulenus' protest would, Thrasea was convinced, prove useless to him and potentially fatal to the young tribune.

"My days are nearing their end," said Thrasea forlornly, "and I must not now abandon a scheme of life (Stoicism) with which I have persevered for so many years." The followers of the Stoic philosophy believed in calmly accepting their fate, whatever it might be. "You are at the beginning of a career in office, and your future is uncertain," Thrasea told the young tribune. "Before you act in a crisis such as this, carefully consider the path to political life that lies ahead."[20]

Thrasea thanked all his friends for their advice, but in the end, he said, he would reserve for his own judgment the question of whether it was becoming of him to enter the Senate on the day of his trial.

The Trial of Thrasea
and Soranus

The next morning, prior to sunrise, most of the senators of Rome made their way from their city homes to the Curia, the Senate House, in answer to the consul's summons. In the Forum, they encountered a group of ordinary citizens who blocked their path. These surly men were armed with swords on sword-belts, which they did not conceal, despite the law that banned the carrying of arms within the city by anyone other than the military—and even then, there were restrictions on what the troops could ordinarily carry within the city walls. The armed men parted to let the senators pass, but followed their passage with threatening expressions. Who had sent them, no one knew, but the fact that they were not challenged by the authorities suggested they were there to intimidate the senators with the encouragement of someone connected with the Palatium.

Then, adjacent to the Curia, in the Forum of Caesar, the arriving senators saw swarms of armed Praetorian troops. Two thousand men from two of the Praetorian Cohorts were scattered in various bodies through the colonnades and courtyards of the Temple of Venus Genetrix. This temple had been erected by Julius Caesar in response to the vow he had made to his patron deity, the goddess Venus, on the eve of the Battle of Pharsalus. If he was given victory over Pompey the Great, he had vowed, he would build this temple. Ironically, Venus was also Pompey's patron deity. Inside the temple, in addition to a statue of the goddess herself, there were statues of Caesar and of his mistress Cleopatra, queen of Egypt.

Obviously sent by the Praetorian prefects Tigellinus and Nymphidius, the Praetorians eyed the arriving senators with menacing looks and with their hands resting in the hilts of their swords. It was another unspoken message to the senators that they should do the emperor's bidding this day. As dawn broke, inside the Senate House the presiding consul, seated in his curule chair, looked around the crowded wooden benches in front of him and noted that Thrasea was absent, having failed to answer his summons. Thrasea had in fact decided to sit out the Senate session with Stoic resolve, relaxing in his gardens while he waited to learn from others the outcome of the debate on his fate. The consul called the House to order, then, when silence reigned, nodded to the emperor's quaestor.

The quaestor came to his feet and read out a speech written by Nero and addressed to the members of the Senate. Nero condemned unnamed senators for neglecting their duties and providing a poor example to their inferiors, then went on: "What wonder is it that men don't come from remote provinces when many, after obtaining the consulate or some sacred office, choose to give all their thoughts to the beauty of their gardens?"[1] There could be no doubt to whom the emperor was referring.

The conclusion of the imperial address was the consul's cue to call on Cossutianus Capito. Tigellinus' son-in-law came to his feet, then gave a speech in which, as expected, he vilified Thrasea. When he had finished, the consul called on another senator, Marcellus Eprius, who used his "pungent eloquence," in Tacitus' words, to also denounce Thrasea. It was a speech that clearly had Palatium endorsement. "We senators have been too lenient in the past in allowing him [the emperor] to be mocked with impunity by Thrasea," Marcellus said, in part.[2]

Marcellus, with the "savage and menacing look he usually wore," then sent shivers of dread around the chamber by unexpectedly implicating three more members of the House in Thrasea's "crimes"—Thrasea's son-in-law Gaius Helvidius Priscus and two others, Agrippinus, whose father had been exiled by Tiberius, and Montanus, a poet guilty of "abominable verses," according to his accuser.[3] When Priscus had served as a tribune of the Plebeians several years earlier, he had gained a reputation for good acts, showing particular attention to the needs of the poor. But now Priscus was being accused of a treasonous association with his father-in-law, an indicted enemy of the emperor. Tacitus characterized the relationship of Priscus and Thrasea as an innocent alliance, but Priscus was, like Thrasea, a Stoic, and like Thrasea, too, Priscus could sometimes be brutally frank.

It was Thrasea who came in for Marcellus' greatest condemnation, for his guilt, if proven, would be enough to destroy the others. "Thrasea openly took on the role of a traitor and an enemy," Marcellus declared, "with rising fury." He wondered why Thrasea had failed to take his place in the Senate, had not been seen at the theater, and had not met his obligations as a priest these past three years. The Senate House, the theater, and the temples had come to be treated as a desert by Thrasea, he said. Thrasea, Marcellus claimed, grieved at his country's prosperity, "and is forever threatening *us* with exile." What, he pondered, was Thrasea unhappy about? "Is it the peace throughout the world or victories won without loss to our armies which vex him?"[4]

After Marcellus suggested, bitterly, that Thrasea "sever his life" from the country that he apparently no longer loved, the accuser took his seat.[5] The consul now called for the Equestrian Ostorius Sabinus, the accuser of Barea Soranus, the second man being impeached on Nero's orders, to be brought into the chamber. The consul's lictors escorted Ostorius in, and the consul gave him leave to speak. Ostorius told the House that Soranus, who was present, had been an intimate friend of the previously condemned traitor Rubellius Plautus and that Soranus, when he was governor of Asia, had fostered seditious movements in the various states that made up the province.

These were stale charges that the senators had heard before, but the accuser now added a new charge, that Soranus' daughter Servilia had recently spent a great deal of money, obtained by selling her wedding presents and jewelry, to employ astrologers to provide horoscopes about her father and Nero. This new claim sent a ripple of low conversation through the chamber. The consul now dispatched his lictors to fetch Servilia and bring her into the Senate to address the charge.

Twenty-year-old Servilia was soon escorted into the House and made to stand in front of the assembled senators. The previous year, her husband Annius Pollio, a member of a distinguished family and a man considerably older than Servilia, had been sent into exile. Pollio had been the best friend of Senecio, the "inside man" in the Piso Plot. When asked to name a single fellow conspirator, Senecio had named Pollio, who had subsequently been banished, leaving his wife forlorn at Rome. As Soranus, an elderly man, stood facing his daughter before the tribunal of the consuls, Servilia could not bring herself to look her father in the eye.

"Did you sell your bridal presents or strip your neck of its ornaments to raise money for the performance of magical rites?" demanded Ostorius the accuser.[6]

Instead of replying, the young woman flung herself down onto the marble floor and wept long and hard. Because Servilia was guilty of employing astrologers, she realized that in doing so, she had exacerbated her father's peril. The Senate patiently waited for her to compose herself and answer the charge.

When the flow of tears had ceased, Servilia crawled up the steps to the altar that stood in the chamber and on which stood a bust of Nero. Clasping the altar, Servilia cried, "I have invoked no impious gods, no enchantments, nor anything else in my unhappy prayers that you, Caesar"— she looked at the marble visage of the emperor—"and you senators, might preserve from harm this best of fathers. My jewels, my clothes, and the signs of my ranks I did give up, as I would have given up my lifeblood had it been demanded of me."[7]

Servilia looked around the chamber at the faces of the senators, some charitable, most solemn, some condemning. "These men must have seen this," she went on, referring to the astrologers and her desperation. "I did not know them previously, or the arts they practice. No mention was made by me of the emperor, except as one of the divinities. But my most unhappy father knows nothing of any of this. And if it is a crime, then I alone am guilty."[8]

Servilia was going to say more, but her father, trying to free her from any blame, interrupted. "My daughter did not go with me to Asia," he declared. "She was too young then to have known Plautus. Nor was she involved in the charges against Pollio, her husband." Turning to his fellow senators, he beseeched them: "Treat separately the case of one who is only guilty of excessive loyalty to her father. As for myself, let me suffer any fate."[9]

As Soranus spoke, Servilia went to run to him, and he to wrap his paternal arms around her, but the consular lictors standing close by intervened and drew them apart. The consul called for witnesses for both the prosecution and the defense to now speak. Up rose Publius Egnatius Celer, one of the architects of the rebuilding of Rome and the construction of the Golden House. Celer had been managing imperial properties in Asia at the time of Soranus' alleged crimes there and was also a client of Soranus.

A professed Stoic and speaking with the slow, deliberate, and virtuous eloquence of a philosopher, Celer added weight to the accusation that Soranus had stirred up revolt in the province, influenced by his friendship with Plautus. Tacitus, later claiming that Celer had been paid to betray his patron, called Celer "treacherous and cunning," a man "wholly entangled in falsehoods and stained with every infamy."[10] In Soranus' defense, another provincial, Cassius Asclepiodotus of Nicaea, reputedly the richest man in Bithynia, was at Rome; he stood before the House and spoke of Soranus' good character.

No one else spoke in favor of either Soranus or Thrasea, yet both had many friends within senatorial ranks. Vespasian, for example, was a friend to both men, although he had little time for Thrasea's son-in-law Priscus. No other man of distinction was prepared to follow the example of Asclepiodotus and speak in favor of the accused. For those who put self-preservation ahead of all else, it seemed a pointless and suicidal act. The Nicaean, a lone voice in support of the beleaguered Soranus, would pay for his loyalty and courage. The Senate would tar him with the same brush as they did Soranus and would impose a stiff sentence on him, stripping him of his great wealth and sending him into impoverished exile.

Late that afternoon, the consul's quaestor, a young man in his late twenties, arrived at the gate to Thrasea's gardens; he had been sent by the consul to convey a message to Thrasea. Escorted into the gardens, the quaestor found Thrasea surrounded by a crowd of distinguished men and women, including Thrasea's wife Arria. The throng was listening intently as Thrasea conversed with Demetrius, a noted Greek professor of the Cynic school of philosophy—Cynics led an austere life, like monks in later times, but were also outspoken and believed in being unconventional and in challenging the social norms of the day. As the quaestor came up to the group, he found Thrasea speculating loudly with Demetrius on the nature of the soul and the separation of body and spirit.

When Thrasea would not halt his discourse, the quaestor spoke with one of Thrasea's friends, Domitius Caecilianus, and imparted the consul's message. The Senate, said the messenger, had found Thrasea, Soranus, and Soranus' daughter Servilia guilty of capital offenses. But the senators had voted to permit all three to choose how they died. Helvidius and Agrippinus had been ordered to leave Italy. Montanus the poet had been saved from similar punishment when his father had stood up in the Senate and proposed that the young man be punished by being banned from ever entering political life, which the House agreed to. The prosecutors in Thrasea's case, Capito and Marcellus, had each been given 5 million sesterces by the Senate for their work, while Ostorius, Soranus' prosecutor, was awarded 1.2 million sesterces and the decorations of a quaestor.

Domitius went to Thrasea and interrupted him, announcing the convictions and sentences to all present. Many of those around Thrasea, men as well as women, burst into tears at the news. Others complained bitterly at the injustice of it all. Thrasea's wife Arria immediately declared that she wished to die with him, taking her own life the same way that her own mother had done some years before.

"No, preserve your life," Thrasea urged his wife, "and don't rob our daughter of her only support." Turning to his friends, he said, "Go quickly now, and don't imperil yourselves by becoming embroiled in the fate of a man who is doomed."[11]

The quaestor was under orders to deliver the verdict to Thrasea in person and to then return to the consul with word of Thrasea's response to his sentence. A failure by Thrasea to take matters into his own hands would result in the consul's consigning the condemned man's fate to the Praetorian prefect. As most of Thrasea's companions hurried away, the quaestor found the man himself beneath a garden colonnade. The quaestor read the consul's message aloud. Thrasea seemed oddly elated, before explaining that he was joyful because the life of his son-in-law had been spared.

After parting from his wife, Thrasea took his son-in-law Priscus and Demetrius the Cynic and withdrew into a room. There, he took out a dagger and sliced open the veins of each arm. Letting the blood flow freely, he sprinkled it onto the floor. He then called in the quaestor, so that he could report that he had seen the condemned man follow the noble course.

"We pour out a libation to Jupiter the Deliverer," Thrasea said to the quaestor, indicating the dripping blood. "Look well, young man—and may the gods ignore the omen—you have been born into times when it is wise to fortify the spirit with examples of courage."[12]

THE NEW ALEXANDER

Thrasea and Soranus were dead, and King Tiridates was on his way back to the East. Nero was feeling on top of the world. At some point during Tiridates' visit to Rome, someone—probably the king himself—seems to have likened Nero to Alexander the Great. Now, Nero was convinced that he could indeed become the new Alexander the Great.

Like Alexander, Nero had eliminated potential rivals and leaders of dissent from within his own camp. Now, Nero would emulate Alexander in other ways. Reputedly, Alexander had sent an expedition south from Egypt into what the Romans called Ethiopia, to search for the source of the Nile River. Nero decided that he would do likewise and issued orders for an expeditionary force to be prepared for just such an operation the following year or, at the latest, the year after that. Nero intended to personally lead this expedition.

In addition to ordering the 15th Apollonaris Legion to transfer to Egypt from Syria to join the two legions already stationed there (the 3rd Cyrenaica and 22nd Deiotariana), the Palatium would partly meet the manpower needs of the Ethiopian operation by reforming an old legion. It was a re-creation of the 18th Legion, one of three legions famously wiped out in the Teutoburg Forest by the German tribes led by Arminius in AD 9. Neither Augustus nor his successors had re-formed any of the three annihilated legions, the 17th, 18th and 19th, because it had been

considered unlucky to do so. Consequently, why Nero chose to re-form
the 18th Legion is a mystery. Making the re-creation of the legion more
difficult, half of its ten cohorts were recruited in Europe, and half in
Libya, adjacent to Egypt.

To provide more troops for the Ethiopian expedition, the Palatium
also called up Evocati reservists in Europe. With these reservists acting
as garrison troops in Egypt, the two legions that had been stationed in
Egypt could march south with Nero in his force of four legions. For the
Ethiopian operation, Nero would make his headquarters in Alexandria,
at the palace of the Egyptian sovereigns of old. That palace's first occupant had been Alexander's general Ptolemy, founder of the Macedonian
dynasty that had gone on to rule Egypt for centuries. The last occupants
had been Cleopatra and Nero's great-great-grandfather Mark Antony.
The palace was grand, but not grand enough for Nero, who instructed
the prefect of Egypt to erect a luxurious new bathhouse in time for his
arrival. Later, after the prefect tried out the newly built bathhouse, an in-
censed Nero would remove him from his post.

Nero would, of course, be accompanied on the Ethiopian expedition by most of the Praetorian Cohorts. It would take the Praetorians'
minds off the loss of half their tribunes following the Piso Plot and give
them the opportunity for action and, more importantly, for booty. In
conceiving this operation, Nero took a leaf from his uncle Claudius'
book. After a revolt among the legions in Dalmatia had been put down
in AD 41, Claudius, who, like Nero, had no military experience, had
initiated the AD 43 invasion of Britain. This aggressive action, which
had added the province of Britain to the empire, had been cleverly conceived by Claudius to prove to his discontented army that he could be
a successful military leader and could give them new sources of blood
and booty.

Nero did not stop at the Ethiopian plan, for he wanted to prove his
military credentials to the army and cement its loyalty. Alexander the
Great had also conquered the Persians, precursors to the Parthians, and
had defeated the aggressive Getae north of the Danube. Julius Caesar,
just before he died, was planning a similar operation, which would have
taken him through the Caspian Gates, around the Caspian Sea, and into

the heartland of the Getae, at the head of a hundred thousand troops. Nero decided that he would both emulate Alexander and take up where Caesar had left off. Movement orders went out to legions around the empire to prepare to move to new bases for the Caspian Gates operation. The 14th Gemina Legion, considered the best legion in the Roman army since it had defeated Boudicca's rebel army, would, for example, leave its longtime base in Britain and relocate to Carnuntum in Pannonia, on the Danube, in preparation for the Getae offensive.

For the Caspian Gates operation, too, Nero ordered the formation of a new legion. The first entirely new Roman legion raised in a century, this unit would also be the first legion recruited in Italy south of the Po River since the days of Julius Caesar. Both aspects were reflected by the unit's title, Legio I Italica, literally, the first Italian legion. It was Augustus who had initiated the practice of raising all recruits for the legions in the provinces, including Cisalpine Gaul (northern Italy), with only the Praetorian Cohorts enlisting their recruits among Italians south of the Po. Nero changed this with his latest directive.

This summer of AD 66, *conquisitors*, recruiting officers, would bustle around southern Italy, consulting with local magistrates as they compiled lists of potential conscripts with an average age of twenty, to fill the ranks of Nero's new 1st Italica Legion. Simultaneously, orders went out for the manufacture of arms and equipment for 5,245 men. By Nero's decree, every man recruited into the 1st Italica would have to be a minimum of six Roman feet tall—around five feet ten inches in today's measurement. This was tall by the standards of the day, with legionaries at that time averaging some five feet four inches in modern terms. Under Nero's decree, too, the troops of his new 1st Italica Legion would be equipped as spearmen. In the ancient Greek fashion, they would carry spears thirteen feet long, and in action they would employ the battle formations and tactics of the Greek phalanx of centuries past. Nero nicknamed his new unit "the Phalanx of Alexander the Great."

In Alexander's army, the cavalry had done most of the hard work in battle, supported by archers, slingers, and javelin men. The nine thousand men of Alexander's phalanx had been his elite infantry troops, like Napoleon Bonaparte's Imperial Guard in more recent times. Held in reserve, the phalanx was thrown into a battle at a critical point as required, driving all before it at the point of its spears. It was Nero's intent that his phalanx would serve a similar purpose, bristling with spears and acting like a giant porcupine. Once the men of the 1st Italica were conscripted, they would be sent to the Adriatic naval base of Ravenna in the province of Cisalpine Gaul to undergo their training and to be ready for service the following year.

Even the centurions transferred from other legions to positions of command with the 1st Italica Legion would have to learn new skills, for the use of the long spear was alien to Roman legionaries, who were accustomed to throwing their six- or seven-foot-long javelins in the first stage of battle and then drawing their swords and moving in for close combat. For the bristling phalanx to work, the long spear must never leave the soldier's hands. Given the boar as its unit symbol, the 1st Italica Legion would be officially commissioned over the winter of AD 66–67, taking the zodiacal sign of Capricorn as its birth emblem.

With preparations for Nero's grand military operations in the works, spies were sent ahead into the regions that were to be penetrated by the two expeditions. According to Dio, Nero was hoping that the barbarians "would submit to him of their own accord" without the need of battles, because he was Nero, emperor of Rome.[1] Now, Nero felt able to indulge his artistic side; he would stay in Greece for the year it took to prepare the army for the Ethiopian and Caspian Gates operations, and he would compete in the poetry and singing competitions and chariot races of the Panhellenic Games as he had long dreamed of doing. It was still spring when he set off for Greece with a vast entourage.

Four main games were held in Greece, and many smaller ones in imitation of them. The Olympic Games, held every four years at Olympia, are the most famous today, but the Pythian Games at Delphi were equally famous in ancient times, if not more so. The Nemean and Isthmian Games, held every two years, were almost as prestigious as the others. Under the normal Greek games calendar, both the Nemean and the Isthmian competitions were held on the first and third years following the Olympic Games, with the Pythian Games held in between, two years before and after the Olympics.

Suetonius would write that to suit his traveling schedule, Nero had the games' timetable altered. It appears that with the Olympic Games due to be staged that year of AD 66, and with the Isthmian Games running in the summer of AD 67 and the Nemean Games over the winter of AD 67–68, Nero probably rescheduled the Pythian Games ordinarily set down for AD 68, bringing them forward to the spring of AD 67. All these events except the Olympic Games always included artistic as well as physical and equestrian contests; Nero commanded that a singing competition now also be added to the Olympic events.

As the emperor set off for Greece, he was accompanied by many of his officials and leading senators. Tigellinus went with him. Nymphidius was left in charge of those Praetorian Cohorts that remained at the capital. Vespasian was also a member of the imperial party. He took along his son Titus, who had recently returned to Rome after several years' military service in Britain. One of many other senators in the party was a Gaul by the name of Gaius Julius Vindex.

To the horror of the Roman establishment, the emperor left the freedman Helius in charge to rule at Rome in Nero's stead while he was away. Helius, whom Nero had inherited from the staff of his predecessor Claudius and whom he trusted above all others, was made senior to the consuls. Nero endowed Helius with the same powers that he himself wielded, "so that he could confiscate, banish, or put to death ordinary citizens, Equestrians, and senators alike, even before notifying Nero."[2]

To noble-born Romans, this was appalling. But, to Nero, rather than risk putting supreme power into the hands of senators who might come to like it and refuse to relinquish it, this was a purely pragmatic step. Snobby Dio would complain about Nero and Helius, "I am unable to say which of them was the worse. In most respects they behaved entirely alike. The one point of difference was that the descendant of Augustus was emulating lyre players and tragedians, whereas the freedman of Claudius was emulating Caesars."[3]

"He sailed off hastily," said Suetonius of Nero's departure for Achaia, "and as soon as he arrived at Cassiope gave his first song recital in front of the altar of Jupiter Cassius, after which he did the round of the contests." The port of Cassiope was the principal town on the Albanian side of the island of Corfu, and the Temple of Jupiter there was many centuries old. "So captivated was he by the rhythmic applause of a crowd of Alexandrians from a fleet that had just put in, he sent to Alexandria for more."[4]

Putting several young Equestrians in charge of these applauders, whom he dubbed "the Augustans," and giving them forty thousand sesterces for each performance, Nero recruited five thousand youths in total. The Augustans were like a giant cheerleading squad for Nero. With the special outfits that were created for them, and their bushy hair, "it was easy to recognize them," said Suetonius. They were divided into three groups. The Bees made a loud humming noise. The Roof-tiles clapped with hollowed hands. The Bricks clapped flat-handed. These Augustans would subsequently appear wherever Nero appeared.[5]

His confidence sky-high now, Nero prepared to enter the Greek games. All of them.

THE APOSTLES AND THE JEWISH REVOLT

While Nero was still entertaining King Tiridates at Rome in the early spring of AD 66, Joseph bar Matthias, the Jewish rabbi, having obtained the release of three fellow priests from Nero, arrived back in Jerusalem. It was just after the year's Passover festival. Joseph found Jerusalem in turmoil.

"There were a great many with high hopes of a revolt from the Romans," he would recall. "They were already in possession of Antonia, which was the citadel."[1] Weeks earlier, the Roman procurator of Judea, Gessius Florus, had come up to Jerusalem from the Roman capital of Judea, Caesarea, to be present for the Passover, when Jerusalem's population was swelled well past a million people by Jewish pilgrims from throughout the ancient world—Josephus put the number of pilgrims one year at three million. Even though Florus had brought extra troops with him to augment the Roman garrison at Jerusalem during the Passover, Zealot rebels had stage-managed such unrest in the city that Florus, in fear for his own life, had negotiated what he thought would be an end to the troubles.

In return for leaving a single cohort of Roman troops at the city and agreeing that these troops would remain in their garrisons and not mix with the people, Florus received a guarantee from the Jewish priests of the Great Sanhedrin that there would be no more trouble. Florus and the majority of his infantry and all his cavalry had then marched back down to Caesarea on the Mediterranean coast, leaving 480 men, apparently from the 3rd Gallica Legion, at Jerusalem. Of those legionaries, 240 were stationed in the Palace of Herod and the rest in the Antonia Fortress—built by Herod the Great and named in honor of his good friend Mark Antony.

Within days, the rebels, against the advice of the Sanhedrin, had taken up arms and launched attacks on the Antonia Fortress and Herod's palace. The Antonia was a vast citadel and much too large for just 240 troops to defend against thousands of attackers. Within days, the rebels had overrun the fortress and massacred all the legionaries inside. It was at this point that Joseph had arrived back home. "I therefore tried to put a stop to these troublemakers," Joseph wrote.[2] Having been at Rome for the past several years and seen the vast resources that the Romans could draw on to rebuild their city from rubble in just a year following the Great Fire, he dreaded what they could do against a rebellious Jewish nation.

Joseph said that he told the rebels "that they were inferior to the Romans not only in military skill but also in good fortune," and that they would only bring "the most terrible disasters down on their country, on their families, and on themselves. And I said this with vehement exhortation, because I could foresee that the outcome of such a war would be most unfortunate for us. But I could not persuade them. For the madness of desperate men was much too strong for me."[3]

The young rabbi realized that "by often repeating these things I would incur their hatred and their suspicion, as if I were on our enemy's side, and would run the risk of being seized by them and killed."[4] So, he joined the priests who barricaded themselves inside the Temple against the rebels. The Zealots, meanwhile, targeted all their efforts on seizing the Palace of Herod. The remaining 240 legionaries were soon reinforced by troops sent by Herod Agrippa II, tetrarch of Trachonitis and Batanaea, a Roman ally. But, after heavy fighting, Agrippa's troops defected to the side of the rebels.

The legionaries, who had retreated to the palace's towers, were now convinced to surrender with the promise that once they gave up their weapons, they would be permitted to leave. As soon as the Roman troops had disarmed, they were butchered by the rebel Jews. Only the centurion in charge was spared, after he vowed to convert to Judaism. At this same time, another party of Zealots was tricking its way into the old Herodian fortress atop the cliffs at remote Masada, beside the Dead Sea. There, the Roman cohort of the garrison was also massacred.

Nothing that Joseph could say now could prevent history from taking its course. The Jewish Revolt had begun, a thousand Roman legionaries had been killed, and Rome would want its revenge. Joseph was now one of three Jewish priests sent to Galilee to coordinate Jewish resistance there, not only to defend against a Roman military reply, but also to guard the Jewish communities against reprisals from the non-Jewish peoples of Judea, who began massacring their Jewish neighbors on the news of the uprising in Jerusalem. Like it or not, thirty-year-old Joseph had just become a general of the rebel Jewish army. He and his colleagues would arm and train tens of thousands of Jewish partisans, knowing that sooner or later, the Roman war machine would have to grind into gear against them.

♾

In May, with Joseph in Galilee building his forces and competing with Zealots for control in the area, while expecting a Roman counteroffensive to be launched from Syria any day, Nero was in Greece attending the Olympic Games and about to compete in them. According to Christian legend, around this same time, two Jews were arrested in Rome. This would have been on the orders of Helius, the freedman left in charge at Rome by Nero during his absence.

One of these Jews was a noncitizen named Simeon of Galilee, who would become known among Christians as the Apostle Peter. Formerly a successful fisherman from Capernaum in Galilee, Simeon, called Simon by the Romans, had become the chief lieutenant of the Jewish preacher whom his Greek-speaking followers called Jesus of Nazareth, or the Christos, or anointed one. The other Jew was Paul of Tarsus, who had made his promised return to Rome. No Roman or Greek historian made any mention of these two Christian apostles, let alone described their time at Rome. All that is known of Peter and Paul at Rome comes from Christian tradition, which is based on later Christian writing.

According to that tradition, Peter and Paul had been preaching in Rome and were arrested and thrown into the Tullianum, or the Tullian Keep, the city prison at Rome, which later became known as the Mamertine Prison. This cavernous underground jail had originally been created, centuries before, as a cistern for the storage of rainwater. Converted into a prison, it consisted of two levels. The upper level was used for the incarceration of general inmates. In the lower level were kept those prisoners who had been convicted of a capital crime and were awaiting execution. It was also in this lower level that high-ranking enemy leaders captured in wartime met their deaths—strangled with a halter after being led through the streets in the Triumph of a Roman general. In this way, Gallic war leader Vercingetorix had been executed here after surrendering to Julius Caesar in 52 BC. Five years from now, one of the senior leaders of the Jewish Revolt in Judea would similarly meet his executioner in this lower chamber of the Tullianum.

The crimes for which Peter and Paul were arrested, convicted, and condemned have never been determined. Paul, in his second letter from Rome to Timotheus, whom he had placed in charge of the Christian church at Ephesus, would complain bitterly from prison that when he stood in court to answer the latest charges against him, "no man stood with me, but all men forsook me. I pray God that it may not be laid to their charge." Paul made no mention of Peter. "Only Luke is with me."[5] Paul said that one of his companions, Demas, who had been with him when first he came to Rome six years earlier, had deserted him once Paul was arrested this second time; Demas had fled to Thessalonica in Macedonia. Two other companions had also left Rome; Crescens had gone to Galatia, and Titus to Dalmatia.

It is likely that Paul had been arrested on the accusation of a local artisan of Greek extraction. "Alexander the coppersmith did me much evil," Paul wrote. "The Lord reward him according to his works." Summoning Timothy to Rome to help him, Paul warned him to be wary of

Alexander, "for he has greatly withstood our words." It seems that until he declared his Roman citizenship, Paul had been found guilty and was about to be sent to the arena to suffer the fate of convicted noncitizens, a meeting with wild beasts, for he told Timothy, "I was delivered out of the mouth of the lion."[6]

Not released into the community under house arrest as he had been the last time he was in Rome, Paul was lodged in the prison in chains. Yet, he was still able to receive visitors, dictate letters to helpers, and receive gifts—he asked Timothy to bring him a cloak that he had left in Troas. Winter was approaching and the temperatures were already beginning to drop when he wrote this letter, most likely in the autumn. "Do thy diligence and come before winter," he instructed Timothy.[7]

Having escaped death in the arena in one of the several annual games in the Circus Maximus that June and July, Paul was being held in the Tullian prison while he awaited the hearing of his appeal to the emperor. The three Jewish rabbis whose freedom Joseph bar Matthias had eventually secured had spent six years in detention awaiting a hearing by the time of their release, and Paul himself had spent two years under house arrest the last time he had been at Rome. With Nero dallying in Greece and not planning to return to Rome for several years, there was every reason to expect that Paul's wait could be a long one.

Peter, on the other hand, was not a Roman citizen. If we accept that Peter did indeed come to Rome and was arrested and executed there—which is a basic premise of the Roman Catholic Church—then as a noncitizen convicted of a capital crime, he had no right of appeal and would either be sent to the arena or be put on a cross and crucified shortly after his conviction. According to one Christian tradition, both apostles were executed within a year of each other. Another has nine months passing between their incarceration and execution. In the case of Peter, a noncitizen, such a long delay between arrest and execution is implausible. This suggests that Paul was arrested first, perhaps before Peter came to Rome, and that Peter was probably not arrested until some months later, during the winter of AD 66–67.

Through the summer and autumn of AD 66, Paul was a lone Christian prisoner in the Tullianum at Rome, awaiting his fate.

In Greece, Nero was competing in the Olympic Games. The news of the revolt by the Jews in Judea had reached him, but it did not concern him in the least. Just as Suetonius Paulinus, one of the consuls this year, had in AD 60–61 put down the Boudiccan revolt in Britain using his own resources as governor of the province, so the emperor expected the governor of Syria, who had four legions at his disposal, to deal with the Judean problem. Judea was a subprovince of the Roman province of Syria, and the authority of the propraetor, or imperial governor, of Syria extended over Judea and its procurator. By AD 66, that governor was Cestius Gallus. Once Procurator Florus in Caesarea had reported the Jerusalem uprising to Gallus in Antioch, the capital of Syria, the Jewish Revolt became Gallus' problem. His expected response would be to march an army into Judea to put down the revolt.

Nero, meanwhile, was competing in the singing contest that he insisted be added to the Olympic program. "Nero Caesar wins this contest," the chief judge subsequently announced, "and crowns the Roman people, and the inhabited world that is his own."[8]

The emperor then competed in the games' four-horse chariot race. Falling out of his chariot midrace, he came close to being crushed to death, but escaped without major injury. Despite his failure to finish, the judges still declared Nero the race winner. After he accepted the victor's laurel crown, Nero presented the Greek judges with a gift of a million sesterces. Flushed with his Olympian victories, Nero moved on. "He competed in every city alike that held any contest," said Cassius Dio, "always employing ex-consul Cluvius Rufus as his herald."[9] The only places in Achaia where he did not compete, for various reasons, were Athens and Sparta.

In the meantime, Cestius Gallus, governor of Syria, had, over many months, put together the force with which he intended to put down the Jewish Revolt. At its core was the 12th Fulminata Legion, a unit that was soon to undergo its twenty-year discharge of time-served soldiers and the induction of a new intake. It was far from the ideal legion for the task. After almost two decades of service, the current enlistment had been drained of men through battle casualties and sickness. Just several years before, Tacitus had commented on the legion's "numerical feebleness."[10]

To the 12th, Gallus added four cohorts from each of several other legions, plus auxiliaries and cavalry. Regional allies, including Herod Agrippa II, answered his call for troops with spearmen, archers, and cavalry, so that Gallus' force totaled twenty-eight thousand men by the time that it reached Ptolemais, in southern Syria just a little north of Caesarea, late in the fall. After relieving the city of Sepphoris in Galilee, which had held out against the Jewish rebels, and destroying the Jewish city of Joppa, Gallus' army pushed up into the Judean hills from the coastal plain. It was October and the time of the Jewish Feast of the Tabernacles when the Roman force arrived outside Jerusalem, having lost five hundred men to harrying partisans over the last days of the march.

Pitching camp on Mount Scopus overlooking Jerusalem, Gallus did nothing for three days, hoping the rebels would surrender. When this did not eventuate, he set fire to the Bezetha region of the city, forcing the Jews to retreat into the old city. For five days, the Roman army attacked the city walls. Then, to the amazement of the defenders, Gallus packed up and marched his army away. Josephus would claim that bribery played a part in the Roman withdrawal. Day after day, tens of thousands of Jewish partisans pursued the withdrawing Romans, attacking them along the entire length of the column.

Only by discarding his heavy baggage and by leaving 400 volunteers at the hill village of Beth-horon on a suicide mission to delay the Jews was Gallus able to escape with the majority of his men. The Jews pursued the badly mauled Roman column as far west as the town of Antipatris. When the bloodied Roman force arrived back in Caesarea and counted its losses, they found that 5,300 infantry and 380 mounted troops had been lost. The Jewish losses, meanwhile, had been minor. And the rebels still held Jerusalem and most of Judea, Galilee, and Idumaea.

Nero was wintering in Greece when the staggering news of Gallus' defeat reached him that December. In addition to the numerical losses, Nero learned that several senior officers including the commander of the 6th Ferrata Legion had been killed during the botched operation. The rebels had also captured the column's wagon train, inclusive of much war matériel, particularly Roman artillery. Worst of all, in the eyes of all Romans, the sacred golden eagle standard of the 12th Fulminata Legion had been captured by the rebels. For a legion, there was no greater disgrace. Cestius Gallus was also dead. Some said that he had perished of natural causes once he was back in Caesarea; others said that he had died of shame. It was even suggested that he had committed suicide.

Nero was shaken by this defeat. Calling in Titus Vespasian, who was in the emperor's large entourage, Nero gave him the task of putting down the Jewish Revolt. Vespasian immediately set off overland for Syria to take command there. At the same time, Vespasian's son Titus sailed for Egypt with orders to lead legionaries and auxiliaries based in Alexandria up to Judea to join Vespasian's new army for the counteroffensive.

Initial news of the revolt at Jerusalem had sponsored similar uprisings among other Jewish communities throughout the Roman world, particularly in Egypt, which a million Jews called home. In Alexandria and at Antioch, capital of Syria and home to forty thousand Jews, Roman troops brutally put down the unrest. Many Jews were killed in street fighting; others were thrown into jail. Nero, made furious by Gallus' failure and the humiliating Roman defeat in Judea, appears to have issued orders for all Jewish prisoners in Roman custody throughout the empire to be summarily executed. This would account for why the apostles Paul and Peter would be executed early in AD 67.

Christian tradition puts Peter's death on February 22. As a noncitizen, he was crucified. At his own request, he was crucified upside down. His slow death on a cross would have taken place on a roadside beyond the city walls. One Christian tradition puts that road in the Vatican Valley, another, on the Janiculum Hill. After Peter's death, according to one Christian legend, Peter's body was for a time interred in the tomb of a Roman senator named Marcellus.

According to Christian tradition, too, Paul was executed several months later. Because of his Roman citizenship, he was decapitated with a sword. The fifty-seven-year-old balding, bearded Paul is said to have been marched from Rome in chains and taken by a squad of Praetorians three miles down the Via Appia to the natural spa of Aqua Salviea. In the Glade of the Tombs, he was forced to his knees before the centurion in charge lopped off his head. In the Roman scheme of things, the deaths of Peter and Paul did not figure at all. No one in the Roman world could imagine that within the span of 250 years, the church that these two Jews helped found would become the official faith of Rome.

∽∽∾

Other disturbing news had reached Nero's ears from Helius, his deputy at Rome. Annius Vinicianus, Corbulo's impetuous son-in-law, had been linked to a new plot against Nero at Rome. The implication was that the conspirators intended to put Corbulo on Nero's throne. The Scribonius brothers, who did everything in public and private life together—they had jointly governed the two Roman provinces of Germany and had jointly put down riots in the port of Puteoli—were also linked to this plot, perhaps as patrons of Vinicianus. Nero's response to Helius' accusations was crafty. Early in the new year, he sent cordial invitations to Corbulo and the Scribonius brothers to join him at Corinth in Achaia, where he would be competing in the Isthmian Games come the spring.

As soon as the sailing season for AD 67 opened in the spring, Corbulo sailed from Syria to Achaia in answer to the emperor's invitation. Corbulo would have been expecting to lead Nero's planned Caspian Gates operation. To give the latest Judean offensive every opportunity of success, Nero had authorized Vespasian to draw on units based in Syria and Egypt—units that had been earmarked for the Caspian Gates and Ethiopian expeditions, both of which were now put on hold. Corbulo, unaware that his son-in-law was in trouble at Rome, came to Achaia no doubt expecting to discuss the future of the Caspian Gates operation with Nero.

On landing at Cenchreae, the port that served Corinth, Corbulo was met by Praetorian troops who advised him to take his own life at once, for the sake of his family, or they would do it for him. Up until this time, Nero had never considered Corbulo a rival to his throne, because of the general's lowly background and apparently unswerving loyalty. Now, although there was not a shred of evidence against him, Corbulo had been found guilty by association.

Corbulo, who was said to curse because he had failed to bring body-guard troops with him to Achaia, was determined to die a soldier's death. Drawing a sword, he exclaimed, "You are worthy of this!" a phrase usually called to triumphants when they took their Triumph.[11] He plunged the sword into his heart.

When the Scribonius brothers arrived in Greece, they were likewise forced to take their own lives. Nero, meanwhile, was competing in the Isthmian Games at Corinth and taking off the winners' pine-leaf wreaths for verse, song, and charioteering. Now, too, he entered the contests for heralds and was awarded the prizes for those as well. Since his initial successes at Olympia, he had also taken to acting in Greek tragedies, even taking female roles—no women appeared on the Roman stage, and as was the case even in Shakespeare's time, men played the roles of female characters. In one play, Nero played the role of a pregnant woman. In another, playing Hercules, he dressed in rags and wore manacles as the part required—a horrified soldier of the German Cohorts bodyguard, seeing his emperor in chains, rushed up to set him free.

Nero also initiated the Corinth Canal, linking the Aegean and Ionian seas, a project envisioned by Julius Caesar. Nero personally turned the first sod. Prisoners then commenced digging the canal, which would be abandoned on Nero's death. Work on Nero's canal would resume in modern times; it was completed in 1893. Once Nero had won his final event at Corinth, he stood in the crowded stadium and delivered a speech in which he announced that the entire province of Achaia would, from that day forward, be free of taxation. This was the province's reward for accepting him as a performer.

In the summer of AD 67, Nero moved on to Delphi, to compete in the Pythian Games, which ran over three months. Since the eighth century BC, Delphi had been famous as the seat of the Oracle of Delphi, at the sanctuary of Apollo on the slopes of Mount Parnassus. Seeking a personal prediction, Nero went through the usual ritual entailed in a visit to the oracle, who was a priestess called the Pythia. Up the zigzag Sacred Way the emperor climbed, bringing a black sheep to be sacrificed in the forecourt of the Temple of Apollo, which was administered by two senior priests, serving in an honorary role accorded leading Greeks of the day. Later this same century, the historian Plutarch would be one of those priests.

As Nero made his way up the road, he paused at the sanctuary's treasury to deposit a gift of four hundred thousand sesterces in gold. Every year, the shrine of Delphi attracted countless pilgrims seeking prophesies. All pilgrims were expected to make a donation, and the larger the gift, the more likely they were to be found a place toward the head of the usually long line. The emperor of Rome did not have to join a line.

Down well-trodden steps went Nero, into a cavern beneath the Temple of Apollo. The role of the Pythia was shared in rotation by three priestesses chosen specially for their gifts. Between spring and autumn each year, the Pythia on duty sat on a three-legged seat above a fissure in the rocks from which rose "the sacred vapor"; modern-day scientists believe this was any one of several naturally occurring mildly hallucinogenic gases. In answer to the applicant's question, the Pythia would go into a trancelike state and provide a cryptic reply, originally in rhyming verse but in later times in prose, which was written down by an assistant.

The question that Nero put to the Pythia was a secret, but according to Cassius Dio, the emperor was so dissatisfied with the response, he abolished the oracle, "after slaying some people and throwing them into the fissure from which the sacred vapor rose."[12] There is no record in any other source of either event, and the Oracle of Delphi would continue to issue her prophesies until AD 393, when Rome's Christian emperor Theodosius I ordered all pagan temples closed across the empire. Dio also claimed that Nero, in his dissatisfaction, had the territory of Cirrha, the port town that served and was controlled by Delphi, taken away and "given to the soldiers"—Nero's Praetorian escort, apparently.[13]

Suetonius' earlier account disagrees with Dio; according to the former, Nero was pleased by the Oracle's prediction, which, Suetonius claimed, warned the young emperor to beware of the seventy-third year. Nero, believing this to refer to his own seventy-third year, felt that his problems were still many years away. The Oracle, said Suetonius, was actually referring to Nero's ultimate successor, Galba, who was seventy-three years old.[14] The only problem with that story was the fact that on December 24, AD 67, Galba turned just seventy.

In addition to footraces and other physical events held at the sanctuary of Apollo's stadium, the Pythian Games included competitions for singers, poets, and heralds, in the sanctuary's theater. There were also horse and chariot races, held in a hippodrome down on the Plain of Crissa. Even today, it is possible to sit on the upper terraces of the Theater at Delphi, which is built into the mountainside, and enjoy a commanding view out over the plain where the equestrian events were held. At Delphi, Nero won the victor's bay laurel wreath, time and again.

Nero was at last living the artistic life to which he had aspired. Meanwhile, his empire was crumbling around him.

THE FALL OF NERO

In the spring of AD 67, new provincial governors appointed by Nero took up their postings. One such appointee was Cluvius Rufus, who up to this point had been introducing Nero's stage performances in Greece; he became governor of Baetica, or Farther Gaul. Gaius Julius Vindex had also left the imperial party in Greece to become Nero's governor of the province of Gallia Lugdunensis. Born in Gaul and the descendant of the onetime kings of Aquitania, Vindex was, according to Cassius Dio, ambitious, shrewd, and passionate.[1] Vindex, like so many other Roman senators, not only had shuddered at the purges of the past three years, but also had been horrified by the news that in Greece, Nero had recently gone through a "wedding" ceremony with a castrated youth named Sporus, a beautiful boy who resembled the late Poppaea Sabina, with Tigellinus giving away the "bride."

By late AD 67, in the Middle East, Vespasian's army had stormed one Jewish city after another in Galilee; the Jewish general and former rabbi Joseph was one of a handful of prisoners taken in the brutal siege of Jotopata. But Jerusalem was still in rebel hands. In Greece, Nero was competing at various games, as he had been for more than a year. In Gaul, Vindex made a decision. Summoning Gallic leaders to a conference, he made a speech about Nero, whom he disparagingly called Domitius Ahenobarbus, the name Nero bore before becoming emperor.

Vindex told his countrymen with disgust: "I have often heard him sing, play the herald, and act in tragedies," (all of which Nero had only done during his current Greek tour, meaning Vindex must have accompanied him on that tour). "Will anyone, then, call such a person Caesar, and imperator, and Augustus? Never!" Vindex saw just one solution. "Rise now against him everywhere. Help yourselves, and help the Romans. Liberate the entire world!"[2]

As the Gallic leaders went away to enthuse their own people and raise and equip a Gallic army, Vindex took control of the 1,500-man 18th Cohort of Rome's City Cohorts, which was stationed at his provincial capital, Lugdunum, modern-day Lyon, guarding the imperial mint. Vindex now turned that mint from producing coins that depicted Nero playing the lyre to coins bearing images of Liberty and the motto "Salvation of Mankind." At the same time, he wrote to the governors of other Roman provinces, urging them to support him in overthrowing Nero.

Several governors forwarded these letters to Rome for Nero's attention; one such governor would have been Cluvius Rufus in Farther Spain. Helius, Nero's loyal deputy at the Palatium, immediately wrote to the emperor to inform him of the problem and to urge him to return to Rome at once and take charge. But Nero was too absorbed in the business of theatrical competition and was looking forward to the Nemean Games over the winter. He ignored Helius' urgent requests, instead writing to ask the Senate to declare Vindex an outlaw, which they did, ordering Verginius Rufus to lead the army of Upper Germany against him and putting a price of ten million sesterces on Vindex's head.

When Vindex heard of this, he countered, "To the one who brings me the head of Domitius (Nero), I offer my own in exchange."[3]

One governor who received a letter from Vindex was sixty-nine-year-old Lucius Servius Galba, who had for the past eight years been Nero's propraetor of Hispania Tarraconensis, or Nearer Spain, which was centered on the city of Tarraco, modern Tarragona in eastern Spain. On receiving Vindex's letter, Galba had written back, offering moral support. Galba also spoke against Nero at a large gathering in his province. His troops hailed him *imperator*, in the style of old, but he refused to accept the honor. Controlling a single legion based in his province (the 10th

Gemina) plus just three cohorts of auxiliaries and two squadrons of cavalry, Galba did not acquiesce to Vindex's call for military support. Meanwhile, Verginius Rufus, governor of Upper Germany, responding to orders from Nero, ordered the mobilization of his four legions, which were in winter camp, for an advance into Gaul.

On January 1, when a crowd assembled at the Capitol gates in Rome to swear the usual vow of allegiance to Nero and offer prayers for his health and safety, the priests declared that the keys to the Capitoline complex had been lost, so that the ceremony and the prayers could not go ahead. Helius, Nero's deputy, concerned by this display of defiance from the priests and worried by news that the Gauls were raising a massive army, gave up writing to Nero. Instead, Helius set off for Greece by warship, ignoring the winter weather, to confront the emperor in person with the threats at home and abroad. Seven days later, Helius arrived at the astonished Nero's quarters and again put his case for his master's immediate return to Rome.

"Yes, you have made yourself quite plain," Nero irritably responded, according to Suetonius. "I am aware that you want me to go home. You will fare far better, however, if you encourage me to stay until I have proved myself worthy of Nero."[4]

Helius persisted, making it painfully clear to Nero that his throne was in danger if he was not seen to return to the capital and personally take charge. Unhappy though he was, Nero agreed. His staff and the members of the imperial entourage began preparations for a return to Italy by sea aboard warships of the Tyrrhenian Fleet.

ᏩᎳᎴ

Nero landed on the west coast of Italy in early March AD 68, then entered Neapolis celebrating his Greek theatrical victories like a triumphant general. Word had been sent ahead to demolish a section of the town wall, and now Nero entered the city through the gap, driving a chariot along streets lined with cheering Neapolitans and with a famous lyre-player beside him, and followed by hundreds of senators chanting his praises. This was how Panhellenic Games victors of ancient times had arrived home to their Greek cities.

Nero lingered there in Neapolis, reluctant to venture further north to Rome, even though, by all reports, the situation in Gaul was worsening. Writing to the Senate, he urged the House "to avenge himself and Rome" for Vindex's insurrection, claiming that an infected throat prevented him from coming to the capital and addressing the Senate in person.[5]

☙❧

An army of one hundred thousand Gauls came together behind the rebel leader. "At last," said Plutarch, "Vindex, plainly declaring war, wrote to Galba" again. This time, knowing that Verginius Rufus planned to march into Gaul with his legions, Vindex suggested that Galba "take the government for himself" with the support of the Gauls and overthrow Nero.[6]

When, shortly after, Rufus came down from the Rhine with his four legions and their twenty thousand supporting auxiliaries, the Gallic city of Vesontio, modern Besancon in central France, closed its gates to him. Rufus surrounded the city and lay siege to it. On hearing this, Vindex marched his army of Gauls to relieve Vesontio. The opposing forces camped near the city while their generals engaged in negotiations. Rufus, it turned out, was not averse to Nero's removal. After an agreement was apparently reached between the two whereby Vindex would control Gaul and Spain and Galba would be given the remainder of the empire, Vindex marched his army up, as if to enter the city.

Rufus' legionaries were chafing for a fight and for booty, and before Rufus could stop them, his legions attacked Vindex's men, taking them entirely by surprise. In the battle that followed, Rufus' forty thousand well-trained and well-equipped professional soldiers crushed the Gauls' hundred thousand raw conscripts, killing twenty thousand of them, for minimal losses of their own. Vindex, trapped inside Vesontio, took his own life. Rufus' men hailed their general *imperator*, tore the images of Nero from their standards, throwing them to the ground, and offered Rufus the throne. But he declined and led his troops back to their Rhine bases.

When Galba, in Spain, learned of Vindex's defeat and Rufus' withdrawal, he was "in great alarm" and wrote to Rufus, "exhorting him to join with him for the preservation of the empire and the liberty of the Romans." Even the cavalrymen attached to the 10th Gemina Legion began talking of returning their allegiance to Nero. Taking a few friends with him, Galba hurriedly retired to the Spanish town of Clunia, "regretting his former rashness," said Plutarch.[7] For now, Galba seemingly stood alone against Nero. Suetonius wrote that news of Vindex's death so unnerved Galba that it "almost turned him to despair and suicide."[8] Anxiously, Galba waited for events to take their course elsewhere.

ᎦᏍᏙᎤ

By the third week of March, Nero was still at Neapolis. It was the week of the Festival of Minerva, the ninth anniversary of the murder of his mother. In the morning, word arrived that Gallus' army had defeated Vindex's Gauls at Vesontio and that Vindex himself had committed suicide. Nero seemed unmoved by the news and in the afternoon attended wrestling contests at the city's gymnasium. At one point, he jumped down from his tribunal and vied with one of the athletes.

That evening, a far more serious dispatch reached Nero while he was at dinner. In this message, Helius apparently informed the emperor that Verginius Rufus' troops had offered their general the throne. Even this seemed not to bother the emperor. He merely threatened to punish the troops involved, then returned to his meal. For eight days, "apparently trying to ignore the whole affair," in Suetonius' opinion, Nero issued not a single order in relation to the upheaval in the west and made no special announcements.[9] At Rome, the Senate, concerned about the security of the state mint at Lugdunum, Vindex's former capital, ordered Nero's new legion, the 1st Italica, to march from Ravenna to Gaul to secure the city. The senator Rubrius Gallus hurried to Ravenna from Rome to take command of the unit and supporting auxiliary cavalry, and then lead them across the Alps.

By early April, Nero had moved a little closer to Rome, taking up residence at his Antium villa. Urgent dispatches kept arriving in quick succession, telling of Galba's troops swearing loyalty to their governor and raising the threat that they would march on Rome. Nero ordered Galba's property seized and put up for sale and had Galba's freedmen at Rome arrested. News would also arrive that once the 1st Italica Legion reached Lugdunum and linked up with the remnants of the 18th Cohort of the City Cohorts that Vindex had left there, the people of Lugdunum, many descended from retired legion veterans, declared their loyalty to Nero. But it was the only city in Gaul to do so. Following Vindex's defeat at Vesontio, the majority of Gauls were bitter and remained resolute in their determination to throw off Roman rule.

Meanwhile, although it was back at its bases in Upper Germany, Rufus' army was unsettled, and there was unrest in the four legions based in the province of Lower Germany, where the locals were generally inclined toward Nero but where the governor, Fonteius Capito, was not. Urged by Helius to act decisively, Nero sent his loyal general Petronius Turpilianus at the head of a flying column of Praetorian cavalry into southern Gaul to put down the unrest and forestall any attempt by Galba's troops to enter Italy. And, at last, the emperor agreed to return to Rome. "He hurried back to Rome in a state of terror," said Suetonius.[10]

Arriving at the capital without ceremony, he did not address the Senate or the people. Distrusting everyone, he dismissed the consuls from office and appointed himself sole consul. One night, he decided to brief the foremost senators and Equestrians on what he proposed to do and summoned them to the still-uncompleted Golden House.[11] He said that he would ask the Senate to conscript all able-bodied men at Rome into an army that he would lead to Gaul to end the unrest.

Nero had already ordered the raising of a new legion from loyal barefoot marines and sailors of the Tyrrhenian Fleet.[12] He had also sent urgent orders to Alexandria for legionaries and Evocati militia transferred there for the now-aborted Ethiopian expedition to urgently come to Rome by sea to join the march on Gaul. This was the extent of his strategy for maintaining his tottering regime. "After a brief discussion of the Gallic situation," said Suetonius, "he devoted the remainder of the session to demonstrating a completely new type of water-organ."

"I have discovered a way by which the water-organ will produce louder and more musical tones," Nero announced. He went on to explain the mechanical complexities of several models. "I will have them installed in the theater," he added.[13]

The senators and Equestrians left the meeting shaking their heads—the emperor seemed to have lost his grip on reality. Over the coming days, Nero dedicated a shrine to his late wife Poppaea Sabina and held lavish banquets, where, according to Suetonius, he entertained his guests with "comic songs about the leaders of the revolt," which he had composed. Nero's songs were witty and catchy. "These have since become popular favorites," said Suetonius.[14]

Emerging from one banquet with his arms around the shoulders of two close friends, Nero declared, "When I reach Gaul, I'll immediately step in front of the embattled enemy and weep and weep. That will soften their hearts and win back their loyalty. Then, the next day, I'll stroll among my joyful troops singing victory songs—which I really ought to be composing right now."[15]

When June arrived, so too did news that Nero's loyal general Petronius Turpilianus, commanding his advance force in Gaul, "had also espoused the cause of Galba," and Turpilianus' cavalry had gone over to Galba. Nero was at dinner at the time. Ripping up the dispatch, he overturned the dining table in his fury. A pair of glass goblets shattered on the floor. With the defection of Turpilianus, Nero "held no more hope in arms."[16] A plethora of schemes entered his head. In one, he would don mourning black and mount the Rostra to beg the forgiveness of his people for his sins; a speech to this effect was later found on Nero's Palatium desk. But escape to Egypt, the land of his dreams, firmed up as a better option.

Sending several of his most trusted freedmen to Ostia to prepare a flotilla of ships for flight to Alexandria, the emperor declared, "Even though we may be driven from our empire, this little talent will support us there."[17]

He was referring to his talent as an artist. Nero seemed to believe that he could live as a private citizen and singer in Egypt. As a last resort, he ordered Locusta the sorceress to make up a draft of poison for him, which he placed in a small golden casket. Feeling insecure in the vast new palace that had arisen from the ashes of the Great Fire, he slipped out of the Golden House and hurried across the Tiber to the Servilian Gardens. There he took up residence in its riverside villa as he waited for a ship to arrive from Ostia and speed him away to Egypt. Summoning those tribunes of the Praetorian Cohorts on whom he felt he could rely, he urged them to flee with him, bringing along troops to protect him. Some answered evasively; other refused outright. All turned their back on him.

"Is it so terrible a thing to die?" called one officer, repeating a line from Virgil, as he walked away.[18]

Matters now moved quickly to a head. While Tigellinus had been in Greece with Nero, his co-prefect Nymphidius had won the loyalty of the men of the Praetorian Cohorts at Rome. Now, Nymphidius instructed Tigellinus to lay down his sword and go quietly into retirement. Finding no support among the Praetorians, the once-powerful Tigellinus did as bidden and slunk away. The source of Nymphidius' newfound power was financial—in Galba's name, he had secretly promised every man of the Praetorian and German Cohorts two thousand sesterces if they would obey him alone and swear allegiance to Galba.

Late on the evening of June 8, having heard this and learning of Nero's plan to escape to Egypt, the majority of the members of the Senate entered the Praetorian barracks and called an assembly of the troops. They then declared Nero an enemy of the State, announced their choice of Galba as emperor in his stead, and ordered the German Cohorts to cease protecting Nero. Led by Nymphidius, the Praetorians then hailed Galba emperor. The Praetorian prefect, who had been raised to his powerful position by Nero, then issued instructions for the now deposed emperor to be found, arrested, brought in laden with chains, and executed.

THE FINAL CURTAIN

A lone near-contemporaneous account of the demise of Nero has come down to us, the one written by Suetonius. This, according to Suetonius, is how the final curtain fell on Nero's life.

At midnight, the young emperor awoke with a start. Though unaware of what had transpired at the Praetorian barracks, he sensed that something was amiss. Wearing the tunic he had been sleeping in, and barefoot, he left his bedchamber in the Servilian Gardens villa. Outside, he discovered that his bodyguards from the German Cohorts had melted away. The Germans had withdrawn to their barracks just inside the Servian Wall to the south of the gardens and murdered their prefect.

Nero sent servants to fetch friends who were staying with him at the Servilian Gardens. When only several came, he went with a few servants to the rooms of the others, only to find the doors closed and barred. Not a soul answered his knock. Returning to his room, he found that while he had been absent, the caretakers of the gardens had slipped in and stolen his bed linen and the golden box containing Locusta's poison— the poison now being more valuable to Nero than the golden casket.

Nero shouted for Spiculus the gladiator or any other trained executioner to come and put an end to him. Messengers bustled away on the errand. But Spiculus was dead, cut down in the Forum by a mob that since the news that the Senate and Praetorians had declared for Galba, had been roaming the streets of Rome in search of anyone associated with Nero. Statues of Nero in the Forum had been knocked down and the pieces heaped over the bloodied body of the famous gladiator. No one answered the emperor's plea for an executioner.

"What? Have I neither friends nor enemies left?" Nero despaired, before dashing from the villa to the riverbank.[1]

His few remaining friends and servants hurried after him and dissuaded him from throwing himself into the river.

"All I want is a secluded spot where I can hide and collect myself," he said.[2]

At this, his freedman Phaon suggested his own villa, four miles northeast of the city, between the Nomentan and Salarian Ways. Nero agreed, even though the course to Phaon's villa would take him back through the city and right by the Praetorian barracks. Five horses were found. Nero strapped on a pair of daggers and then, wearing a faded cloak and a farmer's hat, mounted up, further disguising himself by putting a handkerchief to his mouth—he would pretend that he was unwell. Four men rode with him as he set off from the gardens: Phaon, Petitions Secretary Epaphroditus, the eunuch Sporus, and an unnamed servant.

Probably crossing the Tiber at the Pons Neronianus, a bridge named after Nero, the five riders made their way along Campus Martius streets, which were alive with people. As they rode, a mild earth tremor rocked the city, and lightning flashed in the night sky. Not long after passing through the Nomentan Gate, they heard voices on the still air of the warm summer night. From the northern wall of the Praetorian barracks on their right, Praetorians on guard were shouting about what they expected Galba would do to Nero once he laid hands on him. At this point, Praetorian search parties were on the prowl, looking for the deposed emperor, having found the Golden House deserted. The troops arrived too late at the Servilian Gardens, too: The imperial bird had flown.

Outside the city, the Nomentan Way was crowded with farmers' carts bringing produce into Rome. "Those people are in pursuit of the emperor," one farmer was heard to say as the five horsemen trotted by.

"What news of Nero in town?" called another to the riders.[3]

None of the horsemen replied. They bore on through the night. At one point they encountered a corpse at the roadside. Nero's horse shied at the smell of death, forcing Nero to take the handkerchief from his mouth as he used both hands to steady the animal. A farmer passing at this moment happened to be a retired soldier of the Praetorian Cohorts, and he recognized the exposed face of his emperor.

"Hail, Caesar!" the former soldier called, coming stiffly to attention.[4]

Nero hurriedly returned the handkerchief to its place, and he and his companions rode on. Reaching a lane that led to the rear of Phaon's villa, they dismounted and continued on foot. The lane became a track through bushes and a briar patch that skirted a reedy pond. Nero, barefoot still, had his companions spread a cloak for him to walk on as they crossed the thorny ground. He was clearly distressed, and Phaon suggested he lie low in a nearby gravel pit for a time.

"No, I refuse to go underground before I die," Nero replied.[5]

They reached the villa's rear wall, and as several of the men burrowed a hole in the wall, Nero went to the nearby pond and scooped up a little water in his cupped hands. "This is Nero's special brew," he quipped as he drank.[6]

While waiting for the opening in the wall to be completed, he sat picking thorns from his cloak. When the gap was large enough, all five of them crawled through the fence, and Phaon led them into the house. Nero sank down onto a couch, and Phaon brought him coarse bread and a cup of water. Nero declined the bread, but gratefully took the cup.

"I was still thirsty," he said, sipping the water.[7]

Phaon now bade Nero farewell, saying that he would return to the city and keep his eyes and ears open for information that might help him. After Phaon's departure, Nero sat for a long time, as if in a daze.

"Caesar, I insist that you try to escape the degrading fate that threatens you," one of his three remaining companions, almost certainly Epaphroditus, eventually said. The other two concurred.

Tears were streaming down Nero's cheeks as he instructed them to dig a grave in the garden for his remains and to collect wood for a funeral pyre. "Dead?" he said, half to himself, as the trio set to work. "And so great an artist!"[8]

Toward dawn, a runner arrived from the city, bearing a note from Phaon. Nero snatched the note from the man's hands, impatiently broke the seal, and read the contents. Phaon warned that the Senate had declared Nero an enemy of the state and that he was to be taken alive so that he could be punished in "ancient style." Nero, having left executions up to others, had to ask what "ancient style" meant.

"The executioners strip their victim naked, thrust his head into a wooden fork, and then flog him to death with rods," the learned Epaphroditus informed him.

Terrified by the prospect, Nero drew one of his daggers, tried its point on his finger, threw it down, then repeated the act with the second dagger. "The fatal hour has not yet come," he declared. Turning to Sporus, he begged him to weep for him and to mourn him once he had gone. Then, he implored all of his companions to set him an example by being the first to suicide. All three demurred.

He bemoaned his own cowardice and then muttered, "This certainly is no credit to Nero, no credit at all." He paced about, saying, "Come, pull yourself together!"[9]

A large party of riders was now heard coming up the road to the villa's front door. Peering out the door, one of Nero's companions saw that they were Praetorian cavalry. Perhaps Phaon had informed the Praetorians where to find the object of their quest. Perhaps Phaon's messenger had been followed. Perhaps the Praetorian veteran who had recognized Nero on the Nomentan Way had told someone about it once he reached the city. Perhaps the Praetorians were coming to search the villa of Nero's freedman as a matter of course. Whatever the cause, the troops were just minutes away.

Nero grabbed up one of the daggers. "Help me, Epaphroditus," he pleaded.

As Nero held the knife to his own throat with both hands, his secretary gripped his hands. Nero gave one last instruction: "Don't let them take my head." Then, on Nero's signal, both he and Epaphroditus thrust the dagger into his throat.[10]

A little later, a Praetorian centurion strode into the room. Finding Nero lying on the couch with blood gushing from his throat as the others stood around him, the officer rushed to his side. Kneeling beside the dying man, he used the end of his blood-red cloak in an attempt to staunch the bleeding.

"Too late!" Nero gasped, looking up at the centurion with bulging eyes. "Is this your duty?" he asked.[11] In other words, did the centurion's duty require him to save his emperor's life only to permit Nero to be later subjected to an agonizing death in "the ancient style"?

According to Suetonius, thirty-year-old Nero died in the centurion's arms, this ninth day of June, AD 68. On the centurion's orders, a Praetorian galloped back to the city from Phaon's villa with those tidings. But Dio Chrysostom, a Bithynian philosopher based at Rome and writing around the same time as Suetonius, believed that the truth surrounding Nero's demise never came out.[12] Plutarch later wrote that Icelus, a freedman in the employ of Galba, had been incarcerated at the Praetorian barracks by orders of the Senate until that very evening. He was still there, but a free man now, when the Praetorian messenger arrived from Phaon's villa.

Icelus did not believe the soldier's story. He immediately jumped on a horse and rode out to the villa to see for himself if Nero truly was there, and truly was dead. The house was cordoned off by Praetorians, but Icelus, announcing that he was the freedman of new emperor Galba, pushed his way inside. He found the centurion and Nero's last three companions guarding the corpse. "I went myself to the body and saw him lying dead," Icelus later reported to Galba.[13]

When Icelus saw the body, the centurion was in a quandary. The officer's instructions required him, if he found Nero dead, to take the head back to his superiors. But Epaphroditus, a man with considerable presence, had reportedly argued against defiling the body of the late emperor. Consequently, the centurion asked the freedman of the new emperor to adjudicate in the matter. Icelus advised him not to decapitate the last of the Caesars. The head of the dead man would not go on public display for all to see, but would be hurriedly incinerated with the rest of the body on a funeral pyre.

Icelus hastened back to the city. Staying just long enough to make travel preparations, he set off for Spain to inform Galba that Nero was dead and that the older man was now emperor of Rome. Icelus made the journey to Clunia, where Galba had retired, in seven days. This was record time, and it was not until the official Senate announcement of Nero's death and Galba's elevation to the throne arrived some days later that Galba would believe Icelus.

At Rome, one senator, Mauriscus, warned the House that "in a short time, they might wish for Nero again."[14] How right he turned out to be. Ahead lay a year of turmoil. Within seven months, Galba would be assassinated at Rome by troops dissatisfied by his refusal to pay the bonuses that Nymphidius had promised them for deserting Nero. Galba's short-lived successor would be Marcus Otho, Nero's former best friend, who himself would be dead within another three months after his army was defeated. The leader of the conquering army was Aulus Vitellius, Galba's appointee as commander of the legions on the lower Rhine. Vitellius subsequently succeeded Otho as emperor; this was the same Vitellius who, as chief judge at the Neronian Games in AD 65, had called Nero back to perform in the Theater of Pompey after he had suffered stage fright. Vitellius, who would even celebrate funeral rites for Nero once he became emperor, would be assassinated in December AD 69, to be replaced by Nero's toadying general Vespasian, the first of the Flavian emperors.

As for Nero, his body was reportedly cremated, swiftly, privately, and intact, wearing the gold-embroidered robes that he had used in the January 1 ceremonials on the Capitol. His ever-faithful mistress Acte and his childhood nurses Ecloge and Alexandria carried his ashes and bones in a white porphyry casket to the tomb of his father's Domitius family, on Rome's Pincian Hill. For decades after, flowers were laid on his grave by admirers, every spring and summer. Statues of him mysteriously appeared on the Rostra, and edicts would be circulated about the city in his name by those who regretted his passing, as if he were still alive.

The legend of *Nero redivivus*, or Nero returned to life, persisted until the fifth century. This held that Nero had never died, or that he would be resurrected, would gather a vast army in the East, and would return to Rome to destroy his enemies. Dio Chrysostom, who lived between AD 40 and 120 and resided in Rome during the reign of the tyrannical

Domitian, said this about Nero: "Even now everyone wishes he were still alive, and the great majority do believe that he still is."[15]

Had the body burned at Phaon's villa actually been that of a Nero look-alike? Had Icelus and Epaphroditus conspired to spin a tale about Nero's suicide to permit Nero to escape to a life of anonymity and allow Galba to take the throne? Three times over the two decades after Nero's demise, lyre-playing individuals who looked like Nero would appear in the East and claim to be him. The most famous emerged in Parthia during the reign of Domitian. "Twenty years after [Nero's death], when I was a young man," Suetonius wrote, "a mysterious individual came forward claiming to be Nero. And so magical was the sound of his name to the Parthians' ears that they supported him to the best of their ability, and only handed him over with great reluctance."[16] Once in Roman hands, the pseudo Neros were all executed.

Helius the freedman, who had remained loyal to Nero to the end, was executed by Galba, along with two other of Nero's loyal freedmen, including Patrobius. Even the sorceress Locusta was put to death. Nero's general Petronius Turpilianus was among a number of others executed by Galba; his crimes were having been loyal to Nero for many years and commanding respect among the soldiery. Praetorian Prefect Nymphidius, who had engineered the troops' defection from Nero at Rome, an act that had given Galba the throne, was likewise executed by Galba—for being too powerful. Just as Galba would make numerous questionable appointments, giving powerful, well-paid posts to exiles, former criminals and old men with shameful pasts, he unaccountably protected Tigellinus. But it was only a short reprieve; Tigellinus would be executed during Otho's reign.

Otho also restored to office many of Nero's freedmen. One of the latter, Epaphroditus, who allegedly helped Nero end his life, continued to serve the Palatium for decades. He was petitions secretary to Domitian, a post he held for many years until just months before that emperor's assassination, when the secretary fell victim to Domitian's paranoia and was executed.

Nero continued to fascinate Romans for generations to come. Pliny the Younger would write, early in the second century, of the death of a friend who "was bringing out a history of the various fates of the people put to death or banished by Nero." This friend of Pliny, Gaius Fannius, had by the time he died already published three volumes of his Neronian history. "He was all the more anxious to complete the series when he saw how eagerly the first books were read by a large public," said Pliny.[17]

This fascination with Nero persists to this day, no doubt in part because of his unconventional character and the many famous figures and historic events that figured in his life story. The interest can also be attributed to the fact that as Suetonius wrote, "with Nero, the line of the Caesars became extinct."[18] Nero had no heirs. While many future emperors would include "Caesar" in their name, Nero was the last of the Caesar dynasty, a situation that many Romans lamented.

And as Josephus was to complain, with no descendants to defend Nero's reputation, it became open season for any author who cared to conjure up sensational stories about Nero and his reign and thereby profit from their inventions. Rather than execrating Nero, we might pity him. For most of his short life, he was controlled and manipulated by others: his mother Agrippina, Seneca and Burrus, Tigellinus, and Poppaea Sabina. He dreamed of being an artist and driving chariots. In the end, he realized his dreams, and they brought about his downfall, providing his enemies with the ammunition they needed to destroy his reputation and his support.

Was Nero the cruel and crazy ruler that his detractors claimed he was? Certainly, he was no saint. If his biographers are to be believed—and all can be considered hostile witnesses—blame him for his mother's murder and also for that of his adoptive brother Britannicus. But extenuating circumstances—his mother's insane ambition—might be argued in both cases. Meanwhile, the ambitious Poppaea was probably the person behind the execution of Nero's wife Octavia.

There is no escaping that Nero authorized the executions of men convicted of plotting to kill him. But the governors of various American states today authorize the execution of convicted felons. Does that necessarily make them cruel? If you believe it does, then yes, Nero was also cruel. Did Nero burn followers of Isis following the Great Fire? Some historians believe such a thing never even occurred. If he did burn them, then this was certainly cruel, but no more so than crucifixion, the accepted method of execution for all noncitizens throughout Roman times, yet an execution method that could prolong the victim's sufferings for days. These were cruel times.

Was he a tyrant? If Nero was such a tyrant, how was it that Nerva, who would be rated one of Rome's most wise and just emperors, willingly and actively served Nero and led the hunt for those who plotted against him? Far from possessing a track record of tyranny and cruelty, Nero ordained that no man, gladiator or convicted criminal, should die in the arena. And as Suetonius pointed out, Nero was incredibly tolerant of those who lampooned him, while his patience with Thrasea's years of insulting and royally haughty behavior is almost beyond belief. And when Nero said that he would have spared Torquatus Silanus had the senator not taken his own life, we can believe him. On one occasion, Nero declared that he would not stand in the way of clemency for one of his most bitter critics. In fact, Nero frequently gave the Senate the final say in the fate of his opponents, just as he returned various ancient powers to the House.

Far from being mad, Nero was in many ways a visionary. His plans for massive engineering works were lambasted by the likes of Tacitus and Suetonius as fantastical and impossible, yet the Corinth Canal would be realized and would follow Nero's design. Nero's strict building regulations and clever incentives for the restoration of Rome were innovative and the first of their kind in Rome's history. Tacitus had to agree that through these regulations, Nero created a much more beautiful and utilitarian Rome, yet the historian had to add the ludicrous complaint that some people perceived the city's new, wider streets as unhealthy.

Nero's downfall and the besmirching of his name began with the Great Fire. The emperor's critics and enemies were able to turn that calamity against him, by blaming the fire on him. In the same way, later Christian writers would, falsely, cast Nero as the first Roman emperor to persecute the Christians, in the wake of the fire. He was, after all, an easy target: young, naive, insecure, bisexual, timid, artistic.

Nero was also accused of spending money like a drunkard, yet he reduced a variety of taxes, and the empire was never more prosperous than during his reign, up until the fire. The cost of rebuilding Rome and of constructing his extravagant Golden House did impose a heavy financial burden on the provinces. This certainly contributed to the decline in Nero's popularity in Gaul and exacerbated Jewish unrest in Jerusalem caused by the greed and mismanagement of successive procurators of Judea. No doubt, this rebellion in the East and the struggle that Roman forces initially had in putting it down convinced Vindex that his Gallic revolt could succeed.

Yet, just as Nero's reign was initially made at Rome, it was at Rome that it was undone. The patricians of Rome despised young Nero for his artistic aspirations, just as they despised the provincials and freedmen whom Nero employed in powerful positions. Men like Thrasea actively snubbed their noses at Nero while working against him behind the scenes. As the Piso Plot demonstrated, there were enough malcontents among the upper class and military officers to engineer a concerted attempt to deliver Julius Caesar's fate to the fifth emperor of Rome. And even though that plot failed, it planted a seed in the minds of other ambitious men.

Significantly, the Piso Plot emerged in the wake of the Great Fire. Without the fire, there probably would never have been the courage or the commitment for a Piso Plot. The persistent rumors that swept the city after the fire, the concerted propaganda campaign directed against Nero, gave the Piso plotters the gumption to proceed. The rumor regarding the reading of the Sibylline Books can realistically be traced to Thrasea. And perhaps he inspired some of the other rumors. But it is unlikely that he was the lone rumormonger. There would have been others, men who used the fire to launch bids for the throne.

Why did Galba spare Tigellinus? Could it be that Tigellinus worked behind the scenes on Galba's behalf following the fire, spreading rumors against Nero? And was it the knowledge of Tigellinus' support that gave Galba the courage to launch his bid for the throne from faraway Spain? Certainly, Galba's fearful retreat to Clunia came after Tigellinus lost his power at Rome.

Still another man in authority could have been working against Nero behind the scenes from the time of the Great Fire. There can be no denying that Praetorian Prefect Nymphidius made Nero's downfall possible, and inevitable, by unseating Tigellinus and bribing the Praetorian and

German Cohorts to desert the emperor. If Nymphidius was indeed prefect of the Cohortes Vigiles the night the Great Fire began, as is believed, he may well have been the "one who gives us authority," the man who had sent underlings around the already-burning city to spread the fire. And he may well have been the one to ignite the second fire in the property of Tigellinus, the man he later forced into retirement to gain sole power at the head of the Praetorians.

There had previously been a Praetorian prefect who eyed the throne for himself—Sejanus, Tiberius' slimy underling. To give himself a connection with the imperial family and improve his claim to the throne, Sejanus had married the sister of Claudius and Germanicus. Nymphidius had a similar but even stronger connection, a blood connection, with the Caesars, claiming to be a son of Claudius. It is not unrealistic to imagine opportunistic Nymphidius playing puppet master to a four-year campaign to unseat Nero—a campaign that began the moment the Great Fire spluttered into life. And he succeeded, overthrowing Nero and putting Galba on the throne, no doubt with plans to remove Galba once the prefect felt that he himself could command the loyalty of the army. But his scheme backfired—crusty, suspicious Galba recognized Nymphidius' ambition and saw through his plan, terminating plot and plotter in one fell swoop.

Had there been no Great Fire, Nero would have embarked on his Ethiopian and Caspian Gates operations and may well have become the new Alexander the Great. Hailed by his army, his people, and the writers of history, he might have lived and reigned for another fifty or sixty years, fathering sons with a new wife and propagating the Julian line.

With Nero's demise came the end of imperial Rome's founding dynasty. After Nero, there would sometimes be blood links between emperors, but never would there be a dynasty, or an era, like that of the Caesars. The end of Nero, and the end of his family's dynasty, was one of history's great turning points. Nero's end began with the flames of July 19, AD 64. There can be no doubting that Roman history, and world history, would have been very different had it not been for the Great Fire of Rome.

Notes

Introduction

1. Cassius Dio, *Roman History* 62.16.
2. Ibid. 62.18.
3. Suetonius, *The Twelve Caesars* 6.38.
4. Josephus, *Jewish Antiquities* 20.8.3.
5. Tacitus, *Annals* 13.20.
6. Josephus, *Jewish Antiquities* 20.8.3.
7. Suetonius, *The Twelve Caesars* 6.16.
8. *New Encyclopaedia Britannica*, 18th ed. (Chicago: Encyclopaedia Britannica, 1987), s.v. "Nero."
9. Dio, *Roman History* 62.14.
10. Suetonius, *The Twelve Caesars* 12.10.
11. Tacitus, *Annals* 15.44.
12. 2 Tim. 4:21.
13. Acts 28:15.
14. Suetonius, *The Twelve Caesars* 3.36.
15. Philo, *In Flaccum* 1.
16. Suetonius, *The Twelve Caesars* 5.25.
17. Ibid. 12.1.

Chapter I: The January Oath

1. Based on Vegetius, "The Organization of the Legion," in *The Military Institutions of the Romans* 2.
2. Tacitus, *Annals* 15.46.
3. Ibid. 13.3.
4. Suetonius, *The Twelve Caesars* 6.52.
5. Ibid. 6.20.

6. Tacitus, *Annals* 15.33.
7. Suetonius, *The Twelve Caesars* 6.53.
8. Tacitus, *Annals* 15.33.

Chapter II: The Rival Prefects

1. Tacitus, *Annals* 14.51.
2. Ibid.
3. Ibid.
4. Ibid. 14.57.
5. Ibid. 13.21.
6. Ibid. 14.22.
7. Ibid.
8. Ibid. 14.57.
9. Ibid.
10. Ibid.
11. Ibid. 14.59.
12. Seneca, *Letters to Lucilius* 113.
13. Ibid. 104.
14. Horace, *Odes* 3.29.5–12.

Chapter III: The Poets

1. Martial.
2. Tacitus, *Annals* 15.49.
3. Pliny the Younger, *Letters* 3.21.
4. Seneca, *Letters to Lucilius* 112.

Chapter IV: The Former Chief Secretary

1. Seneca, *Letters to Lucilius* 113.
2. Tacitus, *Annals* 14.65.
3. Ibid. 14.53.
4. Seneca, *Letters to Lucilius* 123.
5. Ibid.
6. Ibid.

Chapter V: The Flame

1. Suetonius, *The Twelve Caesars* 6.28.

2. Tacitus, *Agricola* 6.
3. Ibid.
4. Suetonius, *The Twelve Caesars* 10.3.
5. Pliny the Younger, *Letters* 3.5.
6. Ibid.

Chapter VI: The Water Commissioner

1. Martial, *Epigrams* 9.17.5–6.
2. Frontinus, *Aqueducts* 2.87.
3. Ibid.

Chapter VII: The Singing Emperor

1. Tacitus, *Annals* 15.33.
2. Suetonius, *The Twelve Caesars* 6.20.
3. Ibid.
4. Ibid.
5. Tacitus, *Annals* 15.34.

Chapter VIII: The Gladiatorial Contest

1. Tacitus, *Annals* 15.34.
2. Cassius Dio, *Roman History* 62.15.
3. Tacitus, *Annals* 15.34.
4. Suetonius, *The Twelve Caesars* 5.21.
5. Tacitus, *Annals* 15.34.
6. Dio, *Roman History* 62.13.
7. Tacitus, *Annals* 15.35.
8. Ibid.

Chapter IX: The Jews and the Christians

1. Josephus, *Life* 3.
2. Gal. 1:13.
3. Rom. 15:24.
4. Cave, *Lives of the Apostles* 1, 7.
5. Acts 28:31.
6. Cave, *Lives of the Apostles* 1, 7.
7. Cassius Dio, *Roman History* 61.7.

8. Josephus, *Life* 3.
9. Plutarch, *Galba.*
10. Tacitus, *Annals* 13.45.
11. Suetonius, *The Twelve Caesars* 8.3.
12. Plutarch, *Otho.*
13. Tacitus, *Annals* 13.46.

Chapter X: The Lake Banquet

1. Tacitus, *Annals* 15.36.
2. Ibid.
3. Ibid.
4. Ibid.

Chapter XI: The Charioteer

1. Suetonius, *The Twelve Caesars* 6.22.
2. Ibid.

Chapter XII: The Fire

1. There is no record of these games being scheduled for AD 64. However, Nero, being a member of the Julio-Claudian line and also being a lover of chariot racing, is sure to have planned to celebrate the games of Caesar.
2. Suetonius, *The Twelve Caesars* 6.23.
3. Tacitus, *Annals* 15.38.
4. Ibid.
5. Ibid.
6. Cassius Dio, *Roman History* 62.16.
7. Tacitus, *Annals* 15.38.
8. Dio, *Roman History* 62.16.
9. Tacitus, *Annals* 15.38.
10. Ibid.
11. Ibid.
12. Seneca, *Letters to Lucilius* 114.
13. Ibid.
14. Suetonius, *The Twelve Caesars* 6.38.
15. Tacitus, *Annals* 15.39.
16. Ibid.
17. Ibid. 15.40.

18. Ibid. describes this as "Tigellinus' Aemilian property." This could refer to either of two buildings. The first was the Aemilian Basilica in the Forum; the second, the Aemilian warehouse complex at the docks in Regio XIII. The property in question is most likely to have been the basilica. The fire spread from the Aemilian property up onto the Capitoline Mount and, from it, to the Campus Martius. Had this new fire started at the warehouse complex, it had to pass over districts already razed in the initial blaze to reach the Capitoline Mount, whereas the basilica stood right at the foot of the Capitol.

19. "Fighting Fire with Fire," "Decisions Under Fire," and "Knowing the Enemy," episodes on *Catalyst*, ABC-TV, Australia, October 29, 2009.

20. Tacitus, *Annals* 15.41.

21. Ibid. 15.40.

22. Ibid.

Chapter XIII: The Blame

1. "The Great Fire of Rome," episode 304, *Secrets of the Dead*, PBS, November 27, 2002.

2. Cassius Dio, *Roman History* 62.18.

3. Suetonius, *The Twelve Caesars* 6.39.

4. Ibid. 6.38.

5. Dio, *Roman History* 62.16.

6. Tacitus, *Annals* 15.39.

7. Ibid. 15.40.

8. Ibid. 15.41.

9. Suetonius, *The Twelve Caesars* 6.38.

10. Dio, *Roman History* 62.16.

11. Ibid. 62.18.

12. Ibid.

13. Tacitus, *Annals* 15.42.

14. Ibid.

15. Ibid.

16. Suetonius, *The Twelve Caesars* 6.16.

17. Ibid.

18. Tacitus, *Annals* 15.43.

19. Ibid.

20. Ibid.

21. Ibid.

22. Ibid. 15.44.

23. Ibid.

24. Dio, *Roman History* 62.18.
25. Ibid.
26. Tacitus, *Annals* 15.44.
27. Ibid.
28. Ibid.
29. Ibid.
30. Ibid.
31. Ibid.
32. Ibid.
33. Ibid. 15.47.
34. Suetonius, *The Twelve Caesars* 6.36.
35. Tacitus, *Annals* 15.47.

Chapter XIV: The Conspiracy

1. Tacitus, *Annals* 15.42.
2. Suetonius, *The Twelve Caesars* 6.31.
3. Ibid.
4. Ibid.
5. Ibid.
6. Tacitus, *Annals* 15.49.
7. Ibid.
8. Ibid.
9. Ibid. 15.50.
10. Ibid. 15.49.
11. Ibid. 15.48.
12. Suetonius, *The Twelve Caesars* 6.33.
13. Tacitus, *Annals* 15.53.
14. Ibid. 15.50.
15. Ibid.
16. Ibid.
17. Ibid. 15.51.
18. Ibid.

Chapter XV: The Unraveling

1. Tacitus, *Annals* 15.52.
2. Ibid.
3. Ibid.
4. Ibid. 15.60.

5. Ibid.
6. Ibid. 15.50.
7. Ibid. 15.54.
8. Ibid. 15.55.
9. Josephus, *Jewish Antiquities*, preface, 2.
10. Tacitus, *Annals* 15.55.
11. Ibid.
12. Ibid.
13. Ibid. 15.59.
14. Ibid.
15. Ibid.
16. Ibid. 15.57.
17. Ibid. 15.58.

Chapter XVI: The Suicide of Seneca

1. Tacitus, *Annals* 15.63.
2. Ibid. 15.61.
3. Ibid.
4. Ibid.
5. Ibid.
6. Ibid.
7. Ibid.
8. Ibid. 15.65.
9. Ibid. 15.62.
10. Ibid.
11. Seneca, *Letters to Lucilius* 104.
12. Tacitus, *Annals* 15.62.
13. Ibid. 15.63.
14. Seneca, *Letters to Lucilius* 104.
15. Tacitus, *Annals* 15.63.
16. Ibid. 15.64.
17. Ibid.
18. Ibid.
19. Ibid.
20. Ibid.

Chapter XVII: The Purge

1. Tacitus, *Annals* 15.57.

2. Ibid. 15.66.
3. Ibid.
4. Ibid.
5. Ibid. 15.67.
6. Ibid.
7. Ibid.
8. Ibid.
9. Ibid.
10. Ibid.
11. Ibid. 15.68.
12. Ibid. 15.69.
13. Ibid.
14. Ibid. 15.71.
15. Ibid.
16. Ibid.

Chapter XVIII: The New Stage

1. Tacitus, *Annals* 16.4.
2. Ibid.
3. Suetonius, *The Twelve Caesars* 9.4.
4. Tacitus, *Annals* 16.4.
5. Ibid.
6. Ibid. 16.6.
7. Ibid.
8. Cassius Dio, *Roman History* 62.28.
9. Suetonius, *The Twelve Caesars* 6.35.
10. Tacitus, *Annals* 16.6.
11. Suetonius, *The Twelve Caesars* 6.35.
12. Dio, *Roman History* 62.28.
13. Suetonius, *The Twelve Caesars* 6.35.
14. Tacitus, *Annals* 16.7.
15. Ibid. 16.15.
16. Ibid. 16.8.
17. Ibid.
18. Ibid. 16.9.
19. Ibid. 16.10.
20. Ibid. 16.11.
21. Ibid. 16.13.

Chapter XIX: The Informers

1. Tacitus, *Annals* 14.49.
2. Suetonius, *The Twelve Caesars* 6.39.
3. Tacitus, *Annals* 16.14.
4. Ibid.
5. Ibid. 16.18.
6. Ibid. 16.22.

Chapter XX: The Crowning of a King

1. Cassius Dio, *Roman History* 63.1.
2. Ibid. 63.2.
3. Ibid. 63.3.
4. Ibid.
5. Ibid.
6. Tacitus, *Annals* 16.24.
7. Ibid. 15.43.
8. Dio, *Roman History* 63.4.
9. Ibid.
10. Tacitus, *Annals* 16.24.
11. Suetonius, *The Twelve Caesars* 6.13.
12. Dio, *Roman History* 63.5.
13. Ibid.
14. Ibid. 63.6.
15. Ibid.
16. Ibid.
17. Ibid. 63.7.
18. Ibid.
19. Tacitus, *Annals* 16.26.
20. Ibid.

Chapter XXI: The Trial of Thrasea and Soranus

1. Tacitus, *Annals* 16.22.
2. Ibid. 16.28.
3. Ibid. 16.29.
4. Ibid.
5. Ibid.
6. Ibid. 16.31.

7. Ibid.
8. Ibid. 16.32.
9. Ibid.
10. Ibid.
11. Ibid. 16.34.
12. Ibid. 16.35.

Chapter XXII: The New Alexander

1. Cassius Dio, *Roman History* 62.12.
2. Ibid.
3. Suetonius, *The Twelve Caesars* 6.20.
4. Ibid.
5. Ibid.

Chapter XXIII: The Apostles and the Jewish Revolt

1. Josephus, *Life* 5.
2. Ibid. 4.
3. Ibid.
4. Ibid. 5.
5. 2 Tim. 4:11.
6. Ibid. 4:14–17.
7. Ibid. 4:2.
8. Cassius Dio, *Roman History* 62.14.
9. Ibid.
10. Tacitus, *Annals* 15.10.
11. Dio, *Roman History* 62.17.
12. Ibid. 62.4.
13. Ibid.
14. Suetonius, *The Twelve Caesars* 6.40.

Chapter XXIV: The Fall of Nero

1. Cassius Dio, *Roman History* 63.22.
2. Ibid.
3. Ibid. 63.25.
4. Suetonius, *The Twelve Caesars* 6.23.
5. Ibid. 6.41.
6. Plutarch, *Galba.*

7. Ibid.

8. Suetonius, *The Twelve Caesars* 7.11.

9. Ibid. 6.40.

10. Ibid. 6.41.

11. One of Nero's successors, Otho, resumed work on the Golden House, seeking five hundred thousand sesterces from the Senate for the project, but it never seems to have been completed.

12. This recruitment would form the basis of the new 1st Adiutrix Legion.

13. Suetonius, *The Twelve Caesars* 7.41.

14. Ibid. 7.42.

15. Ibid. 7.43.

16. Dio, *Roman History* 63.27.

17. Ibid.

18. Suetonius, *The Twelve Caesars* 6.47.

Chapter XXV: The Final Curtain

1. Suetonius, *The Twelve Caesars* 6.47.

2. Ibid. 6.48.

3. Ibid.

4. Ibid.

5. Ibid.

6. Ibid.

7. Ibid.

8. Ibid. 6.49.

9. Ibid.

10. Ibid.

11. Ibid.

12. Dio Chrysostom, *Discourses* 21.9–10.

13. Plutarch, *Galba.*

14. Ibid.

15. Dio Chrysostom, *Discourses* 21.10.

16. Suetonius, *The Twelve Caesars* 6.57.

17. Pliny the Younger, *Letters* 5.5.

18. Suetonius, *The Twelve Caesars* 6.1.

Bibliography

Abbott, F. F., and A. C. Johnson. *Municipal Administration in the Roman Empire.* Princeton, NJ: Princeton University Press, 1926.

Adkins, L., and R. Adkins. *Dictionary of Roman Religion.* New York: Oxford University Press, 1996.

Appian. *Roman History.* Translated by H. White. London: Loeb, 1913.

Augustus. *Res Gestae Divi Augusti.* Translated by F. W. Shipley. Cambridge, MA: Harvard University Press, 1924.

Boardman, J., J. Griffin, and O. Murray. *The Oxford History of the Classical World.* Oxford: Oxford University Press, 1986.

Bouchier, E. S. *Spain Under the Roman Empire.* Oxford: Blackwell, 1914.

Boyne, W., with H. Stuart Jones. *A Manual of Roman Coins.* Chicago: Ammon, 1968.

Brogen, J. *Roman Gaul.* London: Bell, 1953.

Buchan, J. *Augustus.* London: Hodder & Stoughton, 1937.

Caesar. *Commentaries on the Gallic & Civil Wars.* Translated by W. A. M'Devitte and W. S. Bohn. London: Bell, 1890.

Carcopino, J. *Daily Life in Ancient Rome.* London: Pelican, 1956.

Cave, W. *Lives of the Apostles.* London: Rickerby, 1836.

Chevalier, R. *Roman Roads.* Translated by N. H. Field. London: Batsford, 1976.

Cicero. *Letters to Atticus.* Translated by O. E. Winstedt. Cambridge, MA: Harvard University Press, 1912.

———. *The Letters to His Friends.* Translated by W. Glynn Williams. Cambridge, MA: Harvard University Press, 1927.

Croft, P. *Roman Mythology.* London: Octopus, 1974.

Cunliffe, B. *The Celtic World.* London: Bodley Head, 1979.

———. *Rome and Her Empire.* Maidenhead, UK: McGraw-Hill, 1978.

Dando-Collins, S. *Blood of the Caesars: How the Murder of Germanicus Led to the Fall of Rome.* Hoboken, NJ: Wiley, 2008.

————. *Caesar's Legion: The Epic Saga of Julius Caesar's Elite Tenth Legion and the Armies of Rome.* New York: Wiley, 2002.

————. *Cleopatra's Kidnappers: How Caesar's Sixth Legion Gave Egypt to Rome and Rome to Caesar.* Hoboken, NJ: Wiley, 2006.

————. *The Ides: Caesar's Murder and the War for Rome.* Hoboken, NJ: Wiley, 2010.

————. *Mark Antony's Heroes: How the Third Gallica Legion Saved an Apostle and Created an Emperor.* Hoboken, NJ: Wiley, 2007.

————. *Nero's Killing Machine: The True Story of Rome's Remarkable Fourteenth Legion.* Hoboken, NJ: Wiley, 2005.

De Boccard, E. *Etudes de Epigraphie et d'Histoire Grecques.* Vol. 1. Paris: 1938.

Delbruck, H. *History of the Art of War.* Translated by J. Walter Renfroe Jr. Lincoln, NE: Bison, 1990.

Dennis, G. *The Cities and Cemeteries of Etruria.* London: Murray, 1848.

Depuy, R. E., and T. N. Depuy. *The Encyclopedia of Military History, From 3500 BC to the Present.* London: MBS, 1970.

Dio, Cassius. *Roman History.* Translated by E. Cary. Cambridge, MA: Harvard University Press, 1914.

Dio Chrysostom. *Discourses.* Cambridge, MA: Loeb, 1939.

Emile, T. *Roman Life Under the Caesars.* New York: Putnam, 1908.

Forestier, A. *The Roman Soldier.* London: A. & C. Black, 1928.

Frank, T., ed. *An Economic Survey of Ancient Rome.* New Jersey: Pageant, 1959.

Frontinus, S. J. *The Stratagems: The Aqueducts of Rome.* Translated by C. E. Bennet. Cambridge, MA: Harvard University Press, 1969.

Fuller, J. *Julius Caesar: Man, Soldier and Tyrant.* London: Eyre & Spottiswoode, 1965.

Gardner, J. F. *Family and Familia in Roman Law and Life.* Oxford: Oxford University Press, 1998.

Goldsworthy, A. *The Complete Roman Army.* London: Thames & Hudson, 2003.

————. *Roman Warfare.* London: Cassell, 2000.

Grant, M. *Gladiators.* Harmondsworth, UK: Penguin, 1967.

————. *The Army of the Caesars.* Harmondsworth, UK: Penguin, 1974.

————. *History of Rome.* Harmondsworth, UK: Penguin, 1978.

————. *Julius Caesar.* Harmondsworth, UK: Penguin, 1969.

————. *Roman History from Coins.* New York: Barnes & Noble, 1995.

Haywood, R. M. *Ancient Greece and the Near East.* London: Vision, 1964.

————. *Ancient Rome.* London: Vision, 1967.

Horace. *Odes and Epodes.* London: Heinemann, 1964.

Jones, A. H. M. *Augustus.* New York: W. W. Norton, 1972.

Josephus. *The New Complete Works.* Translated by W. Whiston. 1737. Reprint, Grand Rapids, MI: Kregel, 1999.

Keppie, L. *Colonisation and Veteran Settlement in Italy, 47–14 B.C.* London: BSR, 1983.

———. *The Making of the Roman Army: From Republic to Empire.* New York: Barnes & Noble, 1984.

Lanciani, R. *Pagan and Christian Rome.* Boston: Houghton, Mifflin, 1892.

Leach, J. *Pompey the Great.* New York: Croom Helm, 1978.

Martial. *Epigrams.* London: Routledge, 1926.

Mattingly, H. *Roman Coins from the Earliest Times to the Fall of the Western Empire.* London: Methuen, 1927.

Mommsen, T. *The Provinces of the Roman Empire.* Edited by T. R. S. Broughton. Chicago: University of Chicago, 1968.

Parker, H. D. M. *The Roman Legions.* New York: Barnes & Noble, 1958.

Philo Judaeus. *The Works of Philo.* Translated by C. D. Yonge. Peabody, MA: Hendrickson, 1993.

Pliny the Elder. *Natural History.* Translated by H. Rackman. London: Loeb, 1938–1963.

Pliny the Younger. *Letters.* Translated by W. Melmoth. London: Loeb, 1915.

Plutarch. *The Lives of the Noble Grecians and Romans.* Translated by J. Dryden. 1683–1686. Reprint, Chicago: Encyclopaedia Britannica, 1952.

Polybius. *The Histories of Polybius.* Translated by P. Holland. 1606. Reprinted, New York: LEC, 1963.

Robertson, D. S. *Greek and Roman Architecture.* Cambridge, UK: Cambridge University Press, 1943.

Rostovtzeff, M. I. *The Social and Economic History of the Roman Empire.* New York: Biblio & Tannen, 1957.

Scullard, H. H. *Festivals and Ceremonies of the Roman Republic.* London: Thames and Hudson, 1981.

Seneca. *Epistulae Morales.* Oxford: Loeb, 1917.

Simkins, M. *Warriors of Rome.* London: Blandford, 1988.

Strabo. *The Geography of Strabo.* Translated by H. L. Jones. Cambridge, MA: Loeb, 1924.

Straus, B. *The Sparticus War.* New York: Simon & Schuster, 2009.

Syme, R. *History in Ovid.* Oxford: Oxford University Press, 1979.

Tacitus. *The Agricola and the Germania.* Translated by H. Mattingly. London: Penguin, 1948.

———. *The Annals and the Histories.* Chicago: Encyclopaedia Britannica, 1952.

Todd, M. *The Northern Barbarians, 1000 BC–AD 300.* New York: Blackwell, 1987.

Valerius Maximus. *Memorable Deeds and Sayings: One Thousand Tales from Ancient Rome.* Translated by H. J. Walker. Indianapolis: Hackett, 2004.

Vegetius. *The Military Institutions of the Romans.* Translated by J. Clark. Harrisburg: The Military Service Publishing Company, 1944.

Velleius Paterculus. *Compendium of Roman History.* Translated by F. W. Shipley. Cambridge, MA: Harvard University Press, 1924.

Vitruvius. *On Architecture.* Translated by F. Granger. Cambridge, MA: Harvard University Press, 1934.

Warry, J. *Warfare in the Classical World.* London: Salamander, 1989.

Watson, G. R. *The Roman Soldier.* Ithaca, NY: Cornell University Press, 1969.

White, K. D. *Greek and Roman Technology.* Ithaca, NY: Cornell University Press, 1983.

Wilkes, J. J., ed. *Documenting the Roman Army.* London: ICS, 2003.

Witt, R. E. *Isis in the Ancient World.* Baltimore: Johns Hopkins, 1997.

Index